YUGOSLAVIAN INFERNO

PAUL MOJZES

YUGOSLAVIAN INFERNO

ETHNORELIGIOUS WARFARE IN THE BALKANS

CONTINUUM | NEW YORK

1994
The Continuum Publishing Company
370 Lexington Avenue, New York, NY 10017

Printed in the United States of America

Library of Congress Cataloging-in-Publication Data
Mojzes, Paul.
Yugoslavian inferno : ethnoreligious warfare in the Balkans / Paul
Mojzes.
p.   cm.
Includes bibliographical references and index.
ISBN 0-8264-0683-1 (alk. paper)
1. Yugoslav War, 1991–   2. Yugoslavia—Ethnic relations.
3.Yugoslavia—Religion—20th century. I. Title.
DR1313.M65   1994
949.702'4—dc20   94-3737
                                                        CIP

Maps designed by Dale Hasenick.
Portions of chapters 9,10, and 11 previously appeared in *The Christian Century.*

This book is dedicated to those
who are endeavoring to alleviate the suffering
and bring an end to the wars
in the former Yugoslavia.

CONTENTS

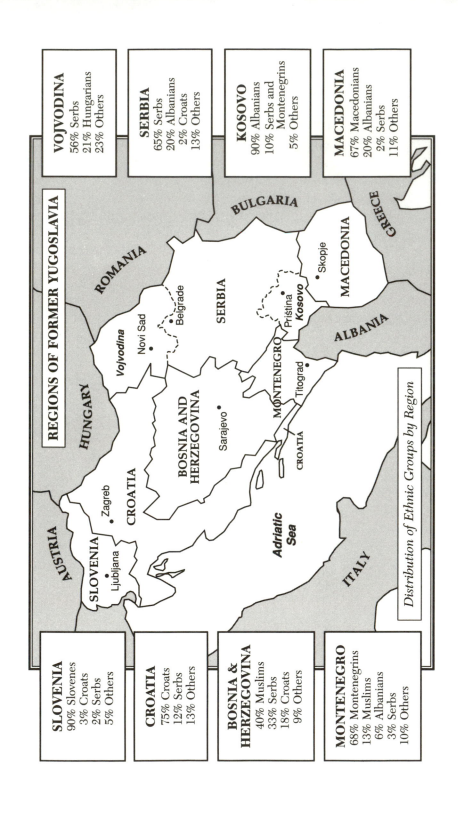

REGIONS OF FORMER YUGOSLAVIA

VOJVODINA
56% Serbs
21% Hungarians
23% Others

SERBIA
65% Serbs
20% Albanians
2% Croats
13% Others

KOSOVO
90% Albanians
10% Serbs and
Montenegrins
5% Others

MACEDONIA
67% Macedonians
20% Albanians
2% Serbs
11% Others

SLOVENIA
90% Slovenes
3% Croats
2% Serbs
5% Others

CROATIA
75% Croats
12% Serbs
13% Others

**BOSNIA &
HERZEGOVINA**
40% Muslims
33% Serbs
18% Croats
9% Others

MONTENEGRO
68% Montenegrins
13% Muslims
6% Albanians
3% Serbs
10% Others

Distribution of Ethnic Groups by Region

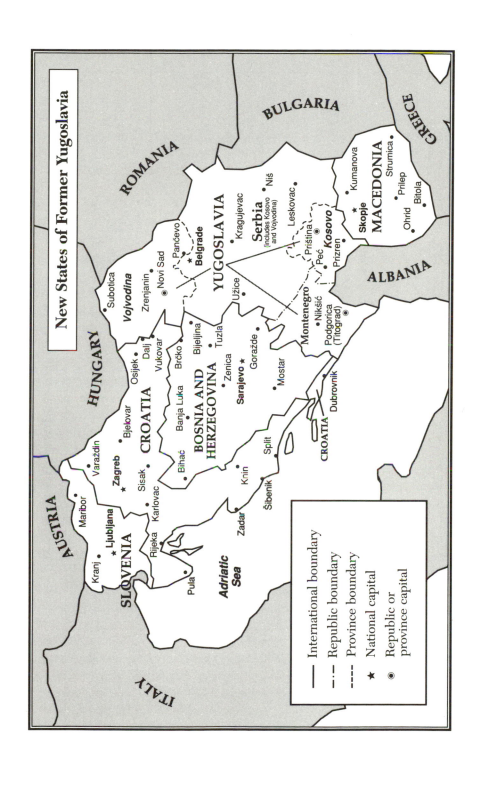

New States of Former Yugoslavia

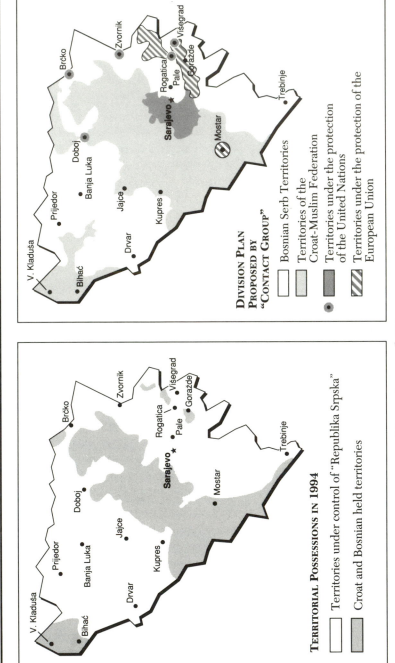

DIVISION PLAN PROPOSED BY "CONTACT GROUP"

☐ Bosnian Serb Territories

☐ Territories of the Croat-Muslim Federation

■ Territories under the protection of the United Nations

▨ Territories under the protection of the European Union

⊙

TERRITORIAL POSSESSIONS IN 1994

☐ Territories under control of "Republika Srpska"

☐ Croat and Bosnian held territories

Bosnia and Herzegovina

PRONUNCIATION GUIDE

A, a = car   I, i = deep

C, c = hats   J, j = yard

Ć, ć = mutual   Lj, lj = million

Č, č = chapter   N, n = no

Dj, dj = ginger   Nj, nj = new

Dž, dž = just   O, o = dormitory

E, e = pen   Š, š = ship

G, g = go   U, u = broom

H, h = loch   Ž, ž = treasure

All other letters generally correspond to the conventional English equivalents.

INTRODUCTION

"Inferno" suggests a situation of real and symbolic conflagration, unrelenting suffering, the prevalence of unmitigated evil, futility, and hopelessness. It can be appropriately applied to the former Yugoslavia, where ethnoreligious warfare has consigned millions to hell and where a return from hell is by no means assured.

The question arises as to the purpose of a book about a country's violent demise and the birth of new order on the Balkan peninsula while the warfare still goes on and the outcome is by no means certain. The present, fluid situation certainly does not call for firm conclusions about outcomes, but there is a great need for understanding the cause of the present great convulsion, especially the role of the religious communities in it that most other analysts have ignored, and to explore the approaches toward a solution.

There is universal concern, along with puzzlement, over the situation in former Yugoslavia. Suddenly most of us are confronted by animosities between peoples whom we barely knew existed. Those who have visited Yugoslavia earlier are baffled that people who used to be so friendly toward them and toward one another could turn so viciously against each other. I share both the puzzlement and concern over the developments in the country of my birth despite the fact that I know the situation intimately. I discovered that the same is true with other emigrants from former Yugoslavia; they are now often alienated from each other and pursuing opposite political aims. Nevertheless, they are all pained and perplexed by the outbreak of a war that is certainly Europe's most serious armed conflict to follow World War II.

There are many contradictory narratives about the present conflict. It is not surprising that interpretations vary according to the background of the author. Serbian authors tend to write pro-Serbian narratives, Croatian pro-Croatian, Muslims pro-Muslim, and so forth. Thus it is important that I lay open my background and biases.

I was born in Osijek, the largest city of the region of Slavonia in Croatia. When I was five years old, my parents moved to Novi Sad, the capital city of Vojvodina in Serbia, which at that time, 1941, was under Hungarian occupation. My father, a Protestant minister, was greatly opposed to the war and moved to Novi Sad out of concern that the then-fascist "Independent State of Croatia" would present a danger to his life. As it happened, he did not escape the fascists' murderous aims—he was killed in 1942 in a Hungarian "labor camp." My mother, who later replaced my father as a minister in the tiny Methodist Church there, taught me love and tolerance even though we were surrounded by hatred and destruction on all sides. Nationalism played no role in our family although a certain religious exclusivism characterized my mother's evangelical fervor.

As a child and young man I came under the influence of Tito's brand of socialism. In particular I found Tito's efforts to build *"bratstvo-jedinstvo"* (brotherhood and unity) very appealing. My generation, at least in the Vojvodina region of Serbia and in Belgrade, did not consider national origin a factor of any importance. When asked our nationality, most of my friends identified themselves as Serb; my only brother identified himself as Serb, and I was a Croat. My best friend was Hungarian and my second-best friend Slovenian. We really did feel primarily *Yugoslav*, an identity which is supposedly artificial but which is no more imaginary than the mythic nationalism of the nineteenth century that created the categories of Serb, Croat, Slovene, and other labels attached to peoples who previously saw themselves as merely related to small geographic regions of the Balkan peninsula and to their religion.

Upon coming to the United States in the late 1950s, my wife and I quickly discarded our Yugoslav identity and eagerly took on an American one in which we saw many of our dreams of a larger human family realized. I reject the notion that we are determined by our past—not *in spite of* being an historian but because I *am* an historian. Human beings desire to shape both their collective and individual lives. They tend to make use of the past in ways that are convenient to their aspirations for the future. Thus, I started regarding myself as an American who was a native of Yugoslavia.

Having become an American citizen and having dropped Yugoslav citizenship, I decided to be in no way politically involved in the life of my former homeland. I took frequent trips to Yugoslavia to keep up links with family and friends, to reminisce about times past, and to see the changes that were taking place in that country—most of which were good. My Yugoslav origin gave me a sense of minor pride: I hailed from a country whose socialist experiment was not slavishly dependent upon the Soviet Union and whose regime was more humane and open to the rest of the world than any of the Soviet-bloc countries. Professionally, my interests were the religious developments in all of Eastern Europe and the Soviet Union, but I always had an interest in the broader developments in Yugoslavia as well. Yugoslavia would be, I thought, the first to reform its Communism into a system more democratic and free than the rest of the Communist countries and would forge the path of gradual relaxation from the system's oppressiveness.

The rapid collapse of Soviet-bloc Communism took me by surprise. I expected that Yugoslav Communism would make an easier transition to post-Communism than others. Mounting nationalist tensions were evident, but I did not anticipate that they would lead to the partition of the country. Just prior to Tito's death in 1980 I wrote an article for *Worldview* entitled "The Hour X," in which I predicted a severe power struggle to inherit his mantle. For the first five years after his death, my prediction seemed amiss; but then the struggle commenced in earnest.

The final result was quite different from what I or anyone anticipated. Since no single person was successful in claiming power over the entire country, the country splintered. The main ideology after the collapse of Communism was resurgent nationalism, which returned to the scene with a vigor that I had not anticipated.

In this book I aim to provide a relatively concise analysis of the issues that brought about the demise of Yugoslavia, along with the ensuing war. In particular I wish to explore the role of religious communities and leaders in this process since some vehemently deny such a role and others simply ignore it. The general survey of developments will be based primarily on my own insights gathered through cumulative experiences, scholarly and journalistic reports, and especially personal interviews with a broad range of former Yugoslav citizens carried out during my several visits, especially in January 1993 and in August/September, 1993.

These visits afforded the unique opportunity to speak with a vast spectrum of people in Slovenia, Croatia, Serbia, and Macedonia. Some exchanges were spontaneous, as with passengers on trains and buses, relatives, former schoolmates, friends, and church members. Others were scheduled with prominent professional people. A few were with government officials, including the President of the Republic of Slovenia, two advisors of a former President of Yugoslavia, a member of the parliament of Macedonia, and two Belgrade political party leaders of very different persuasions. A few were with church dignitaries, including a Macedonian Orthodox metropolitan, two Serbian Orthodox bishops and two priests, a Roman Catholic archbishop, bishop, and priest, a Lutheran bishop and minister, two Methodist ministers, a Muslim *imam*—living in various new states. I talked to journalists, both secular and religious. And most of all I talked to people of my profession, namely professors. Some of them were secular; others belonged to religious traditions—Orthodox, Catholic, and Muslim. All I spoke with have been helpful in helping me to gain a better insight into the situation as well as a better understanding of current events. I took copious notes and reduced myself to a listener rather than an active conversation partner.

Some of those I interviewed held very moderate, reflective, even critical views regarding the origin, development, and culmination of the crisis. Others had been swept into the apologetic mainstream of their nationality. In a few cases I witnessed the tragic transformation of a formerly critical thinker of humanistic Marxist persuasion to a biased replicator of nationalist oratory. Some of the views of those interviewed overlapped; others were very contradictory. On top of all this I ardently followed what the press and media reported and marveled how the same event could evoke such absolutely contrary interpretations by people who profess to report only what actually has happened. Most helpful to me were monographs by insightful scholars of the former Yugoslavia, most of whom I have known personally and who are not cited in footnote form because their writings are in the languages of Yugoslavia. I found their insights most consistent with my own understanding of the situation, but frequently they provided a more penetrating analysis of some aspect of the situation than I could have reached independently.

My views expressed in this book have been formed in the crucible of myriad claims—some reasonable, others paranoid, some deeply analytical, others propagandist. Upon my returns to the United States, I have felt emotionally drained; even my dreams had been drastically changed. All night long my mind was now filled with argumentation. My state of mind simply reflected the conflicts in the former Yugoslavia.

Listening to each individual national claim, one recognizes significant elements of truth and is forced to admit the justice of each. If a traveller were to go to only one particular state, one would return with the conviction that truth had been discovered. But it would not be the whole truth! I would urge prospective visitors to the former Yugoslavia either to make it a point to go to at least two or three republics or not to go at all. Even critical minds can be swept along by the logic of national self-preservation and by the human suffering that is experienced in each of the states. One of the major reasons for the biased reporting by journalists, peace activists, clergy, and professors is that they have tended to be exposed to the claims of only one side in this multifarious conflict, emerging as transmitters of that side's interpretation rather than seeing the larger picture.

I myself have weaknesses in this respect. During my recent visits, unlike my past ones, I did not visit Bosnia and Herzegovina, Montenegro, and Dalmatia. The major reason was a shortage of time. But in the case of Bosnia and Herzegovina it was also a concern for personal safety; it is imprudent to venture into war areas without the structural support of an organization. Of greater concern to me was that if I were to go to Bosnia, I would have wanted to visit the areas under Muslim, Croat, and Serb control rather than only one of them. What is true for former

Yugoslavia as a whole is even truer for Bosnia, where sharply different narratives exist regarding the origin, nature, and development of the war.

Ultimately it is impossible to remain entirely dispassionate, if for no other reason than the sympathy one must feel for the enormous suffering encountered everywhere. Nevertheless, I used all the restraint that I was able to muster in order to remain objective and report truthfully about conditions there. That effort is often not appreciated by some acquaintances from the former Yugoslavia who have taken a more partisan interpretation of what happened and why. They would prefer that I clearly espouse their own or even their opponents' interpretation—with their opponents they disagree, but at least they understand them. My efforts not to take sides appear to them as a copout—a moral failure to make a decision. But I did make a decision, which I still do not see fit to change: namely, to avoid being an advocate of any one of the contentious ethnoreligious groups.

To those who offered me their hospitality, help, meals, time, and, most important, data and insights I owe a debt of gratitude. Their contributions to my understanding were invaluable, and their numbers are too great to be acknowledged. And they are not, of course, responsible for my possible misunderstandings or misinterpretations. Most frequently I have deliberately synthesized a variety of views so as not to reflect solely one person's understanding. I generally tried to give my sources my own personal bent, even to the point of disagreeing with some of them.

Citizens of many countries which espouse the democratic deliberative process are being forced today to make significant decisions regarding conflicts in faraway places that make a claim on the diplomatic, political, financial, and military resources of the rest of the world. It is, therefore, important to offer a book that might be of some help to readers who want to inform themselves about the process of dissolution of a country on the volatile Balkan peninsula and the emergence of several bitterly contentious states there. We cannot avoid doing so even if we wanted, because we have daily watched the destruction there on our TV screens, and our conscience impels us to show concern for such a monumental human tragedy. In addition, we are impelled to judge the action or non-action of our own governmental leaders as well as that of international institutions such as NATO, the

European Community, and the United Nations and must either applaud or disagree. Gradually many nations are being militarily drawn into the Balkan vortex. Public opinion plays a role in democratic societies, but public opinion needs to be more broadly informed rather than to interpret the situation in the former Yugoslavia exclusively in the light of previous engagements such as Vietnam, the Gulf War, Somalia, or even other paradigms, like the Holocaust. Nor must American public opinion be based solely on its own domestic political considerations. To assist the general reader who will need to make political decisions, and especially those readers *to whom religion is significant,* is the purpose to which the book is dedicated.

My wife, Elizabeth, urged me to write the book, and for that I thank her. My sons, Bernard and Leonard, assisted me at several stages of writing the manuscript. I also wish to thank the following people for their editorial assistance: my colleagues from Rosemont College, Dr. Richard Leiby and Dr. Jacqueline Murphy; Dr. John Hunter of Westtown School (PA); Dr. Niels Nielsen of Rice University (Houston); Robert Kotzbauer of Nagg's Head (NC); Donald Ottenhoff and David Heim of the editorial staff of the *Christian Century* (Chicago); and finally, Frank Oveis, my editor, and Donn Teal, the copy editor.

CHAPTER 1

NEVER AGAIN?

Never again. The vow was solemnly uttered by individuals and nations at the end of World War II. Not that there would never again be a war, but that the world would not stand by and watch as entire national and religious groups were systematically destroyed in the name of some higher ideal. Pol Pot's Cambodia destroyed that illusion, but somehow it seemed beyond belief that it would happen in *Europe* again, where genocidal policies tainted much of twentieth-century history but where it seemed that such policies were finally laid to rest.

There is barely a Yugoslav family which did not lose a member to the carnage of World War II. In my family about 30 were killed in a three-day period in January 1942, and that did not include my father, his two brothers, and paternal grandparents, who were killed within the next two years. But my family history was not unique. In fact, we considered ourselves lucky that we did not all die! Some families were completely wiped out. So when the war ended there was hope that it would not happen again.

But even the formal end of the war did not end the bloodshed in Yugoslavia. POWs, those accused of collaborating with the enemy, those perceived as the opponents of Tito's regime were executed and massacred. The remnants of the armies of the Independent State of Croatia (both *ustashe* and *domobran*; i.e., Croatian Nazi storm troops and National Guards) were returned by the British Army to Tito's *partizans* (Communist-led anti-fascist guerrillas) and were wiped out at Bleiburg. The *chetniks* (extreme Serbian nationalist irregulars) were killed and their leader, General Draža Mihajlović, was sentenced and executed. In 1948 and a few years afterward, upon Yugoslavia's break with the Soviet-led Cominform, sympathizers of Stalin were killed or brutally "reeducated" in a number of notorious prisons, especially the one on Goli Otok (Naked Island), a penal colony in the Adriatic Sea whose name betrays its topography. It was a time of "ideological cleansing."

From 1991 onward, ethnoreligious warfare and "ethnic cleansing" rival the worst that transpired in the country during World War II. The official propaganda that a New Yugoslavia had been forged in the national liberation struggle between 1941 and 1945 led by Tito's *partizans* gave us hope that what happened in the past would never happen again. This "new" Yugoslavia was to have settled the interethnic and interreligious problems that characterized the "old" Kingdom of Yugoslavia which escalated to a fratricidal war during World War II. "New" Yugoslavia became a republic rather than a monarchy in which the ethnic group of the Serbian royal family dominated other ethnic groups. Its federal structure was going to ensure that the rights and equality of *all* the small Yugoslav nations were going to be respected. The "Communist internationalism" and a "worker's state" under the slogan "Workers of the world unite" was going to make "bourgeois nationalism" a thing of the past. Communist propaganda effectively promoted *"bratstvo-jedinstvo,"* the brotherhood/sisterhood and unity of the diverse nationalities of this largest Balkan state. Immediately upon the end of the war, "Western imperialism" provided the subterfuge of an external threat that was useful in toning down internal dissensions. It was followed by the Soviet-bloc menace after 1948, which provided another, even more tangible peril to foster unification and pride through successfully resisting the Soviet invasion.

This helped create confidence that interethnic particularism had been eliminated. A group of Yugoslav tourists in Moscow in 1987 sang proudly the song, *"Jugoslavija, Jugoslavija moja najmilija"* (Yugoslavia, My Dearest). Pride would swell my chest, as it did theirs, that this little country found its niche in a world of superpowers by becoming famous for its independence, non-alliance, and unique form of socialism. I recall how as high school pupils and students or scouts from Novi Sad in the Vojvodina, we would travel to Prespa Lake in Macedonia, to Žirovnica in Slovenia, to Sarajevo, Mostar, Dubrovnik, and Split, to my birth-place Osijek, to Belgrade and all of that was "ours" and we were one with the people of the local area, never experiencing resentment or bias. As a sixteen- and seventeen-year-old I volunteered to work as part of the Novi Sad youth brigade for a month of the hardest manual labor I had ever done, building in Bosnia the railway between Brčko and Banovići and then the cable factory in Sevojno, Serbia. Working and living along with us were brigades from Prijedor in Bosnia, Kranjska Gora in Slovenia, Niš in Serbia, Skopje in Macedonia—and we regarded ourselves as of one country. I remember when, with two of my friends, I undertook a perilous hike in Macedonia from Lake Prespa to Lake Ohrid via the Perister Mountain, where we found remnants of barbed wire and bullets from the fighting between the Serbian and Austro-Hungarian battles. We got lost in the barren, rocky terrain and nearly strayed into Albania. A Macedonian shepherd showed us the way to Ohrid. He was "ours" and we thought we were "his." Granted, there were probably people who did not feel that way, but I did not know any. This I mention in order to counter the frequently heard claim today by some of the nationalists that the "Yugoslav idea" never worked and that only brute police force kept the country together.

There was another factor that seemed to guarantee "Never again." Yugoslavia had become a respectable member of the international community—the United Nations, the Helsinki Accords, the Nonaligned Movement—and had signed all kinds of international conventions and agreements in which it bound itself to respect all international legal norms. The country was inching toward a state of law. It never quite reached that goal, but such international involvement increased legality, security, and peace.

At that time "Never again" seemed convincing. Surely no one would ever again set these people against each other considering the many intermarriages, a sizeable movement of ethnically different people settling in one another's areas, the purchase of properties along the Dalmatian coasts by members of *all* our nationalities, the successful integration of sports teams that represented the country in myriad international competitions. Vladimir Beara of Split and Branko Horvat of Zagreb were equally impressive and popular, as were Rajko Mitić of Belgrade or Djemal Hadjiabdić of Sarajevo. Dražen Petrović, a Croat with a

Serbian sounding name, and Vlade Divac, a Serb with a Croat-sounding name, would win world basketball championships for Yugoslavia and play successfully in the NBA. Bojan Križan, the Slovene ski champ, was "ours." A Macedonian played for my hometown soccer team "Vojvodina" and we cheered him on as we did the local prodigy Vujadin Boškov, one of the best European halfbacks of his time. "Crvena Zvezda" (Red Star) and "Partizan" soccer clubs of nearby Belgrade were greater rivals to our "Vojvodina" than "Dinamo" of Zagreb and "Hajduk" of Split. That was so until the 1980s, when nationalism became important again and when big fights would break out at games between fans to whom this was no longer a competition in soccer but a competition between nationalities. When Yugoslavia played Holland in Zagreb in 1989 and the Yugoslav national anthem was heard, fans turned their back to the flag—to the utter confusion of the Yugoslav national team—and cheered for the Dutch. Trouble was brewing. Some of the nationalistic soccer fans quickly became some of the earliest nationalist warriors—and war criminals.

ANTICIPATING WAR

My wife and I were a long way from Yugoslavia and unable to experience the changes firsthand, but we first sensed the change in Philadelphia in the early 1980s. My wife is a dancer, and she used to go folk dancing at the University of Pennsylvania, where folk-dance aficionados loved Balkan folk dances most of all, though few were of Slavic background. A few of our friends, former Yugoslavs, were of various nationalities. A young woman who had just come from Zagreb attended the folk dance for the first time. When approached by my wife with a friendly "I heard that you are from Yugoslavia," she bruskly answered, "No, I am from Croatia. I am from Zagreb." This was the early warning for us that it was not only the old royal Serbian immigrants and the old Croatian pro-*ustasha* immigrants who did not recognize the existence of the "new" Yugoslavia, but that the younger generation also had a different perception.

Whenever an opportunity presented itself to travel on academic business near Yugoslavia, I tried to arrange a visit there, at least briefly. Then, in May of 1991, I took one of my frequent trips to Yugoslavia. I had received an invitation to lecture in Zagreb at the newly founded "Europe House" on the topic of my recently completed book, *Religious Liberty in Eastern Europe and the USSR.* On that occasion I would also visit my hometown, Novi Sad.

By then there was much concern about the violence between the Serbs and Croats. Already during my visit in 1989 I had a distinct impression that a hidden, low-key war was being waged—at that time primarily in Kosovo between Albanians and Serbs. But by 1990 there were tire-slashings; destruction of property (sometimes by local government decree) against buildings allegedly having no "permit," by individuals of another nationality; hostile graffiti; fistfights; and occasional shootings, including killings, resulting in further sporadic and arbitrary violence.

Frequently these outbreaks were accompanied by argumentative questions of language. Would Slovenes be willing to respond to someone speaking Serbian or Croatian or would they insist on pretending to understand only Slovenian, which is not readily understood by the non-Slovenes? What can one say about the relationship between the Serbian and Croatian languages? Serbs and Croats are extremely close to one another; there is no difficulty in communicating, and Serbs and Croats who live in the same city speak the same dialect. Serbian was originally written in the Cyrillic alphabet and Croatian in the Latin, but many Serbs used predominantly the Latin alphabet. Were they essentially the same language, as some maintained? Should one call the language Serbocroat (or Croatoserb, as some sensitive Croats insisted) or Serbo-Croat (or Croato-Serb)? Or were Croatian and Serbian two distinct languages? And was there possibly even a third language, Bosnian, which the Muslims of Bosnia spoke and which also seemed nearly indistinguishable from the other two?

Misha Glenny in his *Fall of Yugoslavia* recounts a tragi-comic story of an attempt to rescue Yugoslavia on the eve of the war in a conference of all the newly emergent political parties. Convened by one of the smaller, democratically inclined Serbian parties, it was to take place near Sarajevo. The Serbian convener apologized that, because of lack of funds, it was not possible to arrange for simultaneous translation into Macedonian and Slovenian and he hoped for understanding and forbearance by the

Macedonian and Slovene colleagues, all of whom spoke fluent Serbo-Croat. Then one of the Croatian representatives angrily demanded that translation ought to have been provided also from Serb to Croat. When a Bosnian Muslim spoke out, too, for translation into Bosnian, pandemonium broke out. They laughed till tears rolled, but essentially the funny part was overshadowed by a realization of the depth of the chasm between the rivals.

Upon receiving the invitation to give a speech in Zagreb's "Europe House," I became concerned about language. Should I speak in English and have someone translate or should I, who has billed himself a Croat but speaks the Serbian version of the language, speak Serbian? My query was answered by "Speak in our language." I found the audience polite and non-resentful of my Serbian inflection, but it was also noteworthy that the moderator stated that I was born in Osijek, Croatia, and studied and taught in the United States but made no mention of my high school education in Novi Sad and law school studies at Belgrade University—as if such information would taint me in the eyes of the audience.

Zagreb in the summer of 1989 was decked out with an enormous number of Croatian flags. Yugoslav flags were not to be seen, though independence had not yet been declared. Almost every window display had a sticker with the Croatian colors and the text *"Bože čuvaj Hrvatsku"* (God protect Croatia), a rather jarring sight after years of no public mention of God and religion during the Communist era. Men in new uniforms, that of the Croatian Guards and Croatian police, had high visibility, apparently to dissuade the Yugoslav People's Army from takeover.

My conversation partners were surprised that I dared to take the train from Belgrade to Zagreb. Was I safe on the Serbian side? they inquired. This was the flip side of the warnings I received in Novi Sad not to take the train to Zagreb because I might be harmed on the Croatian side. The actual trip was rather uneventful, except when a group of high schools boys entered the compartment in Vinkovci, Croatia. They were well behaved and thought I was a foreigner who did not understand the language (a convenient subterfuge to which I resorted frequently when I wanted to listen unobtrusively and yet not have to engage in the conversation). Their entire conversation was about guns; they seemed well informed about caliber, trademarks, and prices. It was quite evident that they were knowledgeable and had access to such weapons long before they became of draft age.

In Novi Sad there had not been such visible nationalist trappings. Outwardly no change was evident as people went about their common chores. But the conversation and the media were focused on a single topic: the outbreak of hostilities. Everyone seemed to be convinced that war was inevitable. Some had grown tired of the nervous expectations and quipped, "Might as well let it start." Much discussion took place as to who was the best politician for Serbia. Miloje, one of my in-laws, a retired director of a trading enterprise and a former prominent Communist favored Slobodan Milošević, but admitted shyly that he found the *chetnik* leader, Vojislav Šešelj, attractive and well spoken. His son, Sasha, an entrepreneur who held two jobs, one in a state-owned enterprise and the other in his private auto body shop, was passionately in favor of Vuk Drašković, the nationalist novelist who emphatically opposed Milošević. The father cautioned his son to be less outspoken against Milošević and to place Drašković's picture less prominently in his house, because "you never know what the future may bring." Apparently the older man had learned certain lessons of life that his son did not appropriate. Democracy would be easier to live in for Sasha than for Miloje, but Miloje could more easily function under a dictatorship than his less-circumscribed son.

THE WAR ARRIVES

In March 1992 my sister-in-law, Mira, visited us in the States. She is a simple, unpolitical housewife. Mira is Croatian and a Catholic. Her now-deceased husband, Milenko, was a Serb and thus Orthodox, but neither practiced their religion. Milenko, however, "practiced" his nationality and their two daughters were raised as Serbs while Mira easily took the Serb side in the conflict.

When she arrived she was very frightened. She recounted stories of half-crazed Yugoslav Army reservists who came to their door in rural Čortanovci, about twenty miles south of Novi Sad, allegedly chased by Croat *ustashe,* supposedly from nearby Croat villages. (I had no awareness of the existence of Croat villages in that vicinity.) She was convinced of the truth of the story and said that they had had to arm themselves against Croat attacks. She was clearly against the Croats and was convinced that the Croats perpetrated the most horrible crimes against humanity—she had seen pictures of what they had done to Serbs in the Vukovar region and elsewhere, as shown regularly on Belgrade TV.

When I mildly challenged some of Mira's interpretations and pointed out Serbian misdeeds, she said those were purely defensive actions. According to her, the Yugoslav Army was forced sometimes to throw hand grenades into Croatian houses because the Croat old folks were so perfidious that they would not report hidden young Croat fighters eager to kill the innocent soldiers. According to her, Serbs had to kill so they were not killed. On numerous occasions she vehemently attacked all Croats and said she wished she were not one and wanted to reject any affinity with Croats. At other times she would moanfully state that it was wrong for people to intermarry, because in a war like this one did not know where one belonged. Her stories stretched the imagination, and it was hard to tell whether they are real or fabrications (not of her own but passed on to her).

The difficulty of distinguishing between reality and fantasy or truth and the lie would be one of the characteristics of this war in Yugoslavia. The newspapers and other media have contributed to this puzzlement—and so has gossip. Sometimes reality is so gruesome that it is worse than the most outlandish fabrication. At other times the stories have been self-serving lies intended to make the enemy look bad and to keep one's own population loyal.

A strange war it is. Zagreb, which I have visited three times since 1991, still seems a picture of Middle European culture, fashion, affluence, and calm. Picture postcards of explosions during the Yugoslav Army air attacks can be purchased, but otherwise one sees no damage from the shelling. Even the many Croatian Guards have disappeared from the streets. Occasionally one still sees the white-colored vehicles of the UN Protective Forces (UNPROFOR). But the calm is deceptive. One can travel thirty to forty miles from there and hear gunfire blasting. And if one were to proceed another twenty miles, one would take great risks not only from artillery shells but from military or paramilitary units. The principle "Shoot first, ask questions later" seems to prevail. Since it is impossible to distinguish ethnicity on sight, people try to survive capture by lying about their identity if caught by the wrong group. ID cards may identify the person. In Croatia there is, for instance, a long process of establishing one's Croatian nationality and permanent residence in order to obtain the new Croatian citizenship without which one can neither find a job nor purchase real estate. In the absence of documents, bands of soldiers may check more blatantly by forcing the male captives to drop their pants. Muslims are circumcised; Christians are not. It is more difficult to tell Croat from Serb judging by the penis. One might have to resort to more religious questions that separate Croat Catholics from Orthodox Serbs. Many are forced to chose sides, sometimes pitting parent against child, husband against wife, sibling against sibling, neighbor against neighbor. Horror stories of killings and rape among people closely related abound as calamity unfolds upon calamity.

WHAT IS THIS WARFARE ABOUT?

While a more precise and detailed account will be given below, we should record some impressions first in order to contrast reality with propaganda claims made by the assailants:

This has been a war about defending national identity and territory. It has not been about protecting the value of human life.

This has been a war about hatred and fear. It has not been about caring for the actual human being.

This has been a war about one's cherished ideas of what was or what is to be. It has not been about compassion for the lives lost at the present.

It has been a war about gaining propaganda advantages. It has not been about telling the truth.

It has been a war about justifying national honor and behavior, allegedly defending one's group from the accusations of others. It has not been about honestly admitting the terrifying atrocities committed by one's own side.

It has been a war of settling old and new accounts. It has not been of building a life based on honesty and decency among human beings.

It has been a war about showing that the others also have

killed, raped, burned, and plundered. It has not been about the ethical sensitivity of knowing that wrongdoing by others does not justify my own wrongdoing.

It has been about group glory and achievement and pride. It has not been about introspection, repentance, and regret.

It has been about revenge but not about forgiveness.

It has been about remembering the evil inflicted by others upon us. It has not been about admitting the wrongs inflicted by us.

It has been about cruelty and survival at all cost. It has not been about acknowledging the terror and the feeling of empathy with the victims.

It has been a war of deeds and words about where we lived, live, or ought to live. It has not about the quality of the life of the individual, which has eroded to mere survival.

It has been a war about differences in religion, ethnicity, and culture. It has not been about faith in God or human beings.

It has been about belittling the name, language, and customs of others. It has not been about respecting inherent human dignity and diversity.

It has been a war to secede, separate, differentiate, "cleanse," homogenize. It has not been about thinking how human beings can live in a community of mutual respect.

It has been about lies, betrayal, and suspicion. It has not been about insight into the larger picture and concern for truthfulness.

It has been about cherished make-believes and illusions. It has not been about admitting that the war means the arrival of the apocalypse for the population.

It has been about euphoria. It has not been about reality.

While the above statements may also apply to other wars, they merit being reaffirmed in the face of so much glorification of war as a means of settling the conflicts in the former Yugoslavia. People are no longer repulsed by the killings and rapes; they try to pass on the responsibility to others. It is always the *enemies* who either openly kill our people or covertly kill their own in order to blame or implicate us. *We* may be wrong but *others* are equally or more wrong. However, we can never itemize our wrongdoing. It weakens the fabric of our group; it can shatter our images of the past. It would tarnish our side if we admit wrongdoing—except in secret, confidentially, perhaps to some trusted friend in the hope that somehow by at least partially disclosing the truth we may be cleansed of the silent complicity with evil. Someday, someplace we may or we will tell the whole truth—but for the time being we must be in solidarity with our group.

This is a war in which a bride is wedded to her dead fiancé soldier at his funeral, so she can bear his child which she carries in her womb. It is a war in which a two-year-old is boiled in a pot in front of his horrified mother. Atrocities are videotaped.

It is a war in which detainees are castrated and in which parts of the anatomy are cut off and forced to be eaten by the amputee or by yet another victim. While sledding on a hill or playing in a schoolyard, children are blown up. Schools, hospitals, libraries, and religious and cultural monuments are specially targeted for destruction. Nothing and no one is sacred. In it, neighbors and classmates of one ethnic group rape acquaintances of another. Children of rape are either rejected by their mothers or nurtured in hatred toward the ethnicity of the rapists. Heads of captives are used as soccer balls. Criminals become heroes, and good people become criminals. Men commute to war as if to go to work. But they do not commute to work, because none is available; the stores are empty and the black market abounds with relief rations and stolen VCRs. Heads of government lie. POWs are sold for hard currency—so are permits to emigrate. The young age prematurely, if they survive the hardship. The old die of hunger and cold. Dishonor becomes honor. Moderates are pushed to the margins. Twenty-five million people are pushed both into social psychosis and moral bankruptcy.

As in every war noble actions also spring to the fore. People sacrifice for family and neighbor. Lovers die embracing as they are cut down by snipers. Doctors perform heroic surgeries with no electricity, surgical equipment, or anesthesia; the wounded may incredibly survive the ordeal. Women stoically raise children amid utter privation—or lose their sanity. The memory of happier times nurtures the determination to survive. Some avoid hate even though they are victimized by the enemy.

The list of horrors exceeds the list of honors, however. The bottom line is cataclysmic. An American journalist, Peter Brock of El Paso, TX, wrote in October 1991:

All of the landmarks of my meager visitations are amidst cal-
umny, brothers seeking out the shadows . . . behind shattered
walls and then going about this acceptable business of extermination, annihilation, holocaust. And we are quite comfortable with
the consequential, daiiy body count of one here, one there, a
mother and two children killed by a cluster bomb near Vukovar.
And in Vinkovci, Serbs [are] now experts in lofting a barrage of
mortars to further decimate the skeletal shell of . . . what? A
municipal building? Police offices? Desks that were days ago the
little station of clerks, administrators, functionaries?

One marvels at the lyrical sensitivity of young people who are
forced to grow up amid the madness.

A letter from a seventeen-year-old boy from Zagreb dated September 17, 1991, related:

I wanted to write to you yesterday a letter which would be full of
words such as democracy and liberty. I wanted to write that at
last we printed a periodical which young Europeans would read.
I wanted to write that until yesterday I believed completely
that there will be no war here. We lived during bombardments,
snipers, with hunger and the wounded. For a long time there are
barricades in front of my house. Two snipers were eliminated
from the roof of my house. I spent many nights on the floor of a
suffocating shelter.

But yesterday, yesterday around midnight, the telephone rang
and a voice said quietly and clearly: our friends were killed although only yesterday we together succeeded in putting together
the periodical out of nothing. Already by midnight all those words
[of cooperation] that are in the periodical turned into a senseless
piece of paper. All these human tragedies, exiles, arson, killings
dispersed at these words: "They died." You should know that until recently I approached all these words calmly as if they were
words from some other planet. Yes, planet. Not of my house, not
of my friends or neighbors. All of us look in front of our yards.
We look and watch CNN and view wars around the world. But
CNN can be viewed from a comfortable armchair . . . Alarm . . .
But I stay upstairs. I want to tell you that the only light visible
now is the moon. Observe, please, the thoughts of a common man
here. A person lives surrounded by sirens and explosions. You go
to the store—alarm. You go to buy the papers—alarm. Do you
know that we are all here an enormous lunatic asylum with men-
tally sick? People from an asylum have only two possibilities, to
die there or to run away. A shot. Two shots. It is not hard to die.
But how to run away? Because there is no return. There will never
be the old Zagreb which you visited. Maybe Zagreb will look like

in World War II. This room will be punctured by an accurate grenade. And I, probably by an accurate bullet.

So this is the average occupation of each person here: counting shots, talking about shelters, tanks, airplanes. It seems to me that all of this looks like a German concentration camp. But those murderers did not succeed to kill all of their guests. And if they did not, neither will these.

You should know that no matter how often this land is trampled upon, Croatia cannot disappear. It would continue even if it had only five inhabitants.

I hope to hear from you.

Igor Smailagić

Another letter was written by two nineteen-year-old Bosnian Muslim twin girls regarding their feelings about having to flee from Sarajevo, while their parents were obligated to remain behind:

April 4, 1992, Saturday. On this sunny early spring morning automatic weapon fire breaks out bringing with it two short but fateful words: CIVIL WAR. The war began unexpectedly and rapidly. So rapidly that we did not observe when it came through the door that was left ajar. It was the door of our previously peaceful and happy lives. The war came as an unknown stranger whom no one invited or loved. With him he brought his inseparable friends: DEATH, HUNGER, DISEASE, MISERY, and MISFORTUNE.

April 17, 1992. As children of well-to-do and well-known parents we were "lucky" to depart from the Dante-oid hell of Sarajevo. We left in hope for a quick return to this, for us, the most beautiful city in the world.

This unique city of Olympic Winter Games [1984] fame is a place of the collision and intermingling of three faiths and cultures: Islam, Christianity [both Orthodox and Catholic], and Judaism. All this is now gone; destroyed by heartless barbarians who only sow death and hate. But we retained our soul, the soul of that Sarajevo, of that Bosnia which consists of its inhabitants.

If it were not for this damnable, insane war which happened in our homeland everything would be different. Surely, we would have continued to be strong and honorable persons from whose face smiles never parted. Now we have the feeling that we have been diminished in every regard and lost much: home, friends, and homeland.

Fleeting memories of happy times, joy, peace, and family life surface by themselves. Now we are alone in a strange world, with strange people whom we are trying to love and receive love from. But what once was can never come again. What remained is only the memory of our happy childhood, our Sarajevo, our Bosnia, which is now being ravaged from all directions as they want to destroy it so it will exist no longer. Now we are all dispersed, each in her or his own direction, all over the world. Only now we know what we had and what we lost.

But sometimes in moments of happiness a defiant self arises which does not allow us to surrender to despair. It prods us further and further and further because the hope remains in all of us—that Bosnian spirit—believing that despite all the savagery and horror our Bosnia remains in our hearts in the way we loved it and the way in which we saw it the last time on April 17, 1992: HAPPY, PURE, and UNBLOODIED.

Munich, Germany, December 29, 1993

Anesa and Leila Hrustanović

The enormity of suffering during war is such that one is tempted not to describe it, research it, analyze it, theorize about it. Yet if others are to understand and be able to respond, we must go beyond the personal, the anecdotal, the emotional, the horrible, the lofty. This will be our task in the following chapters.

CHAPTER **2**

MYTHO-HISTORY

Long before the warfare broke out, someone once remarked that Yugoslavia was "the despair of tidy minds." Indeed, *many* people, bewildered by media reports, were looking for someone to simplify and clarify what seemed to be a complex problem. However, the danger of simplifying is that it may lead to distortion. Those who look for simplicity need read no further, because this attempt to explain what has been going on is bound to be far more complex than what can be gleaned from journalists. Nevertheless, the extremely complex issue is ultimately understandable if we build our knowledge upon a fine foundation of basics.

Who are these former Yugoslavs who are locked in a struggle over sovereignty, territory, independence, and national pride? Even this question is more complicated than it seems. Simply put, they are Slovenians, Macedonians, Croatians, Montenegrins, Serbians, Albanians, Hungarians, Gypsies, and myriad others. Each group represents distinguishable national and linguistic characteristics; and some groups are related to each other and some not. Nor are the groups easily defined. Are Montenegrins a separate nationality or are they simply Serbs who live in the land of the Black Mountains (the native name for the country is Crna Gora, meaning Black Mountain)? Are Macedonians a distinct Slavic group or are they rather southern Serbs, or western Bulgarians, or northern Greeks—or are they a mixture of ethnicities defined by the territory which they inhabit? Are Dalmatians and Slavonians ethnically identical to Croatians, or were some of them in the past a different nationality until defined by a common religion and a common ruler? Why are 30 percent of the population in Serbia non-Serbs, while a third of all Serbs live outside Serbia?

History alone does not yield clear answers to these questions. Nationalism is a modern tendency. The predecessors of these modern "nationalities" were not organized along ethnic lines, but were instead under the feudal claims of powerful overlords or religious affiliations that united diverse clans and tribes, and for whom ethnicity and language were of small concern. In any case, the reader ought to be aware of the many contradictory nationalist claims because nearly all of them are based on tendentious reinterpretations of past history. To quote the Macedonian scholar, Vladimir Gligorov:

> . . . history is still on the level of mythical storytelling, so that every generation reinvents its collective memory. Not only current but also historical identities are contested territory. The same arguments over the names, origins, defining criteria, territories, cultures, religious contributions, and heritage are exchanged in historical as well as contemporary terms. History is perceived as primarily supplying the required justification for the current national and political interests.[1]

The impunity with which scholars, journalists, politicians, and clergy use their freewheeling imagination to rewrite this or that segment of history is shocking. Their sometimes bizarre interpretations are made plausible by past repressions of certain events and persons or by the demands of certain rulers. Presently, large segments of the population gullibly accept a variety of contradictory new pseudo-historical interpretations which answer some deeply felt psychological needs to bolster their positive self-image or cast aspersion on their ethnic rivals. For that reason no extended discussion of the history of that part of the Balkan peninsula which later came to be united into Yugoslavia will be attempted here beyond the most rudimentary information needed to understand and identify the nations that play a role in the present warfare.

Prior to the sixth and seventh century there is little evidence of Slavic tribes in the Balkans; the population was Illyrian,

---

1. Vladimir Gligorov, "Balkanization: A Theory of Constitution Failure," *East European Politics and Societies*, Vol. VI, No. 3 (Fall 1992), p. 301.

Greek, Roman, Avar, and various other peoples. They were generally controlled by the Roman and later the Eastern Roman, i.e., Byzantine, empires. As the hold of the Roman Empire weakened, a "power vacuum" was created which was conducive to the settlement of migratory tribes. The Slavs migrated southward from their presumed land of origin beyond the Carpathian mountains in what is today Ukraine and southeast Poland. Their settlement was largely peaceful, although occasional wars were waged, particularly against the Greeks. They were organized in numerous clans and tribes that were gradually united by war and absorption with the more dominant Croat, Serb, Slovene, and similar tribes.

A short survey of the major historical events of each of the six former republics which made up the Yugoslavia federation follows.

SERBS

The Serbs[2] are numerically the largest and have been politically the most potent in the last two centuries. That is a good enough reason to start with them. It should be mentioned that the present area inhabited by Serbs is vastly larger than the states which they consider to be the origin of their national identity.

The Serb *(Srbi)* tribe (or amalgam of tribes) migrated south of the Danube river to the sources of the Morava and Vardar rivers, the former flowing north into the Danube and the latter south into the Aegean Sea. Some tribal chieftains evolved into rulers who took on the title of *knez* (duke), and their descendants the title of kings or even emperors. After their settlement in the seventh century they fell under Byzantine cultural and religious influence and were converted to Christianity around 870 by Saints Cyril and Methodius or their apostles. The form of Christianity which the Serbs acquired does not fundamentally differ from Greek Orthodoxy except that the liturgy is in Old Slavonic. This was the language bequeathed to nearly all Slavs in common by these two Greek missionary brothers, who, it should be remembered, had the blessings not only of the Patriarch of Constantino-

---

2. Terminologically, I am using the word "Serb" to designate the nationality and "Serbian" to designate the land, the language, and the Serb inhabitants of Serbia. The same distinction applies to "Croat" and "Croatian" and "Slovene" and "Slovenian."

ple but also of the Pope in Rome to spread Christianity in its Slavic form among Slavs both East and West. Early Serbian kings sought papal blessing and coronation as much as they did Byzantine and patriarchal. Though great stress is placed today that they embraced the eastern branch of Christianity, called Orthodoxy, it should be noted that all the diplomacy of Serb royalty for blessing by Constantinople or Rome happened well before the Great Schism, which tore apart Orthodoxy and Catholicism in 1054. Nowhere has this schism had more fateful and tragic effect than in the Balkans, even to the present day.

Originally there were two states, Zeta (later called Dukla) near the Adriatic Sea roughly where Montenegro lies today, and Raška to the east in the southern part of contemporary Serbia. Steven Nemanja (1169–96) is regarded as the founder of the first stable Serbian state, and his third son, Sava, is credited as the founder of the autonomous Serbian Orthodox Church. Both are regarded as saints by the Serbian Orthodox Church. Thereafter there was no longer a clear separation between the interests of the Church and those of the Serbian nation. These Orthodox Serbs adopted the Cyrillic alphabet (named in honor of St. Cyril), based on Greek. Thus their orthography is the same as that of the Bulgarians, Russians, Ukrainians, and Byelorussians.

Another characteristic of Serbian Orthodoxy is *"Svetosavlje,"* veneration of the above-mentioned St. Sava. *"Svetosavlje"* is devoid of concrete doctrinal content. It is not a deviation or augmentation of Orthodox doctrine but is primarily a celebration and glorification of the Serbian Christian identity. Interestingly, the idea of *"Svetosavlje"* began long after the death of St. Sava and it took on an aura of martyrdom and suffering that would reflect Serbian suffering in later centuries. By and large, it has been a way of shrouding the Serbian identity in a cloak of mystery that is called upon to protect the Serbian people in times of crises. Lately, Serbians have taken their *Serbian* identity far more seriously than their *Orthodox* identity. Leaders of the Serbian Orthodox Church generally promote a close identity of the two terms, seeing that they feed upon each other.

After several kings, some of whom tried to play Rome against Constantinople, the mightiest of the Serbian rulers, Tsar Steven Dušan the Mighty (1333–55), chiseled out an empire in which he claimed to be the emperor of Serbs and Byzantines and hence master of Bulgaria, Greece, and Albania. He promoted the leader of his church to the patriarchal level. The irony is that soon after his death this empire fell apart. In 1389 the Serbians were routed in the battle of Kosovo Field by the Ottoman Turks. For the next four centuries the destiny of the Serb people was to be in various forms of Turkish dependency.

In the earlier periods of Turkish dominance the well-being of the Serb population was not good but it was tolerable. As the Turkish Empire deteriorated, greater abuses of power by local Turkish overlords took place, thus shaping the image in the Serb psyche that the entire period of Turkish control had been horrible. Therefore, in the Serb mind, the greatest threat to their nation comes from the Muslim Turks, closely rivaled by the threat from Catholicism. Interestingly, the Turks were religiously the more tolerant, whereas the Christian allies, the Austrians, believed that it was their duty to convert the Orthodox Serbs to Catholicism—something the Serbs resented bitterly. Serbs to this day feel threatened by both Catholicism and Islam. Simultaneously, under the Turks the Orthodox and Serbian identity coalesced even closer because the Turks allowed the Orthodox clergy to serve as surrogate rulers in certain local matters, no Serbian secular leadership being permitted.

Several incidents are imbedded in the collective memory of Serbians. One is that they lost a closely contested battle at Kosovo, during which both the Turkish sultan and the Serbian king were killed. The second is a memory of bitter Turkish overlordship, during which time the Serbian nobility became extinct and Serbians became a nation of peasants led by a small cadre of clergy and merchants. The Serbs have nurtured heroic folk poetry in which their heros, especially Prince Mark (quite contrary to the historical record, which shows him to have been a Turkish vassal), regularly beat the Turks. They also developed a special brand of brigandry, named *hajduk*, which allegedly has preyed upon Turks in order to divide the spoils among the poorer people and has been lauded as heroic up to the present day.

The great migrations of Serbs, led by their patriarch and clergy from Kosovo and southern Serbia, to Hungary and Croatia also figure large in Serb memory. Since the northern Balkan peninsula was contested by the Hapsburg and Ottoman empires, a *cordon sanitaire* between the two feuding empires, called the *Vojna Krajina* (Military Frontier) was created. For several hundred years the Serbs and Croats living in this border region constituted a permanent fighting force against the Muslim Turks on behalf of Christendom. They felt that they protected Europe from Turkization and Islamization. To this day they consider themselves to be the last bastion of European civilization against the "dark forces" of Islam.

In the meantime, Kosovo was being repopulated by the northward migration of Albanians. These great migrations, forced by Turkish or Islamic colonialism, are the reason for the great intermingling of populations. This forced ethnic mix has given rise to contradictory claims and efforts to separate themselves from each other by means of what is today called "ethnic cleansing."

The tide began turning in Serbia's favor beginning with the First Serbian Uprising in 1804, under George Petrović, nicknamed Karadjordje. During the nineteenth century, more and more Serbian territory was liberated as formerly Turkish-occupied lands were relinquished piece by piece. This process was hampered by the great powers, which frequently denied Serbs at the negotiation table what they won on the battlefield, and has engendered much bitterness. Indeed, it has fueled the feeling that the world is against Serbia and that the Serbs can rely only on the tenacity of their soldiers and the force of their arms. Only the Russian Empire, another Orthodox power, has provided steady support to the Serbs and Montenegrins, thereby nurturing a mutual friendship. Belgrade became the capital, thus shifting the focus of Serbian statehood from Kosovo and southern Serbia to the north, and the Danube River basin. Many Serbs in the meantime also settled the southern regions of the Panonian plains, which were controlled by the Austro-Hungarians.

During the nineteenth and early twentieth century two rival families, the Karadjordjević and the Obrenović, rotated in a power struggle. Meanwhile, toward the end of the last century Serbia was placed into almost a vassal dependence upon the Hapsburg Empire, a development that was greatly resented and fuels even to this day a great suspicion of Germanic intentions to dominate the Balkans. Ultimately the Karadjordjević family led Serbia through two Balkan wars, in 1912 and 1913, and World War I and emerged as the royal family of the newly formed Kingdom of Serbs, Croats, and Slovenes.

During the two Balkan wars, the Turks were nearly pushed out of Europe by an alliance of Greece, Montenegro, Serbia, and

Bulgaria, Bulgaria falling out, however, against the others in the second Balkan war—which gave the Serbs a victory and preeminence in the newly liberated lands of Macedonia. Thus, at the outset of World War I Serbia had already emerged as the predominant Slavic state in the Balkans, poised to lead other Slavic states to independence. The tragedy was that the finally independent united state of southern Slavs was perceived differently by the Serbs, who saw themselves as the agents of liberation, and the other Slavic peoples, who envisioned a different process of unification. More about this in Chapter 5.

Between the two world wars the Serbian monarchy, officials, and bureaucracy (both civilian and military) were dominant. No stable government could be formed because of irreconcilable party differences, and in 1929 King Alexander I proclaimed a royal dictatorship. After a brief flirting with the Axis powers under Prince Regent Paul, the Serbs rejected Hitler's overtures and consequently suffered the military invasion of Yugoslavia in 1941 by Germany, Italy, Hungary, and Bulgaria and a partitioning of the country into about ten units.

Several months after the invasion, the Serbs began a revolt against the Nazi occupation which initiated a war of national liberation. Since this led to the reunification of a liberated Yugoslavia in 1945, the Serbs considered themselves as champions of the effort, having sacrificed the most for victory, while the Croats, Slovenes, and Macedonians were viewed as having collaborated with the enemy. But the multinational Communist Party, under whose leadership the war of liberation took place, claimed full credit for the victory and described the process of liberation to be a socialist revolution of all of the peoples of Yugoslavia rather than giving most credit to the Serbs.

When World War II ended, Tito, a Croat Communist, imposed internal borders between the six states without benefit of any discussion or negotiations.[3] Serbia was assigned a smaller territory than it had traditionally aspired to. Not only that, but Serbia was the only republic in which two autonomous regions were established. One of them was Vojvodina and the other Kosovo.

---

3. I agree with Bogdan Denitch that these borders were the fairest possible. See his *Ethnic Nationalism: The Tragic Death of Yugoslavia* (Minneapolis and London: University of Minnesota Press, 1994), p. 26.

These provinces have characteristics somewhat different from those of Serbia proper.

Vojvodina is a fertile area in the Panonian plain north of the Danube river. For most of its history it had been a fairly uninhabited part of Hungary, although for a while it was under Turkish rule. It was later incorporated into the Austrian Empire. Under the Austrian empress Maria Theresa all nationalities were encouraged to settle the marshes of Vojvodina; these drained, one of the most fertile areas of Europe emerged. Vojvodina is even more ethnically mixed than the rest of the Balkans. In it live Hungarians, Germans, Serbs, Croats, Slovaks, Ruthenians, Romanians, Jews, Gypsies, and others. Serbs, however, became the most numerous group, and after the fall of the Austro-Hungarian monarchy the land was bequeathed to Serbia. During World War II, Vojvodina was partitioned: Bačka fell under the control of Hungary, Srem under Croatia, and Banat was administered directly by the Germans. After World War II, Tito declared it to be an autonomous province within the Serbian republic. In 1989 the government of Slobodan Milošević carried out a *Putsch* and eliminated the autonomous status without consultation with the other republics, claiming that this was an internal matter of Serbia's.

The Serbs of Vojvodina were among the best educated and most industrious and had a different sense of identity from the Serbs south of the Danube River. Some of that difference was erased by the large number of migrants from Montenegro, Kosovo, and Bosnia-Herzegovina who were resettled there after the war's end.

Kosovo is a smaller province located in a plain in the southwestern region of Serbia. It was the cradle of Serb civilization in the Middle Ages, and some of the most significant Serbian religious and cultural monuments are located there. The Serbs' patriarchal seat was, in fact, for centuries in Peć. And it was on Kosovo Field that in 1389 the Serbian Army was defeated by the Turks, becoming a landmark of great mytho-legendary significance, a kind of defining moment for Serbian self-awareness. However, during the seventeenth century, in response to Turkish depredations, large Serb migrations to the north and west took place. The vacuum was quickly filled by Albanian Muslims (and some Catholics), who spread northward from Albania proper and called the province "Kosova." Interestingly, it was one of the last pieces of land that the eventually retreating Ottoman Turks ceded to the Serbs. There has been no end to the debates about who should rightfully control this land.

During World War II Kosovo was given to Albania, at that time under Italian military rule; but it was returned to Yugoslavia following the war. Between 1945 and 1948 it appeared that Albania might be annexed by Yugoslavia, in which case Kosovo would not have been such a contested land. But this did not take place. Instead, Albanians in Kosovo were held in strict control by the Serb personnel of the secret police. When that control was relaxed in the 1970s and Yugoslavia became decentralized, the Albanians there requested more autonomy and a severe conflict broke out in which both nationalities claimed that genocide was being carried out by the other.

The population ratio of Albanians to Serbs in Kosovo since the 1980s is 9:1. Albanians claim they have been in the majority for centuries. A 1921 census does, indeed, support the contention that they were in a slight majority. Nevertheless, Serbs claim that they were *once* in the majority and were driven out by Albanians; the Albanians say they were always in the majority and that the Serbs are now trying to push them out. None of the population figures are accurate; each side produces its own. Since 1989, Kosovo has been under Serbian martial law. A condition of virtual apartheid exists, which is likely to explode in the foreseeable future.

CROATS

Geographically adjacent to the Serbs and linguistically their closest kin are the Croats *(Hrvati)*, who established a homeland west of the Serbians. The second-largest association of southern Slavic tribes, the Croats settled the northwestern region of the Panonian plains and Dalmatia, the land along the Adriatic coast, forming a boomerang-shaped territory. After migration there, they fell under the sway of the Romans, who had numerous settlements in Dalmatia.

Originally there were two Croatian states, Panonian Croatia in the north and Dalmatian Croatia in the south. The Croat people were converted to Christianity around the year 800 A.D. by Frankish missionaries who were loyal to Rome; henceforth the country became steadfastly devoted to the papacy. In the ninth century an independent Croat kingdom emerged which blossomed under the kings Tomislav (925–28) and Zvonimir (1076–89). From the outset the kingdom maintained close relationships with Rome and after the Great Schism in the eleventh century saw itself as the southeastern outpost of Roman Catholicism. It is hard to overestimate the importance of the Great Schism in creating a rift between the Serbs and Croats both religiously and culturally. Croats gravitated to Rome and the West; Serbs to Constantinople and the East. History separated them even further when the last Croatian king died without an heir. The Croat nobility selected king Koloman of Hungary as their own, thereby creating a union by which they maintained a quasi-independence under the authority of the Hungarian ruling house. When the Hungarian royal line died out, the Hungarians and Croats selected the Austrian Hapsburgs as their kings and emperors.

During the Turkish expansion toward Vienna in the sixteenth century, large sections of Croatia were also under Turkish control, the demarcation line between the two rival empires moving back and forth. Occasionally Croat nobility rebelled against Vienna; best remembered by Croats was the unsuccessful anti-Hapsburg rebellion by *ban* (governor) Nikola Zrinski and nobleman Krste Frankopan in the seventeenth century. During the uprising Vienna purposely permitted the Turks to inflict damages upon Croatia and Hungary in order to weaken the nobility of these two countries. Thus the Croats, like the Serbs, also remember a defeat which they have turned into a mythical affirmation of the courage of their nation and the deceptiveness of their neighbors. By the end of the eighteenth century the Croats were no longer under Turkish rule. Turkish control did, however, continue for Croats who lived in Bosnia and Herzegovina, but eventually, by 1878, those Croats became also a part of the Austro-Hungarian Empire.

The Croats as well as the neighboring Slovenes were impacted by the Reformation and even more so by the sweeping Counter-Reformation. Segments of the Croatian nobility were attracted by the Protestant promise of greater independence from the staunchly Catholic Hapsburgs, but the Hungarian hegemony in

Croatia tended to sway many Croatian noblemen toward a pro-Austrian and therefore Counter-Reformation position. The playing off of Vienna against Budapest was typical of the Croats well into the twentieth century as they sought the greater advantage to themselves. Thus, for instance, during both the famous 1848 Hungarian Revolt and the 1868 negotiations that resulted in the agreement to form a dual monarchy the Croats played the pro-Viennese card, hoping to gain more autonomy for themselves. The Croats hoped for concessions similar to those the Hungarians received from the Hapsburgs.

The main threat to Croatians were, then in 1868 and earlier, the Germanizing and Hungarianizing tendencies emanating from Vienna and Budapest. Of the two, the more immediate threat was Magyarization. Hence the Croats under Ban Josip Jelačić helped Vienna crush the Hungarian Revolt of 1848. But they were not rewarded for their loyalty and came to realize by the early twentieth century that neither the Austrians nor Hungarians were willing to make significant concessions to their own aspirations for autonomy. The Austrians were not willing to give Hungarians what (in effect) they had, the Hungarians were not willing to give Croats what they sought from the Austrians, and the Croats were not willing to give to Serbs in Croatia what they asked for themselves from Hungarians. Ultimately, however, Croats oriented themselves toward an alliance with other southern Slavs, particularly the ever more victorious Serbians. There *was* a faction among the Croats which was explicitly anti-Serb, but the Yugoslav idea promoted by the great Catholic archbishop Josip Juraj Strossmayer prevailed and Croats ultimately opted for unification with the other southern Slavs.

The history of Dalmatia has been quite different from Panonian Croatia. Here Italian—that is, Venetian—influence was paramount. The city of Dubrovnik, like Venice, was a city-state with a republican form of government. For years it rivaled Venice in successful trade relations, but eventually the Venetians were able to subdue the entire Dalmatian coast and stamp upon it distinct Italian cultural features, including making Italian the fashionable language among influential citizens. In time Austria replaced Venice as the master of the Adriatic shoreline and islands, although significant pockets of Italian population remained in the cities. As late as 1923 there was an Italian fascist takeover of the city of Zadar (Zara) and in World War II Italians again occupied the entire Dalmatian coast. Dalmatia was finally united with Croatia proper (the area around Zagreb) and Slavonia (northeastern Croatia) in 1918, forming a single Croat state.

Almost from the beginnings of the newly created Yugoslav state, many Croat politicians were in radical opposition to the Belgrade government. Especially uncooperative was the leader of the Croatian Peasant Party, Stjepan Radić. The conflict in the parliament escalated so sharply that in 1929 a Montenegrin member of the parliament killed him, his brother, and two other Croat deputies. While the moderate Croat leaders found some ways of cooperating with the Serbs, particularly those living in the former Austro-Hungarian regions, an extreme right-wing movement, called *Ustasha*, was being organized by Ante Pavelić. It was supported by fascist Italy and Nazi Germany. After the quick collapse of Yugoslavia under the onslaught of the Axis forces, Hitler and Mussolini permitted Pavelić to form the Independent State of Croatia. There were Croats who distanced themselves from and opposed this puppet regime, but for many Croats the creation of an independent state was the culmination of a national dream, and they were willing to overlook the atrocities committed in its behalf.

The collapse of Nazism brought about the collapse of the Independent State of Croatia. Croatia became one of the republics in the new federal Yugoslavia led by a Communist of their own nationality, Josip Broz, more commonly known as Tito. The majority of Croats accepted this for about three decades. However, since the late 1970s (Tito died in 1980), an increasing number of Croats revived the hope for a sovereign state, a condition which they achieved in 1991 but at the cost of the breakout of the Serb-Croat war (see Chapter 6).

SLOVENES

The Slovenes *(Sloventsi)* are the earliest-mentioned Slavic people (because their name is synonymous with the generic name for all Slavs, *Sloveni*), but they had the shortest period of independence. Upon migration to the northwestern regions of the Balkan peninsula and the southern Alpine district, they were first under the Avars, then around 630 became part of the Slavic kingdom of King Samo, then came under the rule of Bavarian and Friulian dukes until they finally fell under Frankish domination. Under Charlemagne in the early ninth century they were Christianized. Later, as part of the Holy Roman Empire, they were organized into the provinces of Carinthia, Carniola, and Styria. For a brief period in the thirteenth century they were a part of the Slavic kingdom of Bohemia of King Ottokar, but then they fell under the rule of the Hapsburg dynasty, under whose control they remained until 1918.

Having been under Germanic domination for over a millennium, the Slovenes were naturally Germanized and might have been completely absorbed into Germanic culture had not religion and literature played a role in raising their national consciousness. The religious moment was short but decisive. In the sixteenth century the influence of the Protestant Reformation reached Slovenia and had a strong following among both the nobility and the townspeople. Primož Trubar translated the New Testament into Slovene, and thus, as Luther did for Germany, founded the vernacular culture. Other reformers, especially in cooperation with the like-minded Croats, worked on a grammar for the language, a translation of the Old Testament, a catechism, and a variety of other books. Despite the effort of the Protestants, however, the Catholic Counter-Reformation was soon almost completely successful and the Slovenes became Roman Catholic once more, except for a few parishes in the Prekmurje part of this small country. Nevertheless, although most of the Reformation books were destroyed as heretical, the memory of the use of the Slovene language remained and was clandestinely nurtured. Empress Maria Theresa and her son Joseph II permitted the use of Slovene literature during their enlightened rule.

Another boost to Slovene national self-consciousness was Napoleon's conquest of Slovenia and Dalmatia and the creation of the Napoleonic province of Illyria. Local customs of the area were respected and economic prosperity greatly increased. Ideas of the French Revolution arrived and the Napoleonic Code was introduced. The teaching of Slovenian was encouraged in schools and the works of the priest Valentin Vodnik spread ideas about the relatedness of Slovenes with Croats and Serbs.

Upon the defeat of Napoleon, Slovenes were again denied their local autonomy and the Slovene identity was kept alive primarily by poets like Jernej Kopitar and France Prešern. In the late nineteenth century the Slovenes put some pressure on Vienna to establish a kingdom of Slovenia within the Hapsburg Empire, but this came to naught and only the status of Hungary was raised to the level of Austria. Slovenes grew increasingly restless with persistent policies of Germanization and started to look more and more to some sort of alliance with the neighboring Croats and Serbs. During World War I the Slovene representatives in the parliament of Vienna urged that all southern Slavs be united in a Yugoslav kingdom that would remain within the Hapsburg Empire. But events outstripped that proposal. When the Empire collapsed after the war, the idea of a *separate* Yugoslav state became the dominant one. Slovenia became part of the newly founded Kingdom of the Serbs, the Croats, and the Slovenes (which was the first official title of the country, to be renamed as Yugoslavia in 1929).

During the volatile interwar period Slovenia was dominated by a conservative clerical party led by the Catholic priest, Anton Korošec, who had been briefly prime minister just prior to King Alexander's proclamation of royal dictatorship in 1929. The Slovenes, like the Croats and the Serbs living outside Serbia proper, were generally not happy with policies generated in Belgrade. Increasingly a sense of alienation from Yugoslavia occurred, so that when the country was conquered in 1941 by the Axis powers quite a few Slovenes favored this turn of events.

During World War II Slovenia was partitioned between Germany and Italy. A struggle against these occupying forces was mounted by the Liberation Front, which consisted of a coalition dominated by Communists. The Liberation Front led Slovenia back into the "New Yugoslavia" upon the end of the war. Then, in the 1980s Slovenia spearheaded the drive to gain independence and sovereignty and in 1991 became the first Yugoslav republic to secede. Thus, in 1991, Slovenia—for the first time in more than a millennium—became a sovereign, independent, internationally recognized nation. One need not be surprised that the Slovenes were euphoric.

BOSNIANS AND HERZEGOVINIANS

Contrary to the claims frequently heard from Western politicians and journalists, Bosnia and Herzegovina is not a well-established nation. There was never a Bosnian nation, although there was briefly a Bosnian state in the Middle Ages. It is debatable whether a functional Bosnian state was established, except in a *legal* sense, since its precipitous international recognition in the spring of 1992—the wisdom of which will be argued by politicians and scholars for years to come.

Bosnia is the land that is located in the middle of the former Yugoslavia. Its borders are fairly undefined except in the north, where the Sava River separates it from Croatia, and in the east, where the Drina River defines a border with Serbia. The extent of Bosnia has varied greatly over the centuries and this land was ruled by a bewildering succession of nations: Byzantines, Hungarians, Croatians, Serbians, Turks, Austrians, and several native Bosnian dynasties. For most of its history it was ruled by outsiders and, hence, there never developed a distinct Bosnian nationality. Bosnians and Herzegovinians are Slavic peoples, but there has always been a tug-of-war about which ethnicity is the most Bosnian, the primary two claimants being Serbs and Croats, but, later, Slavic Muslims asserting themselves along with the other two.

Herzegovina, which in the last three centuries has been increasingly linked with Bosnia, is the former region of Hum, an inhospitable mountain area to the south of Bosnia and bordering on Montenegro and Dalmatia. Herzegovina shared Bosnia's destiny of being ruled by all the same nations. In the sixteenth century, Hum was ruled by a duke, which title in German is *Herzog*, hence the name Herzegovina.

Bosnian statehood came later, compared to that of the other Yugoslav states. The first native ruler of Bosnia was the legendary Kulin-ban, in the twelfth century. The Christian population had already been split up by the Great Schism of a century before, when some segments of the population declared their loyalty to the Orthodox Church while the rest committed themselves to the Catholic. Concurrently, the arrival of the Bogumil heresy from Bulgaria further complicated matters.

Bogumilism had a great impact on both the peasantry and nobility of Bosnia and soon became the predominant faith. It was a Christian faith that rejected hierarchy, sacraments, pomp and circumstance, and was ruled by ascetic semi-monastic elders who held a somewhat dualistic theological view in which the material sphere was regarded as evil and the spiritual as good. Bogumils became so influential that some of the Bosnian kings accepted this religion and established the "Bosnian Church." Thereby they incurred the wrath of both the Orthodox and the Catholics, who attacked them as heretics. Older historiographers saw the Bogumils as part of the Patarene, or Paulician, heresy, but more recent historiographers argue that it was not the theology of that church which was unorthodox, and therefore objectionable to the Orthodox and the Catholics, but that this church wanted to maintain independence from the churches of neighboring lands and would not take sides in the Great Schism. The Catholic Church waged battle against the Bosnian Church, the Hungarian king even leading crusades as a pretext for occupying Bosnia.

Following short periods of Croat, Hungarian, and Serbian rule over Bosnia, several very able local rulers emerged. One was King Stephen Kotromanić and another was his nephew, Tvrtko I (1353–91), who, by the successful expansion of his domain, had proclaimed himself king of Serbia, Bosnia, and Croatia, including large regions of Dalmatia, and was thus the first king to unite the South Slavic heartland. His kingdom suffered the same fate as the empire of Tsar Dušan of Serbia; it collapsed almost immediately upon his death. By 1463 the last Bosnian king surrendered to the Turks, who controlled Bosnia-Herzegovina until late in the nineteenth century with only sporadic challenges to their rule.

The arrival of the Turks was not entirely unwelcome to the Bosnians. While large numbers of Orthodox and Catholics fled Bosnia at that time, the majority of the people who had belonged to the Bosnian Church regarded the Turks as more tolerant than Christians. Many of the Bogumil nobility were willing to accept Islam not only because the two religions were not terribly different from one another but because thereby they could share in the benefits the Turks were willing to offer all Muslims. Thus, ever since the fifteenth century a very sizable portion of the Bosnian population became Muslim, retaining no memory of their ethnoreligious ancestry. The remaining Catholic and Orthodox population was subjugated and reduced to near-serfdom and to life in the countryside as farmers and shepherds. They were leaderless, except that the Franciscan Order kept a semi-secret presence, sharing the poverty of the local Catholic population and ministering to them. To this day, therefore, Franciscans are very popular among Croats. The Orthodox Serbs were ministered to by Orthodox parish priests who were often not much better educated than their parishioners. The Muslims, on the other hand, inhabited the cities and made up the civil and military bureaucracy, landowner, merchant, and craftsmen classes. They were ruled by Shariate law and had an educated leadership as well as strong Sufi mystic orders. The Bosnian towns were built on the Near Eastern model.

During the height of the Ottoman Turkish Empire, Turkish colonial oppression was not excessive. With the decline of the empire the local Muslims, because of their proximity to the borders of the Christian states, became ever more conservative and oppressive, and frequently defied Istanbul. They regarded the attempted reforms in the Ottoman Empire as anti-Islamic and considered the Sultan an apostate. They therefore frequently rebelled against the central authority. These rebellions were always eventually suppressed after much bloodshed, and so were the frequent rebellions by the Bosnian Christian populations—encouraged by neighboring Christian states—against their local Muslim overlords. Bloodshed and cruelty are thus no strangers to Bosnians and Herzegovinians.

Under the pretext of helping the Christian population in Bosnia, the Hapsburg emperor succeeded in taking over Bosnia-Herzegovina in 1878 although it remained *figuratively* under Turkish sovereignty. The Austrians brought with them large numbers of Catholics of various nationalities, which made the ethnic composition of Bosnia even more complex than it already was. Catholicism became the religion favored by the new government, while the Muslims and the Orthodox were in retreat. The emergent Serbian state was very upset by the Austrian presence, and it cooperated with the local Bosnian Serbs in resisting the Austrians.

When, in 1908, Austria-Hungary fully annexed Bosnia and Herzegovina with no prior negotiation, Serbian dissatisfaction more sharply increased. Various nationalistic Serb clandestine groups, some of which were directly linked with the Belgrade government, increased their plotting against the Austrians. When, on June 28, 1914, the Archduke Ferdinand and his wife visited Sarajevo, a young Serb nationalist student by the name Gavrilo Princip assassinated them. The shots that rang out in Sarajevo were "heard around the world," for they became the pretext for Austria's subsequent ultimatum to Serbia which began "the Great War." The war devastated Serbia and Macedonia because many great battles were fought on the soil of these lands. The southern Slavs frequently found themselves drafted into opposing armies, thereby turning the conflict for them into a fratricidal war.

Upon the eventual establishment of the Yugoslav state, it was the Orthodox religion that replaced Catholicism as the most influential in Bosnia. Now it was the Muslims' and Catholics' turn to retreat, and the Muslims fared worse, for there was a strong feeling by both Orthodox and Catholics that sooner or later the Slavic Muslims ought to be reconverted to Christianity. The Christians now revenged themselves for the centuries of Turkish oppression, often taking it out on the local Muslim Slavs whom they called "Turks" or *poturice* (those who abandoned their ethnicity and became Turks). In the nineteenth and twentieth century, Christians massacred Muslims in retaliation for earlier Muslim massacres. The ancient but still valid customary law of the Balkans is vendetta—"eye for an eye"—or better yet, "two of your eyes for one of mine."

When World War II broke out, many of the Croatian Bosnians immediately opted to be joined to the collaborationist Independent State of Croatia. Parts of Herzegovina were turned over to Italy. It was from Herzegovina where Ante Pavelić and many of his most extremist *ustashe* came. Like right-wing Croats, many Muslims joined the *ustashe* and some of them were drafted by the Germans into special SS divisions. (It is generally believed that the most irreconcilable and fiercest fighters come from Herzegovina, the land of barren rocks where even the snakes are the most poisonous. "Similar plants grow on the same arid soil" was a remark by an Orthodox Bosnian priest as he sought to explain why Serbs, Croats, and Muslims from Herzegovina show the same determined hostility toward those not of their own ethnicity. Herzegovinians, regardless of ethnicity and religion, fight mercilessly.)

Throughout the entire war Bosnia-Herzegovina became a land of tears. One bloody battle after another took place in which the participants were German and Italian armies, *ustashe* and *domobran* (home guard) Croat units, Muslim SS and irregulars, Serbian *chetniks* (nationalist irregulars) and Communist-led *partizans* (guerrillas). They engaged each other in every way but peaceful. They burned, raped, pillaged, massacred entire villages and towns. Ravines were filled with thousands of bodies, some shot, others knifed, and still others simply pushed over precipices. No one was spared—no babies, no sick, no octogenarians, no pregnant women. No one. It was for that reason that everyone in Yugoslavia knew that if a war ever broke out again in this land it would be another holocaust.

When Yugoslavia started to fall apart, the Muslims (over 40 percent of the Bosnian population) and Croats (nearly 20 percent) favored the establishment of a sovereign state; the Serbs (about 33 percent of the population) would not hear of this and wanted to remain within Yugoslavia. Believing that the Muslims and Croats were conspiring against them so that they would have the majority in any election, the Bosnian Serbs decided to boycott and declare the elections non-binding. The Muslims and Croats and some of the Serbs went ahead anyway and elected a government headed by Alija Izetbegović, one which the Serbs relentlessly opposed. That government, without negotiations with the local Serbs, declared Bosnia sovereign and independent. The newly formed government envisioned itself as having the right to form Bosnian statehood, which it had lost in the fifteenth century. The Serbs on the other hand did not want to be separated from fellow Serbs. The precipitous international recognition of Bosnia-Herzegovina angered the Serbs of both Bosnia and Serbia, and the war commenced at once. (For details see Chapter 6).

MACEDONIANS

The southernmost republic of the former Yugoslavia was called Macedonia. The name is an ancient one even going back to before Alexander the Great of Macedon. It designates an area of land of uncertain borders currently located adjacent to northern Greece, southwestern Bulgaria, and southern Serbia. In antiquity it was, of course, Hellenistic and then, subsequently Byzantine. In about the seventh century Slavic tribes migrated as far south as the Aegean port of Salonika and settled throughout Macedonia. It was from the Salonika Slavs that Saints Cyril and Methodius learned the language which they used in order to spread Christianity among the various Slavic peoples.

Macedonia has been one of the most contested lands. Just about everyone in the region ruled it at one time or another—and, currently, makes claims that it therefore belongs to them. When the Bulgars arrived in the Balkan peninsula and integrated themselves with the local Slavs in the seventh century, they soon challenged Byzantium. Under the first Bulgarian dynasty of Simeon the Great (893–927), Bulgarians ruled over Macedonia. Tsar Samuel (976–1014) ruled in western Macedonia until his army was routed by the Byzantines (see Chapter 3). After a Byzantine period of rule, the second Bulgarian period took place in Macedonia in the twelfth century but it was short-lived. After a confusing period during the Fourth Crusade, when Macedonia became part of the so-called "Latin Kingdom," it became a part of the Serbian empire of Tsar Dušan in the fourteenth century. Then came the Turks, who controlled Macedonia until the First Balkan War in 1912.

During Turkish rule, additional population migrations were encouraged and Macedonia's population became one of the most mixed and amorphous in the Balkans. There were many Turks, Albanians, Greeks, Vlachs, Jews, and Gypsies in addition to the Slavs. Each major group claimed that its ethnicity was in the majority and that therefore it should rule the region. The nationality question was actually unimportant until the nineteenth century, when Greeks, Serbs, and Bulgarians all rebelled against the Turks and each stated its claim for the territory.

As Turkey kept retreating, countless local rebellions broke out particularly during the latter part of the nineteenth century and just before the Balkan Wars. Many brigands operated both against the Turks and against each other; the general population suffered the consequences. As a Western historian wrote in 1906, "A word from a Greek bishop would often condemn a whole Bulgarian hamlet to the flames. A Bulgarian band, descending by night upon a hostile village to murder a spy-priest and to burn his house, was not always careful to save his widow and his children from the conflagration."

Most famous of the revolts was the Ilinden Insurrection of 1903 led by the legendary local hero, Gotse Delchev. Over 5,000 people were killed and 3,000 women were raped by Turks as they crushed the two-month-long rebellion. For a brief period the Young Turk rebellion of 1908 gave hope that all these mixed ethnic groups could unite behind a joint program of reform, but the hope was illusory and the fighting continued even more viciously. One of the groups in what later became Yugoslav Macedonia, the Internal Macedonian Revolutionary Organization differed from all the others not in the degree of its violence but in its claim that the Slavs of Macedonia were neither Greeks, nor Bulgars, nor Serbs—but Macedonians. The three neighboring countries, however, continued their respective acquisitive claims, enforced by brutality against those who professed a different ethnic origin.

The First Balkan War, in which Serbia, Bulgaria, Greece, and Montenegro drove Turkey almost out of Europe, placed Macedonia in Bulgarian hands. The Serbs, Montenegrins, Greeks, and Romanians were not happy with the dividing of the spoils, and attacked Bulgaria in the Second Balkan War, of 1913, under which Macedonia fell into Serbian hands. It was not to remain under Serbian control for long, because Bulgaria joined Austria in World War I and wrested control of Macedonia from the Serbs—but only for the duration of the war. After World War I, western Macedonia was proclaimed to be southern Serbia, Bulgaria got a part of eastern Macedonia and declared that Macedonians were Bulgars, while southern Macedonia came under the rule of Greece. Greeks vehemently insisted that Macedonia was Greek and that only a very small and fully Hellenized Slavic population lived there. The Macedonian Slavs claimed that the Hellenization was forced upon them and that the number of Slavs was much greater than the Greeks were willing to admit.

Between the two world wars Macedonia was a part of Yugoslavia as an integral part of Serbia. During World War II Bulgaria again reclaimed Macedonia as a reward for joining the Axis in partitioning Yugoslavia. After World War II, for the first time a separate Macedonian republic was created with the express purpose of being the state of the Macedonian people. Tito and the Communist Party of Yugoslavia promoted the process of ethnic solidification of the Slavs in Macedonia, the capital of which would be Skopje. A Macedonian literary language was created, the political scene was dominated by local politicians, and the Orthodox Church of Macedonia was encouraged to break away from the Serbian Orthodox Church and establish an autonomous Macedonian Orthodox Church in the 1950s (which as yet has not been canonically recognized by other Orthodox churches).

In 1992 Macedonia was permitted to secede from Yugoslavia as a sovereign and independent nation. The Yugoslav Army withdrew without incidents. The Macedonian Orthodox Church is seeking to become autocephalous (completely self-ruling) but has not found much support in the Orthodox world. Among the newly established political parties is the reborn Internal Macedonian Revolutionary Organization, which obtained a majority in the parliament and which has rashly proclaimed that its ultimate purpose is the reunification of all Macedonian lands, including those presently under Greece and Bulgaria. The country was recognized by Turkey and Bulgaria, although the Bulgars do not relish the thought of an expanded Macedonia. But the country has encountered a vociferous opposition by the Greek government and by Greek people both in Greece and abroad, demanding that Macedonia not be given international recognition until it renounces the use of the name "Macedonia" which the Greeks claim is theirs exclusively. They insist that the name of the country be "Skopje" (name of the capital city); the UN finally decided on a temporary name for the country: "The Former Yugoslav Republic of Macedonia," alphabetizing it ridiculously under "T." The United States gave Macedonia diplomatic recognition in 1994 despite Greek opposition. Another problem for Macedonian Slavs is that approximately 25 to 40 percent of the population are ethnic Albanians, who live alongside the Macedonians. The ultimate aspiration of the Albanians seems to be unification with Albania—along with the land on which they dwell.

Therefore, the new country has serious political problems. Its poor economic condition due to lack of resources, capital, a skilled labor force, mountainous terrain, insufficient rainfall, and landlocked location—as well as being surrounded by hostile neighbors—do not bode too well for the new state. Nevertheless, the Macedonians are quite euphoric about their independence and hope to make a go of it.

MONTENEGRINS

The smallest, least populated, poorest, most mountainous, and most isolated former Yugoslav republic is Montenegro (Crna Gora, or Black Mountain), so named for the appearance of some of its mountains from a distance. Much of it lies close to the Adriatic Sea nestled between Albania, Serbia, Bosnia-Herzegovina, and Croatia. During its early history it was a part of the medieval Serbian kingdom, and to this day there are heated discussions of whether Montenegrins are simply Serbs dwelling in the Black Mountains or whether a distinct Montenegrin nationality has emerged. In any case, Serbs and Montenegrins feel a strong affinity for each other and are the two republics which still call themselves Yugoslavia. Its earliest local dynasty at the time when it was still called Zeta, and then Dukla, was the Balša (1355–1421) followed by the Crnojević (1421–1516). By the fifteenth century it had become entirely surrounded by the Turkish conquerors, who, however, were not able to conquer entirely this remote section of the Balkan peninsula, though they tried again and again. The terrain is ideal for guerrilla fighting, as is that of Bosnia-Herzegovina. While the Turks would from time to time capture some of the small towns and fortresses, they could never pacify the mountain-dwelling local clans who were fiercely independent and uncooperative even with each other.

From 1516 to 1851 Montenegro became a theocracy. It was ruled by the bishop, who was named *"vladika,"* or ruler, in both religious and secular matters. At first the bishops were selected at popular assemblies, but from the eighteenth century the office became uniquely hereditary among members of the Petrović family. Since bishops must be celibate, they passed the office to a near relative, usually a nephew, who was groomed to become the next *Vladika*. The best known bishops were Danilo I, Peter I, and the most famous Peter II Petrović-Njegoš (1830–51), who was a poet, a warrior, and ruler. Like his predecessors he made good use of assistance from Russia, Serbia, and even Venice (the latter of which he had to hold at bay), as he fought the Turks and those Montenegrins who had converted to Islam. His poem "Mountain Wreath" is used as an inspiration by many who would eradicate all traces of Islam from the Balkans.

His successor, Danilo II, decided to separate the ecclesiastic and the secular facets of reigning and became a prince. His son, King Nicholas, ruled from 1860 until 1918, at which time he abdicated in favor of the Serbian king due to Montenegro's voluntary incorporation into Yugoslavia. Montenegro became a close ally of Serbia in most things. The Montenegrin Orthodox Church was completely absorbed into the Serbian Orthodox Church after World War I and lost its autonomy—which some Montenegrins begrudge even today.

During World War II the small country was first occupied by Italians, with some German units. A popular revolt broke out quickly, but soon the Montenegrins divided themselves into *chetniks,*—i.e., Serbian/Montenegrin nationalists—who fiercely fought the pro-Communist *partizans.* Montenegrins are regarded as habitual fighters, because waging war is the only occupation worthy of a male. They fought the occupying forces as well as each other with gusto. Many of them became famous in Tito's guerrilla forces, the best known among them being Milovan Djilas, at first an heir-apparent of Tito and then the first and most famous ex-Communist dissident, who wrote the famous analysis *The New Class* published in 1957.

Montenegrins were very much oriented toward the central government in postwar Yugoslavia and went in large numbers to Belgrade, where they distinguished themselves in the Communist Party and in the Yugoslav People's Army bureaucracy. They were dedicated to the Yugoslav idea and steadfastly rejected secessionist plans. Yet in 1990 they opted to go with Slobodan Milošević all the way; both Milošević and Radovan Karadžić are of Montenegrin ancestry. Montenegrins fight on behalf of what they call "Great Serbia." Their foray into Croatia as they laid siege to Dubrovnik and vicinity did not serve their reputation well as they stood accused of looting defenseless towns and nearly destroying one of the greatest cultural monuments in Europe. The economic difficulties brought on by the UN embargo have caused some Montenegrins to have second thoughts about the alliance with Serbia, but on the whole the alliance is firm.

THE MYTHIC ELEMENT

Four myths are especially prominent in the memories of Balkan groups. The first is the *myth of land and blood.* The land is perceived as sacred wherever and whenever people of a given ethnic group lived. One hears of "pure-blooded" members of this or that ethnic group, as if this makes a person more patriotic and better than one who has people of other ethnicities in her or his family. One's respective nation-state is great and it exists in essential continuity with a powerful medieval state of one's ethnic ancestors. The assumption is that the people in the Middle Ages experienced ethnic nationalism in the same manner as their modern-day contemporaries. Foreign rulers are inevitably and consistently evil as they temporarily impede cultural and civilizational progress of people who are of one's own blood; it is the foreigners who are responsible, to this day, for every present-day evil. They have caused nothing but suffering to one's own ethnic and religious group. There is little readiness to admit that some foreign rules may have connoted civilizational advances at least in some areas of life. Nor is there willingness to recognize that the periods of the decline of the foreign empires may have worsened conditions for the local population. *Their* rulers are evil and *our* rulers are good, except those of our rulers who fall under their influence. The myth is that every local ethnic group has had to defend itself against the continuous attempts to rob it of its ethnic and religious identity.

The second important myth is the one that turns defeats into victories. One may call this *the crucifixion and resurrection syndrome.* Because of steadfastness despite suffering we rise as victors. Most Balkan people have learned about the past through heroic epic songs rather than through the study of history. The epic songs always glorify the local ethnic hero and vilify the stranger and traitor. Epic songs alter defeats into victories.

The normal study of history is tainted either because of the narrow, romanticized nationalism in which one's own history is glorified out of proportion or because of the Marxist historians who have had no taste for national heroes at all but tended to denigrate them as members of former ruling classes so that they could pay attention only to class analysis and provide only a

Marxian interpretation of history. Since Marxist historians have obscured and repressed ethnoreligious history, upon their discreditation today a powerful rush back to romantic, nationalistic exaggerations has become the rule.

The third, and perhaps most important, mythic element is that *time is understood mythologically rather than chronologically.* As Nebojša Popov, a Belgrade dissident philosopher, expressed it at a meeting of Serbs and Croats in Zagreb, December 20–22, 1993, thinking in the Balkans is governed by a powerful mythomania that destroys the sense of real time. Concepts of the past and the present are so intermixed that a grievance of long ago is perceived as a present affliction. Likewise, it is believed that a present action may not only vindicate but actually eradicate and reverse a past defeat. It is as if one can repeatedly take a make-up test for past failures.

This author had witnessed, at the Tomb of the Patriarchs in Hebron, people weeping uncontrollably for a legendary person who may have lived six thousand years ago and who is totally unrelated as if he or she was a next of kin who died just hours before. The same inability to tell time is present among many people in the Balkans. Past villains are still rumored to plot territorial acquisitions at our expense, regardless of the fact that conditions have radically changed. Once an enemy, always an enemy. But once a friend, one is not necessarily *always* a friend—because when the friend no longer agrees uncritically, then it is time to perceive him or her as an enemy. A case in point is an article by a little-known Montenegrin journalist residing in Sarajevo who directed a vicious attack against Serbs for their barbaric behavior toward the Muslims. He states that as a Montenegrin he feels no solidarity with these Serbs because he does not have the same need to even out the score with Muslims; Turks did not rape his mother as they did the mothers of these Serbs, they did not control Montenegro as they did Serbia, nor was he ever a Turkish serf as Serbs were. All the while he writes as if the Turkish indignities toward the Serbs are of a most recent vintage and are being presently experienced by his intended readers.

Popov also pointed out the inability to experience a catharsis over past traumas and crimes, which might enable people to free themselves for the future without the constant need to relive traumas and add new ones. Thus there is a continual demand for

payment in blood for what others have done since time imme-
morial. Tito's regime had placed a tabu on the retrieval of memory of the traumas caused during World War II. The present nationalist leaders have released the floodgates of memory without
any selectivity, so that many untraumatized citizens get caught
up in wanting to avenge themselves for real and imaginary
wounds of the past.

The fourth myth is *the glorification of war and violence as the
best way to keep or reclaim one's freedom.* The Balkan economies are perpetual war economies. People are ready to sacrifice
everything in order to win a new round of fighting. There is no
tradition of nonviolent resistance or pacifism. The great heroes
are always those who inflict the greatest damage to the enemy.
Past and present warriors are promoted indiscriminately into
"the Great Warrior Hall of Fame" of respective nationalities,
their names written into history books as if they have been the
greatest contributors to national welfare.

CONCLUSIONS

Even from this greatly simplified summary of the history of
the six states of former Yugoslavia (and without having gone into
the history of the occupational forces, which greatly affected local happenings) several conclusions are evident.

First, that the various states which came to comprise Yugoslavia had vastly different political, social, economic, and religious
histories. While adjacent areas often shared common destinies
and ethnic similarities, a journey from one end of the former Yugoslavia to the other is a trip through entirely different worlds.
A highlander from the Slovenian Alps on the Austrian border
would find little in common with a dweller at Lake Ohrid in
Macedonia on the Greek-Albanian border. A citizen of Dubrovnik, Croatia, on the Adriatic Sea would have a completely different milieu than a person living in Sarajevo, in central Bosnia. A
Montenegrin shepherd from Cetinje would find little affinity
with a farmer from the Vojvodina or Slavonia.

Slovenians say they have more in common with Western Europeans than with Central Europeans. Macedonians say they belong to a Mediterranean culture. Bosnia has distinct Near Eastern

characteristics, while Serbians gravitate eastward toward Orthodox countries, especially Russia. Even within Serbia, Vojvodina is regarded as Central European, Serbia proper Eastern European, and Kosovo Near Eastern. It is not surprising that the peoples of Yugoslavia did not have a strong traditional sense of bonding, or that, in a period of approximately seventy years of living together, they were unable to unite what for over a millennium was fragmented.

Second, that throughout history there has been great political, economic, and social discontinuity in the region which caused an extreme sense of insecurity in its population. Not only did armies, governments, and religions change in the domination of an area in a period of a century, but they also sometimes changed within a decade, a year, and even in a day. One could simply not be certain that one's relatives on the other side of the river would have the same government and experience the same changes. Foreign colonial empires ruled supreme for centuries, the only novelty being that they often replaced each other rapidly. Politically the Balkans was and continues to be fractured and contentious, contributing the word "balkanization" to our vocabulary. Another of our words, "byzantine," stems essentially from the same region connoting a particularly devious, circuitous, and convoluted form of politics.

Economically such discontinuity is ruinous. Discontinuity breeds resentment and chaos. There has never been enough economic stability to make it worth saving money or working hard to obtain it. Too much depended on luck and fate, and therefore little self-reliance could be nurtured. Many people feel that greater powers than one's own govern existence, so that one's decisions will not bring noticeable change. The result is a heavy dose of fatalism.

Third, there have been exaggerated expectations of greatness, backed up by far too little historical evidence of it. Though they are perennially small, weak, and downtrodden the people's dreams of greatness are persistent. Paradoxically, they may be persistent perhaps because of feebleness. Reign over a sizable part of the Balkans by a native ruler or dynasty was fairly rare and certainly not synchronized. When one tribe or nation was "up" the others were "down." Thus most of them had *periods* of "greatness." Fondly they have remembered the expansion of their importance, wishing to repeat it. Thus there are claims of "Great Serbia," "Great Croatia," "Great Bosnia," "Great Macedonia," "Great Bulgaria," "Great Hungary," "Great Albania," "Great Greece," etc. But there is simply not enough real estate for all these claims of greatness; their territorial ambitions are mutually incompatible.

Fourth, there exists a sense of *hubris* as a collective character trait, such as is revealed in Greek tragedies. The famous Belgrade philosopher Svetozar Stojanović, an advisor to the former president of Yugoslavia, Dobrica Ćosić, wrote that this trait consists of a disdainful and ostentatious mockery of fate by exceeding one's abilities. This can also be described as an inability to back down from a disaster. He wrote, about the Serbs: "They fall into this chasm pretentiously and arrogantly defying fate, extending themselves beyond their available means, power, and limits—a defiance perhaps best expressed in [the bishop and poet] Njegoš' command: 'Let there be what cannot be!' "

This characteristic is, indeed, applicable to Serbs, but it is my experience that the other nationalities share the same attitude. Most peoples of the Balkans oscillate between extremes, with little propensity for moderation. It is either freedom or slavery, either mutiny or loyalty, either war or capitulation, either love or hate, either hospitality or rejection, either self-denigration or narcissism. One may hear, practically at the same time, "We are better than others" and "We are the worst." National leaders, many of whom are imbued with such traits, have a tendency to resort not to diplomacy, negotiation, or compromise but, rather, to gamble for all or nothing!

Fifth is the role that religious conflicts have played in political confrontations in the Balkans. (The close identity between religion and ethnicity will be discussed in more detail in Chapter 7.) It is here that Eastern Orthodoxy, Roman Catholicism, and Islam met and collided with each other (Judaism and Protestantism are also present but are numerically marginal, and they do not affect the larger picture). Religious leaders became national leaders and used and misused people's national adherence. Politicians, on the other hand, have frequently used and abused people's religious sentiments. Some Serbs make claims that they are the "Heavenly People" and that "God Protects Serbs." Many Croats and Slovenes claim that God protects *them*, and that they are under the patronage of the Holy Virgin Mary. Catholics (Croats) have long considered the Eastern Orthodox (Serbs) as having broken away from the true Church of Christ; and vice versa. Both Orthodox and Catholics have believed that it was desirable to return the others into the fold of the One, True, and Apostolic Church. Both considered the once-present "Bosnian Church" as heretical, as they did Protestants. All were contemptuous of Jews. Muslims were considered heathens by Christians; Muslims felt that it was *they* who were doing Allah's will, whereas Christians were infidels.

Last, short periods of unity and cooperation are almost always succeeded by extended periods of conflict and strife. "Times of troubles" are so frequent that it is unnecessary to call any specific period by that name. Only several decades have been without war and then new wars have broken out. Nor were the periods between wars trouble-free; on the contrary. People are long-suffering and have an incredible endurance for misery. The Balkan people's struggle for sheer survival is perennial and the belief that life is a constant trouble gives them a dismal sense of despair. Since one never knows how long one will live or how much one will have, the tendency is for immediate gratification of desires. Hence, amid pain there will be outbreaks of joy or ostentatious consumption; the next hour, it may all have been in vain. Today, as always, fate dwells on these people heavily and oppressively because it is clear that a long period of struggle lies ahead, with few solutions in sight. Time itself has proven that alternatives are almost always bad, and therefore most nationalities search to find solutions that are the most advantageous for themselves. The question most Balkan people generally ask is: "Which alternative is the least destructive for myself? Let the others cope the best they can."

CHAPTER 3

THE DESTRUCTIVE USE OF MEMORY

THE HERITAGE OF HORROR

A few miles outside of the southeastern Macedonian city of Strumica on the slopes of the Belašica Mountain lies the small village of Očevad (Dig-out-Eyes). It commemorates the battle in 1014 in which the Byzantine Emperor Basil II routed the army of Emperor Samuel of the Bulgarian-Macedonian state. About 15,000 captured soldiers were blinded in both eyes. Every hundredth man was blinded in only one eye so that he could lead the others home. Seeing this, Samuel fainted and two days later died.

The first Serbian ruler of some significance, King Stevan Nemanja (1168–95), is largely responsible for the Christianization of his realm. He silenced the adherents of the Bogumil heresy (see Chapter 2) in his territory by cutting their tongues out.

Starina Novak, the celebrated hero of epic songs, and his son Grujica were cruel not only to their enemies but their own family. One of the old songs describes how Grujica with his father's permission killed his own mother by cutting off her right breast and both arms, covering her with tar, and burning her while the two of them warmed themselves at this fire.

In Imotsko, in Croatian Herzegovina, Franciscan friars recorded in the seventeenth century how people fought among themselves. They kidnapped their own brothers and sisters along with their cattle and sold as many as one hundred of their kin at a time to Venetians as galley slaves.

Karadjordje, the leader of the first Serbian rebellion against the Turks, in 1804, in order to foment support for his rebellion burned down entire Serbian villages. He slit the throats of his own father and brother. He killed captured Turks in front of other people's homes so they would have to join the rebels.

Turkish and Slavic Muslim overlords terrorized the masses of the Balkan peninsula by publicly impaling "wrongdoers" upon wooden spikes, causing a slow but agonizing death. Even as late as World War II a case of impalement was recorded in the territory of Yugoslavia.

The 1913 Carnegie Endowment Inquiry into the Balkan Wars contains around 400 pages of documentation of unspeakable savagery perpetrated equally by Turks, Greeks, Bulgarians, Serbs, Macedonians, Albanians, and Montenegrins. Pillaging (one of the favorite pastimes of both the military and civilians in these wars), rapes, arson, mass murder of entire villages, and flogging were only the most frequent atrocities documented by the Carnegie commission. An Austrian officer records that, ten days after the peace treaty was signed ending the 1913 conflict, Greek soldiers burned down numerous houses in Strumica (today in Macedonia) and raped the wives of a Turk, a Jew, and a Bulgarian. The Turkish woman died of it while her child was abducted never to be seen again.[1]

Vladimir Dedijer records in his *Dnevnik* (Diary), which was written during World War II, that a Serb in Bosnia was so angry at another Serb whom he suspected of having betrayed him that he sent a message to two of his own friends ordering them to seize the man and his wife and rape her, forcing the husband to hold her down during the rape. He concluded, "that will hurt him the most . . . and then I will come and kill him."

Milovan Djilas recounts that among Montenegrins a distinction is made between theft and robbery. Theft is minor, concealed, cowardly, and unethical; robbery is major, open, heroically violent, and ethical. When a Montenegrin *chetnik* leader was captured during World War II and sentenced to execution by a firing squad he requested to die by having them cut his throat because he felt that this is the only honorable way to depart from this life.

---

1. *The Other Balkan Wars: A 1913 Carnegie Endowment Inquiry in Retrospect, with a New Introduction and Reflection on the Present Conflict by George F. Kennan* (Washington: Carnegie Endowment, 1993), p. 204.

In January 1941 the Hungarian occupational authorities massacred approximately 3,000 civilians in Novi Sad by digging holes in the ice on the Danube River and then pushing them under it, most of them alive.

While the exact number of Serb, Jewish, Gypsy, Muslim, and even some Croatian victims of the death camp in Jasenovac, organized by the Independent State of Croatia during World War II, is still hotly debated among Croat and Serb writers (they range from 60,000 to 800,000), the deaths inflicted in Jasenovac were not as expeditious as the Auschwitz annihilation. Often the camp guards carried out the mass killings by mallets and knives.

During World War II the military and paramilitary units of Serbs, Croats, Muslims, and the Communist-led *partizans* burned, killed, and looted each other's villages. Frequently they carried out cruel mass murders. To this day trenches full of hundreds of victims are being discovered. When the British Army returned thousands of captured Croatian *ustashe* and other soldiers at the end of World War II, they were slaughtered *en masse* by the *partizans* and were unceremoniously tossed into ditches.

As a prelude to the present warfare, mass graves of executed Serbs from World War II were discovered in Medjugorje, Herzegovina. It is alleged that they are close to the world-famous pilgrimage sites over which a Roman Catholic Church was erected. Fact or fiction, the important thing is that Serbs believe it is so.

Should it come as a surprise that in the current war a tank unit of Serbian soldiers gang-raped a twelve-year-old Muslim girl, tied her bloody body to the tank, and drove around for months until only the skeleton remained?

As we have watched the constant artillery, mortar, and sniper attacks on cities such as Vukovar, Dubrovnik, Zadar, Sarajevo, Tuzla, Mostar, and Goražde, pounding them either into total or near-oblivion, or as we have gazed at the charred bodies of children and old people piled up after a flash attack of "ethnic cleansing" we wonder whether this war is really dirtier or whether the combatants are more cruel than in other wars? Though it is unclear what a study of comparative cruelty would yield, it does seem that the people of the Balkans do not have a monopoly on destructiveness either in previous centuries or in this, the most destructive of all centuries. The Hitlers, Stalins, Pol Pots, and other mass butcherers and individual killers of this century have not been surpassed in the Balkans.[2] In other countries the death tolls have run higher. In Rwanda in April 1994 in just a few days of fighting between the Hutus and the Tutsis it was reported that nearly 100,000 people died; it took former Yugoslavia more than a year to run up such casualties. Later estimates from Rwanda quickly exceeded the calculated number of those killed in the former Yugoslavia. Nevertheless, it is certain that the battlefields of the former Yugoslavia are places where monstrous human behavior is made manifest with regularity and without letup.

What is distinctive about the Balkans is the mixture of cruelty and warmth, destruction and outreach. There is a kind of maniacal descent into the depths of depravation by people who are outlaws in every sense of the word, outlaws who are celebrated as heroes in their own settings. The Balkans have bred a special kind of outlaw—the *hajduk* and *uskok*—two variant words connoting a combination of the notions of brigand and freedom fighter. Such men became celebrated for their adventuresome violence against the enemy, but they were not loath to turn against their own kin and loved ones if they were crossed. Their twentieth-century equivalents are just as short-tempered, with precisely the same mixture of sentimental love and fierce hatred. Such people have been objects of fascination, celebrated in spontaneous folk songs, though by the standards of civilized society they are war criminals and mass murderers. Twentieth-century paramilitary groups, such as the *chetnik* (Serbian), *ustasha* (Croatian and Muslim, though the latter may use the Arabic term *mujahedin*), and *partizans* (Communist guerrillas), built upon the heritage of *hajduk* and *uskok* "freedom fighters" of a previous era in the taking of the lives of enemies and "traitors" with a viciousness the memory of which had survived centuries.

Currently such terrorists as *"Vojvoda"* ("Duke") Vojislav Šešelj, Željko Ražnjatović-Arkan, Dobroslav Paraga, Miroslav Lazanski, and Ismet Bajramović are accompanied by an entire legion of "commanders" known only by their first name, such as

---

2. The portrait painted by Robert D. Kaplan, in *Balkan Ghosts* (New York: Vintage Books, Random House, 1993), of the Balkans as an exotic and mysterious cradle of varieties of evil, ranging from terrorism to Nazism, strikes me as overdramatized. An analogy would be to view an account of the sinister racial and ethnic strife in American cities as adequately depicting American life.

Captain Dragan. This group contains Serb, Croat, and Muslim war criminals. These are the folk who will use the decapitated heads of their victims for soccer balls. Most of them were, in previous private lives, either criminals or workers in bakeries, pizzerias, and other non-glamorous jobs. Šešelj, who has a Ph.D. in philosophy, is an exception in education but not in behavior.

When the war began, the Yugoslav prisons were opened and criminals, some of them multiple murderers, were allowed to go to the front to be "rehabilitated" by fighting for their fatherland. Their reputations skyrocketed. Arkan received a standing ovation when he appeared at a soccer game. He was subsequently elected to the Serbian parliament. Šešelj, the head of the Serbian Radical Party, for which nearly a third of the Serbian electorate voted in the 1991 election, is known to personally beat those whom he dislikes. Reports claim that people have witnessed him personally killing POWs. He makes election speeches waving a pistol in his hand and is always surrounded by menacing "gorillas," or bodyguards. Such men as these men are unafraid to threaten publicly the extermination of entire ethnic groups. A Bosnian Muslim professor recounted that Vojislav Šešelj stated in front of him that all Muslims in Bosnia and Herzegovina ought to be exterminated in forty-eight hours.[3] When the Muslim professor thanked him for the advance warning so that he could depart in a timely manner, Šešelj jovially assured him that those present would be exempt from the annihilation.

Ismet Bajramović, twenty-six, nicknamed "Baldy," is a Muslim in the tradition of the gangster-hero. The Sarajevan 6-foot-5-inch giant is a convicted rapist, robber, black-marketeer, drug dealer, and gangster but also a war hero to many in the Bosnian capital. For a while he headed the Bosnian Army's military intelligence. When he was critically wounded by a would-be assassin, a team of doctors worked diligently to save his life. His recovery was the stuff of legends in the eyes of many Sarajevans.

With alarming frequency, local authorities have freed jailed criminals, armed them, and given them the unsavory tasks of

---

3. This threat had been issued previously by the leading Serbian general and later Prime Minister of Yugoslavia, Nikola Pašić, at the end of World War I in which he said that Bosnian Muslims would be given 24, or at most 48, hours to convert to Christianity or they would be killed or exiled.

threatening unwanted ethnic minorities. Thus, for instance, in Nikšić, Montenegro, jailed criminals had the task of frightening the population of predominantly Muslim town of Metković. Sometimes they bungled the task by shooting indiscriminately, inadvertently killing members of their own ethnic group.

Armed criminals take over roadblocks to monitor traffic, control fuel distribution (at $60 a gallon in Sarajevo), and manage large scale black market food distribution. When a can of Coca-Cola can bring $10 and a glass of instant coffee $2 in hard currency in Sarajevo, it is clear that much money can be made in such trafficking. Even policemen and UN peacekeeping troops get corrupted and cooperate in these criminal activities. The population often believes that these gangsters control their fate more than politicians, police, and peacekeepers, and develop a fear-and-fascination attitude toward the mobsters. The combination of charm and wit with utterly detached cruelty and intense hatred displayed by the gangsters-rulers-outlaws perpetuates the heritage of horror.

REVENGE AND SPITE

The desire for revenge may be universal. Nevertheless, not every culture, especially not a predominantly Christian one, makes it the cultural norm. Yet in the Balkans even the old and infirm vouch that they would revenge themselves on those who did harm to their family or people. There are sections of the country, especially Kosovo and Montenegro, where vendettas have been carried out through the centuries. Such revenge is not always the result of any direct harm that has been inflicted upon a member of the nuclear family; it is often merely a matter of defending one's own honor for injuries real or imagined.

"Near" and "far" coalesce in the mind of many peoples of the Balkans; they do not have the same reckoning of either time or distance as most contemporary peoples. Even elderly folk in the countryside will walk for hours through mountains and perceive the distance to be short. Likewise, there is a sense that centuries are no more than a few years; the distant past is like yesterday. People will cry at the graves of individuals who died five hundred years ago. Such is their ability to empathize.

Another typical feature is *prkos*, which can be translated by the words obstinacy, spitefulness, and defiance. All three of these behavioral patterns are deeply embedded in the majority's character. These traits developed as necessary weapons for surviving adversity and enemy oppression but have become permanent features in the peoples' behavior.

Defiance of authority—all authority—has characterized the general behavior. In the past it was directed toward foreign invaders, and such non-cooperation was extolled as patriotic. But it was internalized as a cultural trait to such an extent that even when the foreigners were driven out and one's own government ruled, people disobeyed it and rather casually dismissed even reasonable rules. An attitude of devil-may-care can be frequently encountered, especially after a few drinks. And drinks are imbibed frequently, in particular the 90– or 100–proof *shlyivovitsa* (plum brandy) drunk with equal enthusiasm by Orthodox, Catholics, and Muslims. In the current war, as in past ones, both soldiers and commanders are often drunk. As a matter of course they defy commands from above. A relative told me anecdotally that some young Croatian artillerymen, defenders of the city of Osijek, when surrounded by Serbian forces were plied with brandy by the local citizens who came to encourage them. In their drunkenness they fired upon the Serbs who immediately fired back on the city. The Serb gunners were probably just as drunk.

Spitefulness is nearly universal. It is not unusual that from childhood onward many people commit certain acts only in order to spite others, even if these acts result in distinct disadvantages to themselves.

Obstinacy, stubbornness, loathing, and inflexibility are also quite widespread. Predrag Tašić, a journalist who is a Serb, says that he personally shares the characteristic stubbornness, and unyielding spite, and that these lead to a struggle with all and everybody, without fear, and to the end. This mindset may be more intensely seen in Serbs, but the Croats and others betray it, too—proving thereby that all Yugoslavs, all Balkan peoples, are sibling nations, despite the current efforts to split them up. Frequently for no apparent reason, quite contrary to sound judgment, a group of people will set out to prevent another group or person from doing something or accomplishing something. Sometimes this is to simply show to others that you are able to carry out your own intentions, no matter how arbitrary they are toward others. Sometimes the reason is envy—another vice that has been elevated to a virtue.

Even though the peoples of this region recognize obstinacy, spite, and defiance as both virtues and vices, they generally excuse themselves by saying that they are Balkan traits and that people around the world will simply have to make an attempt to understand this mentality if they want to deal with them. It does not occur to the locals that *they* may be in need of making some adjustments so that the rest of the world can understand *them*. It is always that the rest of the world must understand and adjust to the Yugoslav and/or Balkan idiosyncrasies. This is recognized as a trait of teenage mentality. Perhaps, therefore, it would be accurate to say that collectively many peoples of the Balkans, despite their age-old history, behave in an immature way, as if their growth were stunted by deprivation and oppression. Unresolved childhood traumas, which may lead individuals to abnormal behavior and an inability to mature, may also be displayed by ethnic groups. The peoples of the Balkans have been in colonial dependency for so long a time that now, when they are in a position to control their own destiny, they act belatedly like juvenile delinquents.

An American journalist recorded the following story of local obstinacy:

> Božidar Paunović, a gaunt Serbian man with deep-set blue eyes and a wispy blond beard, had crossed the divide that separates obstinacy from madness. But no one in the village of Vučitrn, not even his wife and two daughters, seemed to take notice. . . . The other Paunovićs have done his crazy bidding without the slightest hesitation, following him to Vučitrn [in Kosovo] on foot from their former home in Bosnia-Herzegovina, ninety miles to the west, and erecting a forty-square-foot army tent in an abandoned Orthodox cemetery. . . . He was at great pains to explain why he and his family were there. The conversation meandered fitfully through half a dozen rounds of brandy . . . "Vučitrn used to be a place for Serbs and must be again. How our ancestors fought for it a thousand years ago." . . . He came there on behalf of all Serbs, the dead and the living, to bear witness to the truth. He says he will not leave until Vučitrn is Serbian again.[4]

---

4. Frank Viviano, "The Balkan Tribe," *Mother Jones*, Jan./Feb. 1993, pp. 33–34.

It so happened that Vučitrn had become purely an Albanian village, the Paunovićs being the only Serbian family that took up this precarious residence. Even more frightening was that an educated friend of the American journalist who helped interpret the event opined that Paunović's words did not sound crazy. In my own experience thousands, if not millions of Serbs, from the uneducated to the journalists and politicians, state with conviction that despite Albanians' outnumbering them in Kosovo nine to one, the Serbs will never surrender Kosovo. They are, indeed, capable of exterminating over a million Albanians in pursuit of this goal.

While observing Balkan destructiveness, it is helpful to distinguish between anger and rage. Anger has a specific cause, is directed toward a specific target, and is usually limited in duration, having accomplished the elimination of a specific threat. Rage is usually caused by accumulated frustration and anxiety, a sense of loss of control over one's own destiny, and it results in undirected or misdirected fury and destructiveness. Rage can outlast the destruction of a particular threat because its source is lodged *within* rather than *outside* oneself. Entire ethnic groups in the Balkans are experiencing rage rather than anger, from accumulated frustrations and the longtime inability to control their own destinies.

PROPAGANDA: GOOD GUYS VS. BAD GUYS

It might well be a universal human trait to give preferential treatment to one's own group and be suspicious or even hostile to others. Jesus urged people to take the log from their own eyes before trying to remove the splinter in their neighbor's, but it appears clear that a splinter in the eyes of another is always more visible than a log in our own. We are used to the metaphor of the good guys vs. the bad guys; our films and novels overflow with them. This dualism has become particularly pronounced— even brazen—during the disintegration of Yugoslavia.

An outsider will have great difficulty in seeing physical differences between peoples of the Balkans, because they are nonexistent. Even cultural differences frequently escape the eye of observers who look at people of different ethnicities/nationalities residing in the same location. There are often great differences between cities and their residents located within a national territory while those situated in a different Balkan state sometimes display obvious similarity. The people in the former Yugoslavia, themselves, are, however, rather convinced that they are each very different from the others. They dwell far more often on what separates them than on what they have in common. Their diversity has often been seen as a liability rather than a strength and they have often apologetically said that they succeeded in something not because of their diversity but in spite of their diversity.

After Tito died, the enormous propaganda machine which had obediently cranked out slogans of "brotherhood and unity," idealizing common Yugoslav achievements, disengaged itself from this program. First, the society started to create space for more critical, professional journalistic reporting and, for a short time, engendered some refreshing social criticism. Yet there remained always those who would serve as any regime's sycophants, and the secret police always took a keen interest in the ideas of free thinkers. But as freedom increased, so did the abuse of freedom. Given freedom, of course, most people tended to push its limits to the extreme.

An unholy alliance between nationalistic political leaders and the media and the press began to blossom in the late 1980s. Political leaders continued to show an appetite for a monopoly or near-monopoly of communications. One after the other, the liberal editors or program directors who with much difficulty had asserted themselves in the period of Communism were now rudely or cleverly removed from their positions by the new nationalist political elite. For a short time such journalists could still find jobs in other sympathetic enterprises. Slowly but surely, however, the takeover became complete, especially in television, which is the sole source of information for the majority of the population. The radio stations and the largest publishing houses followed.

The reputable and formerly independent Belgrade daily *Politika* (Politics) became the most servile mouthpiece of Milošević. In a strange twist of irony, *Borba* (Struggle), the former official daily of the Communist Party, which had once been terribly dull and loyal, became a far more independent, investigative, and analytic newspaper. *Vjesnik* (Messenger) in Zagreb, became the instrument of the Tudjman government. *Slobodna Dalmacija* (Free Dalmatia) in Split resisted takeover by the Croatian government but was finally subdued by Tudjman's people.

There were refreshing exceptions. One of these was *Oslobodjenje* (Liberation), from Sarajevo, in which journalists of all three nationalities continued to chronicle daily the heroic suffering of that city despite great odds. A few new publications appeared, such as the Belgrade *Vreme* (Time) which continued independent journalism; in the meantime, unfortunately, the population had become so impoverished that few could afford to purchase it. Once the most interesting magazine in the entire country, Zagreb's *Danas* (Today) was forced to close its doors several times, primarily due to pressures by the Croatian government; it was ultimately taken over by pro-government forces.

Having taken over the major newspapers and other media, the nationalist leaders launched shamelessly chauvinistic propaganda. Some journalists out of financial necessity, others out of nationalist convictions, started a vitriolic campaign against alleged "enemies." These journalists kept poisoning readers with slanted interpretations that were served up as facts. Many journalists simply prostituted themselves. This is admitted in private by those who have retained a guilt feeling that they became, to quote one of them, "executioners in the hands of the regime who write 90 percent lies and 10 percent truth."

Particularly venomous was the Belgrade press. Its journalists created a barrage of misinformation. They would impute statements to their opponents which they had never made and then ferociously criticize them for allegedly being "anti-Yugoslav" or, even more sinfully, "anti-Serbian." As one of Belgrade's remaining critical journalists has characterized it, it was journalism of "spitting,"—namely, denigrating, distorting, humiliating, and clearly libelling people, including the federal premier, without giving those people the right to retort. Leaders of other nationalities were demonized, Serbs' own glorified. In the Serbian press the Croatian leader Franjo Tudjman and the Slovenian leader Milan Kučan were described as fascist; the reverse was the case with the Slovenian and Croatian press, which could not find any good in the "Communist" Serb, Slobodan Milošević. Entire nations were indicted. The Serbian press and government leaders called the Croat people *ustashoid* and genocidal, while the Croats and Slovenes thundered that all Serbs everywhere and at all times were hegemonistic, byzantine, imperial, and "Communist."

Most people were receptive to this steady barrage of slander. Latent suspicions and hostilities were now "documented" by the press. The readers, with relatively few exceptions, enthusiastically accepted and transmitted such feeling. The body politic of all the new nations was thus poisoned. They became hypercritical of the others, "the bad guys," and totally uncritical, defensive, self-congratulatory, and self-righteous of—"the good guys."

Democracy does not thrive in such an atmosphere. It will take a long time to detoxify the atmosphere and to educate for self-criticism, tolerance, and dialogue, which are prerequisites of every democratic society.

LIES, LIES, LIES

Lying is almost endemic in cultures that have almost completely relativized the Ten Commandments. It is so widespread that from childhood onward nearly every claim made by a person is challenged by other persons who ask that one give a word of honor and swear an oath, such as "It's true; may my eyes fall out if it is not" or "May my mother die if this is not true." A casual attitude toward keeping one's word only when it is convenient is prevalent. Exceptions are rare even in journalism, scholarship, or government.

The expeditious is more important than the truthful. The source of this attitude may have been that lying to foreign oppressors seemed justified as an act of non-cooperation and defiance or even as part of the art of survival. It was certainly reinforced during totalitarian Communism, at which time everyone had to say what was expected of her or him and not what she or he truly believed. Thus people were able, as the Czech playwright and president Václav Havel pointed out in his writings, to separate life into two realms: one *private*, shared only with confidants, and one *public*, in which one said what was expected.[5]

---

5. Walter Sawatsky, "Truth Telling in Eastern Europe: The Liberation and the Burden," *Occasional Papers on Religion in Eastern Europe*, Vol. XI, No. 4 (August 1991), pp. 15–37.

In Yugoslavia, furthermore, the Near Eastern mentality encountered the Communist totalitarian mentality and the two were fused, making it possible to lie brazenly and without pangs of conscience. Of the press this certainly was and continues to be the case. Perceptive people often automatically consider that what is published is a lie. From the moment the nationalists took over the press in the new republics, the articles have been written to be of advantage of one's own side, no matter what the facts were. Facts have been distorted, invented, and obstructed, in order to serve one's own nationalistic interests. Journalists do not seek to report, but write opinionated commentaries typified by hyperbolic language designated to inflame readers' opinions. If it were not tragic, it would be amusing to compare various nationalistic journalistic accounts of a single event. One gets totally different versions of what took place, depending on which national paper one may read. The nationalist press and media also blockade news that they do not want their readers or viewers to know about. The manipulation by the press and media all across the world is obvious to most of us; but what is encountered in the Balkans goes far beyond the customary manipulation. The press and media here are simply perceived as legitimate tools in a wider conflict in which no holds are barred.

Even scholars are not reluctant to place themselves in the service of the powers that be (which might simply be an ideology such as Communism or nationalism or fascism, rather than a specific boss). Pretending to write "objective," scholarly treatises, many shamelessly distort data; they have, indeed, even contributed significantly to the outbreak of the warfare—which, in fact, started as a war of words, exaggerated historical claims, in short, a war of maps. Driven by nationalist ardor, the region's scholars began inventing theories, some extremely far-fetched, as to who inhabited which territory at what time, who has the legitimate claim over it, who was responsible for forcible migrations, who are the heroes and who are the villains.

What was particularly damaging about the lies of the professors is that they were among the few really trusted sources of information. One knew that journalists and politicians lied, but one reasoned that scholars were disinterested, serious pursuers of the truth. In Eastern Europe the intelligentsia has had considerable prestige and power, and its betrayal of the trust of the people is a moral catastrophe. Just as did their predecessors in Nazi Germany Balkan scholars have allowed themselves to be recruited into the service of diabolical forces; their intellectual education was not bolstered by a moral education. They have been all the more dangerous as liars because they could camouflage their lies with pseudo-logical and pseudo-factual arguments.

Recall how many cease-fires and agreements have been signed by the leaders of the various states and armed forces in the wars in the former Yugoslavia. All these agreements collapsed, some immediately without being implemented at all, others only after a very short period of time. The international mediators have noticed, by now, that signatures by Balkan leaders mean nothing; they are barely worth the cost of the ink. Even the Russian special envoy to the Balkans, Vitaliy Churkin, was beside himself in April 1994 when he was brazenly deceived by Bosnian Serbs toward whom he was well-disposed; they gave him assurances which were concurrently violated. Nor do political leaders or scholars know when to believe each other. The various regional leaders are surrounded by officials and staff many of whom they dare not trust. A cursory examination of the newspapers reveals many scandals in which it is almost impossible to distinguish lies from truth in ongoing confrontations between the politicians. This situation is not always noticed by the international press because foreign journalists do not fully understand what is happening—and why. Telephones and rooms may be bugged, people trailed, information leaked, videos doctored, false testimonies obtained, and physical threats issued, tortures inflicted, all quite routinely. Even the highest officials in the republics are not exempt from such treatment. People—leaders, as well—under these circumstances say what they need to say, not what they want to say.

Even more unnerving is the practice of simply denying that one said what one said, even in the presence of witnesses. Promises and verbal agreements have been made, sometimes even in the presence of stenographers, which are later negated. This makes it impossible to know *when* one has an agreement. One can imagine how confused foreign dignitaries are when they have thought they had obtained a consensus or assent to a policy, only to discover that the players from Yugoslavia do not play by the customary rules.

Lest the reader think that the above opinions are merely

claims by an expatriate disillusioned by and alienated from his native land, here is a quotation by Predrag Tašić, former press secretary of the Federal Executive Council of Yugoslavia, who participated in many of the negotiations between political leaders during the years of crisis:

> This agreement, like many before and after, was not honored. Europe has, in its contacts with the leaders of the Yugoslav republics, increasingly come to experience what Marković [the federal premier] did. It discovered the strategy of resistance. Prolonged negotiations would take place at which, finally, concessions would be made, the proposed solution would be accepted, and solemn promises would be made to carry them out. The moment they left the hall, the participants in the agreement would even more emphatically devote themselves to achieving their crazy ideas which necessitated the negotiations in the first place. So they lied to Marković, then to Carrington, then to Vance, then . . .[6]

THE RETURN OF PRIMITIVISM

Having been held under colonial domination by great empires for centuries, only a very small number of people in the Balkans have been afforded the opportunity to raise themselves from oppressive conditions to a level above the mere struggle for survival. Only in the nineteenth and twentieth century were conditions introduced, but then only sporadically, for the transcendence of "primitivism." In Yugoslavia this word, which is in some sense identical to its English equivalent, does not connote "simple" or "early" or "original" (as in "primitive Christianity") but has the primary connotation of traits that are barbaric, coarse, wild, savage, uncivilized, and destructive. Such behavior could, until recent decades, be encountered almost constantly in some environs, but slowly progress has been made in uplifting the behavior of considerable segments of the population to levels of civility, courtesy, mutual respect, and good manners.

The process of industrialization after World War II was accom-

---

6. Predrag Tašić, *Kako sam branio Antu Markovića* (How I Defended Ante Marković) (Skopje: NIP "Mugri 21," 1993), p. 148. Translation from the Serbian by P. Mojzes.

panied by an equally rapid process of education and urbanization. Huge numbers of young people were transferred from villages where their behavior had been circumscribed by very traditionalist strictures that kept in check the most destructive forms of behavior. But in new, often squalid, and certainly impersonal urban environs many of these new settlers lost their moral bearings. Some of them drifted dangerously in and out of anti-social or even criminal behavior. They learned quickly what was to their own and to others' detriment. The totalitarian nature of the Communist regime, however, kept the excesses of detrimental behavior in check by threat of police punishment, which could be rather brutal. On the surface many citizens believed that the time of primitivism has been left behind and that the outbreaks of primitivism that were displayed in the civil conflicts during World War II had been left behind. Many in Yugoslavia, seeing the savagery displayed in Lebanon, Vietnam, Cambodia, Biafra, and Uganda, were convinced that such behavior could ever reappear in their own land.

They were in for a big surprise. The civilizing process did not last sufficiently long and it took place simultaneously with anti-civilizational trends. As it turned out, only a very thin veneer of civilization masked the still underlying primitivism. Pressures of nationalist passions were far too strong, causing primitivism to erupt violently. Hence, in many parts of the former Yugoslavia the law of the jungle is now a fact of life.

Beginning around 1985, huge numbers of people began obtaining arms and there seemed little reluctance to use them on friend or foe. Life in the Balkans has never been intrinsically respected, because the individual is relatively unimportant in a collectivist climate; and the traditional culture of the Balkans was *collectivist*, reenforced for a few decades by Communist collectivism. Although for about a decade in the 1970s to the 1980s there appeared to be an early budding of a civil society in which the *individual* was the crucial ingredient, the passions of reawakened nationalisms plunged the regions of Yugoslavia right back into collectivism. The survival of the group again became so important that the individual could be sacrificed.

In the defense of the collective, all is once again allowed. No act is too cruel, no killing too horrible in order to bring about the goals of the collective. As mentioned earlier, criminals have been released from jail, sent to the front lines, and encouraged to spread terror among the enemy. Peer pressure and nationalistic enthusiasm have quickly induced even previously decent people to repeat horrors, the memories of which have obviously been fastidiously perpetuated and nurtured in the Balkans. Thus, this generation could not allow itself to be less destructive and primitive than previous ones. This generation has advanced the diabolical spiral to new heights of inhumanity.

Vukašin Pavlović, a professor of political science at Belgrade University, has pointed out that the reason for the singular degree of intolerance and cruelty in these Balkan wars is that they are not the typical "conflicts of interests" (for which one can find some common denominators) but are "conflicts of identities."[7] Identities are difficult to define and achieve. When one experiences a threat to one's identity one is willing to sacrifice even one's own economic and material interests because, in defining one's identity, far more decisive factors are culture, emotion, morality, religion, and values. The nationalist euphoria in post-Communist societies is the expression of disorientation which takes place when one value system is being replaced by another. Both individual and collective identity become threatened by the dissolution of a lifestyle or by governmental dictates. In the search for the lost identity, the masses take hold of those *past* identities that have been repressed and which are easiest to mobilize. These turned out to be national, or ethnoreligious, identities. The most primitive attachments to land, blood, heritage, and mythology have today become, once again, ways of appropriating identity. What's more, in the Balkans the most frequent manner of appropriating one's identity is by rejecting and destroying the identities of others. The heritage of horrors is therefore perpetuated in the insane vortex of death and destruction that is the Yugoslavian inferno.

THE LOCKSMITH WAS BETTER

A bit of graffiti in New Belgrade proclaims, "The locksmith was better." Locksmith is a reference to Tito. It is a sign that some are becoming disillusioned with the advancement that has

---

7. From a speech by Vukašin Pavlović at the Serb-Croat Round Table, in *Erasmus*, No. 5 (Zagreb, February 1994), pp. 26–27.

supposedly been achieved by Tito's heirs. Tito had undergone a number of transformations in his life—from locksmith to soldier, to POW, to professional Communist agitator, to the clandestine General Secretary of the Communist Party, to the legendary guerrilla leader in World War II, and to the President of postwar Yugoslavia. His reputation underwent some transformations following his death: from the limitlessly glorified and beloved superman and then posthumous iconographic adulation, to a sudden sobering when his many blemishes were discovered after it was allowed that he be scrutinized, and finally to a vilified source for all that has gone wrong in the destinies of the various peoples of the former Yugoslavia. But currently there are some signs of nostalgia. Croatian newspapers derisively call it "Yugo-nostalgia"; and if one is tagged by it, it may be the end of one's career. Yet nostalgia for Tito's time is setting in, at least in some minds.

There is no absolute measurement of how anyone feels about his or her situation. We measure ourselves relatively, partially against the well-being of the rest of the world, but primarily by comparing our present with our own past and that of our neighbors. When Tito died, there were prospects of emerging out of the Communist totalitarian mold and into the sweet life of the capitalist West, even hope of being admitted into the affluent European Economic Community. This gave rise to anti-Tito sentiments. One of the interesting features of the late 1980s was that he was no longer referred to by his legendary nickname Tito, but by his real name Josip Broz. When someone started saying "Broz did such and such," we could anticipate a criticism of Tito's action.

The newly established successor states are ruled by men who did not start out as lowly locksmiths. They were bank presidents, generals, directors of enterprises, lawyers, authors, educators—all successful. One would expect improvement in people's lives. At first it seemed that this improvement might happen, and some still hope it will. But by now these former Yugoslavs have been pushed over the precipice into an abyss of self-destruction. A comparison between Tito's times and today is inevitable. It is true that he contributed to the present situation, and that much of the increase in the standard of living in the 1970s was the result of his squandering international loans on consumerism; but the common people are unable to take that into account. They compare the peace and stability and the standard of living which they had while Tito ruled and know that they are worse off today. No subtle economic indicators are needed to arrive at this insight. It was better under Tito, everyone concludes. And if a people are forced to look back at a better past, that means that a better future eludes their imagination. Nostalgia is a sign of despair over the present and of hopelessness about the future.

CHAPTER 4

LAST CHANCE FOR A UNIFIED YUGOSLAVIA

In the late 1980s Yugoslavia faced four options: first, that Yugoslavia might indiscriminately surrender to unregulated Western capitalist economic takeover; second, that a military or Communist dictator might grab power; third, that the country would fall apart, possibly accompanied by great violence; and fourth, that reforms might succeed. Prof. Srdjan Vrcan, the former dean of the Law School in Split, put it more picturesquely. In 1986, he said, that three undesirable alternatives were the Americanization, the Polandization, or the Lebanonization of Yugoslavia.

The Americanization of Yugoslavia would be a surrender to Western capitalism and an economic takeover by foreign capital, national policies being dictated by Western political and economic interests. Polandization would be for the Communist Party or the Army to follow the example of General Wojcieh Jaruzelski of Poland, installing martial law to quell "Solidarity." Lebanonization would be the state of permanent warfare between factions/regions with little hope of a settlement. Vrcan feared Lebanonization the most. Ultimately, Yugoslavia followed precisely this final option. However, in the late 1980s a glimmer of hope still existed that a fourth, more desirable alternative—of reforming the country into a modern democracy—might succeed.

Prof. Zdenko Roter, a sociologist from Ljubljana, wrote in 1988 that Yugoslavia was at the crossroads[1] between political authoritarianism (the forces in the federation tending to concentrate

---

1. Zdenko Roter, "Yugoslavia at the Crossroads: A Sociological Discourse," *Occasional Papers on Religion in Eastern Europe*, Vol. VIII, No. 2 (May 1988), pp. 11–24.

power in the federal government), the trend toward greater independence in the republics, and a trend toward a multi-party system without real democratic political pluralism. He concluded that Yugoslavia was in a crisis and that hardly anyone could be satisfied with the current arrangement, but to him the option of warfare did not seem a likely alternative.

A global transformation from Communism to post-Communism was taking place. In Yugoslavia it took place earlier than in other Eastern European countries, but the actual breakdown of the Communist system occurred here less decisively than in Poland, Hungary, East Germany, and Czechoslovakia—countries which had lagged far behind in the liberalization process.

Vesna Pusić, a sociologist from Zagreb University, analyzed the reasons for the timidity of change, at least in regard to Croatian Communist rule.[2] She pointed out that the very fact that Yugoslavia was not a member of the Warsaw Pact and was the most liberal Communist regime in the world made the systemic contradictions appear less acute. The reformist and dissident groups were made up mostly of intellectuals, journalists, and some Marxists who had been expelled from the Communist Party, but few of them had practical experience on how to assume power in any multi-party elections—which seemed so desirable to the population and which now loomed close. These thinkers had moral influence but no political influence. Reform-oriented Communists, on the other hand, were a strong force in Yugoslavia, and it appeared that they would be able to carry out the transformation of the system and bring Yugoslavia to a higher level of social development, as a post-Communist nation. As it turned out, however, not even these figures were strong enough to carry out the transitions. In the meantime, "a revolution of symbols" spontaneously took place in which distinctly Croatian symbols of the past had been resurrected. In other republics a comparable process took place. The political maturity to deal with these potent symbols, which indeed were reminiscent of some destructive nationalist periods in the region's past did not exist in those political parties that received a decisive plurality in the first multi-party elections.

---

2. Vesna Pusić, *Vladaoci i upravljači* (Rulers and Managers) (Zagreb: Novi Liber, 1992).

A culture of democracy was lacking; to build it one needed time. But time was running out quickly. The nationality issue was far more difficult in Yugoslavia than in most other Eastern European countries (see Chapter 5). The nationalist ideology therefore entered the scene explosively, rather than slowly or in a nuanced way. The reform Communists did not get the chance to lead a gradual transformation into democracy. Instead, elected politicians—the anti-Communists in Croatia and Slovenia and the dedicated Communists in Serbia and Montenegro—badly mishandled the nationalist euphoria. It burned brightly because it was fanned so vigorously by these politicians who later were unable to restrain them.

After the collapse of the Communist Party of Yugoslavia (as described in Chapter 5), there was one chance that Yugoslavia could still make the transition into post-Communism in an orderly and creative way. It was the election of Ante Marković as federal Premier in January 1989.[3] Marković had been a successful director of one of Yugoslavia's largest industrial enterprises. He was a pragmatic, well-educated reform-oriented Communist who believed that a "new socialism" was possible. Economic reforms, according to Marković, were the preconditions for the further democratization of Yugoslav society. He believed that the national question could be dealt with more successfully by means of privatization. New entrepreneurs would emerge in all the states who would jointly defend their own economic interests, and thus would defend the federal government, which created these business opportunities for them.

Tito's legacy was different. Tito and his circle espoused the "self-managed" economy, which in theory belonged to everyone but concretely to no one and was therefore actually managed and disposed of by the Communist Party by means of a bureaucratic system of orders from the top ranks to the bottom. Members of the party had an enormous vested interest in the inviolability of this basic arrangement. The outward form could be, and was, tampered with as long as the essence remained unchanged. The resistance to Ante Marković's reforms would ultimately come

---

3. Important insights in the section on Ante Marković were gained from the memoirs of a Serbian journalist who was the press secretary of the Federal Executive Council headed by the Premier, Ante Marković. See Tašić, *Kako sam branio Antu Markovića.*

from the Communists in the civil service and the military, in other words, from those who were the most privileged segment of society. Milovan Djilas, the most prominent ex-Communist dissident, has called these "the new class."

By 1988 the Yugoslavian economy was already in a deep crisis, with a galloping inflation of 1,000 percent annually, 90 percent of the federal expenditures being for defense, with colossal industrial enterprises that were inefficient and failing, and with a quickly deteriorating nationality problem. Marković nearly pulled off a miracle. With bold fundamental measures he brought about a rapid privatization. Nearly 50,000 new private enterprises were formed in a year, and a clever fiscal policy halted the inflation and created an internal convertibility of the dinar. The exchange of dinars for German marks (or any other hard currency) was guaranteed to every citizen at the stable rate of seven dinars to a German mark—after having slashed four zeros off the previous domestic currency. Speedily, a large convertible currency reserve developed that could spur the growth of the economy. Salaries soared to near-European levels, productivity increased, and a sudden air of satisfaction could be felt. But this turned out to be both illusory and short-lived.

Marković had the mind but not the will to deal with the other cutthroat Balkan politicians. The Communists immediately realized that they would lose their privileges and power, and they resolutely ambushed the Premier at virtually every level. This was particularly true of the Serbian politicians. And by this time the interests of the leadership of the various republics were so divergent that it took most of the Premier's time and ability to try to work out a consensus. He tried to use reason, but reason cannot be used toward those who do not recognize its validity. His plans were torpedoed first by the Serb Communists; Milošević had recently monopolized power in Serbia and decided that he would not permit Marković to succeed, because this would be an obstacle in his own bid for dictatorial power over the entire country. The Slovenians and Croatians, observing Serbian obstruction, also sabotaged Marković's reforms. They preferred a very loose confederate model of governing that would be advantageous to their economic interest. Marković, on the other hand, was convinced that a genuine democratic federal model provided the best alternative.

Milošević had secured Serbia's control over both of its autonomous provinces (Vojvodina and Kosovo) and now engineered a takeover of the Montenegrin leadership by means of the so-called "anti-bureaucratic revolution" (see Chapter 5), placing in all the key positions people who were blindly devoted to him. Thus, secure in his power and with the unified support of all Serb Communists behind him, he made his move to bury Ante Marković. The latter did not recognize that Milošević, like so many other Balkan politicians, would pledge support of federal government initiative but then would either totally ignore this pledge or oppose it, saying that the policy had never been agreed upon in the first place.

First, the Serbian government—"secretly," but brazenly misusing the National Bank of Yugoslavia—printed billions of dollars' worth of Yugoslav currency to pay for its political bribes of the Serbian workers, peasants, and officers during the election. This totally undermined the economic reform and constituted a blatant Serbian aggression against all the other republics. When the plunder was discovered, the Serbian government defended itself with the lame excuse that fraud also existed elsewhere.

Next, Serbia, Slovenia, and Croatia refused to make their payments to the federal treasury—thus bankrupting the federation. The top Army brass complained now that the federal government had not paid the armed forces for over a year and that unless officers were paid salaries the following month, they might mutiny. Initially Gen. Veljko Kadijević, then defense minister, was inclined to see in Marković an ally in holding Yugoslavia together. But he switched to Milošević when he saw that the federal government was at the mercy of financing by the republics, which were enmeshed in a bitter tug-of-war on economic and political issues, and when he became convinced that Milošević was not reluctant to manipulate fiscal matters in the Army's and Serbia's favor. Hence, the Army generals, who were in any case dogmatic Communists, realized that their ambitions coincided with those of comrade Slobodan Milošević rather than with those of Mister Ante Marković. From then, they began following a distinctly Serbian interpretation of what was in the interests of Yugoslavia.

From 1989 onward, the Army saw eye to eye with Milošević's aspirations to create a Great Serbia, realizing, nevertheless, that the other republics were unwilling to buckle under to Milošević's bid for power and that consequently the federation would be unable to solve its problems. Thus, a *Putsch* had been carried out jointly by the Serbian Communists and Yugoslav Army, no punishment being meted out to those subverting the federation! This would, of course, encourage the nationalist leadership of the other republics to engage in similar actions destructive of the union.

A spate of arms purchases from abroad followed. First, the Yugoslav Army bought enormous amounts of very advanced Soviet missile technology; these equalled five years' normal purchases. Slovenian and Croatian governments, meanwhile, secretly imported automatic infantry weapons from Hungary, though the Army and Customs became aware of this. Ostensibly this importation was to protect themselves from local Serbs, who were given armaments by the Army, secret services, and the Serbian government—again ostensibly for *their* self-defense against the *Croats*. All of this happened without the knowledge or approval of the federal Premier.

From 1987 onward the Serbian government and media had been carrying out a hysterical campaign claiming that Serb minorities were gravely threatened throughout the country. There was some truth in that claim in respect to Kosovo, but it was untrue and unrealistic in Croatia and Bosnia-Herzegovina. With the uprising of the Serbian population in the Knin Krajina region of Croatia, came a Serb psychosis of fear that was a threat to themselves, a self-fulfilling prophecy. According to Vesna Pešić of the Belgrade-based anti-war Civil Union, the legitimate political role of the Republic of Serbia should have been the protection and guarantee of Serb minority rights in the other republics. Instead, tragically, Serb minority leaders proclaimed that they simply could no longer live alongside other ethnic groups if these republics were to declare independence. Milošević and his allies then started espousing the idea of a Great Serbia, i.e., the annexation of all lands in which Serbs live (or lived in the distant past) in any appreciable numbers. It was allegedly a policy to defend all Serbs.

This was an idea inspired by the ill-famed Memorandum of the Serbian Academy of Sciences and Arts, issued in 1986 by top Serbian scholars. In the Memorandum they warned that Yugoslavia was in danger of disintegrating. They also maintained that Tito and the Communist Party of Yugoslavia had ruled to the detriment of Serbia, which was the most exploited republic in Yugoslavia.[4] Serbs everywhere, said the scholars, must unite in order to end this totally undeserved victimization, because it was they, and not the other Yugoslav nationalities, who had shed the most blood for the creation of both the first and the second Yugoslavia.

Thus, by 1989 there was in place the ideology of the "defense" of Serbs everywhere, coupled with the alliance of Milošević's monopoly over Serbian politics and the awesome might of the Yugoslav Army led by a predominantly Serb officers' corps. There was also in place the determination of the political leadership of the other republics to escape the steel embrace of the Serbian leadership, preferring a confederate arrangement. A collision was on the way and Ante Marković's government was too weak to prevent it as the middle got squeezed out by both ends.

---

4. Slobodan Selenić and other participants of the round table discussion between Serb and Croat independent intellectuals in December 1993 in Zagreb pointed out the relentless media abuse of claims that each of the republics was exploited by the others in order to turn people against each other and increase national intolerance. See *Erasmus*, No. 5 (Zagreb, February 1994), pp. 45–49.

CHAPTER 5

THE UNRESOLVED NATIONAL QUESTION

The single most important reason for the dissolution of Yugoslavia was the inability of this multi-national country to solve the national question. While many persons and groups can be blamed for exploiting and exacerbating the issue (see Chapter 8), also at blame were some profound structural issues that had lasted throughout the turbulent history of Yugoslavia.

THE STRUCTURAL PROBLEM

One problem was that the various national groups *united* with each other with different notions as to what would take place. Likewise, when they experienced difficulties working with each other, they also disagreed as to whether, why, and how they might *separate*. To put it succinctly, after World War I Yugoslavia was created following the Wilsonian principle of self-determination of peoples[1] who were previously subject nations of crumbled empires; in Yugoslavia's case, the Austro-Hungarian and Turkish.

The Serbs thought of the process as an *accession*. Croats, Slovenes, and others were to be joined to the victorious Serbian state so that Yugoslavia would not be an entirely new entity but

---

1. Julie Mostov (in "Democracy and the Politics of National Identity," *Studies in East European Thought*, Vol. XLVI [1994], p. 23) points out the confusion in Eastern Europe as to what constitutes peoples, nations, and ethnic groups, which makes the concept of self-determination slippery and easily manipulable.

be an expanded continuity of the Kingdom of Serbia. In the mind of many Serbs, Croats and Slovenes were part of that Hapsburg empire which waged war on Serbia and lost. Serbia's reward for its suffering during the war and for being among the victorious allies was its ability to bring together all Serbs and other southern Slavs (with the exception of Bulgarians) into their state. The Slovenes and Croats thought the union was a voluntarily *associ-ation*, a free affiliation of a number of south Slavic nations to create an entirely new entity of related nations, by which all would benefit.

The national crisis came to a final head in the late 1980s, when the Serbs perceived the efforts of the other nationalities, especially the Slovenes and Croats, as unconstitutional *seces-sions* from a permanently unified federal structure. The Slovenes and Croats regarded it as a process of *dissociation* from a structure that did not serve them well.[2]

Serb nationalism was *hegemonistic*, while the nationalism of the others tended to be *separatist*. Serbs saw in the idea of Yugo-slavia the opportunity to have all Serbs living in a single state and, in addition, gathering around them the other nationalities in such a way that Serbs would play the dominant role. They saw Yugoslavia as their state in its entirety and assumed that the territories of the other nationalities were, like their own, a part of the Serbs' Yugoslavia. The Serbs, from the beginning, took pride in the power and position of the Yugoslav state and as-sumed that the others shared this feeling.

The Serb approach to the Yugoslav idea has been determined by this people's historical experience as a Byzantine Orthodoxy indigenized by Serbs shaped in a five-century-long resistance to Turkish Islam and nurtured primarily in epic poetry and reli-gious festivals. Folk saying verbalized that resistance as a strug-gle for "the honor of the cross and for golden freedom." The Christian masses under Turkish domination had few rights and the result was a "patriotism of warriors" who were forced to pro-

2. The Bosnian Muslims were not directly involved in these controversies but watched from the sidelines to see which side would prevail so that they could join the winning side. However, they were forced to make a decision before they were ready. They opted westward toward Europe (i.e., concretely toward Croatia and Slov-enia) rather than eastward, i.e., the stronger Serbs. It remains to be seen whether they miscalculated in the long run.

fess loyalty to oriental despotic dynasties, according to the phi-losopher-sociologist Andrija Krešić.[3] A constant aspiration was the assembling of all Serbs in one kingdom, either a Great Serbia or a Serb-dominated Yugoslavia.

What most of the Serbs were not aware of was that the other southern Slavic nationalities, especially those who had lived in the former Austria-Hungary, did not share in this feeling. Under the Hapsburg monarchy the Croats and Slovenes enjoyed the sta-tus of citizenship in one of Europe's most cosmopolitan em-pires.[4] They also were of the same religion as that of the empire. By the nineteenth century, under the influence of the French Revolution, the idea swept over them, too, to unite all Slavs in a single state structure. It would be a country guaranteeing equal status to the constituencies, united by common economic and cultural interests. When the Serb troops marched into their terri-tories upon unification in 1918, they were perceived as a rag-tag primitive Eastern army that came to replace the glittering and well-organized Hapsburgs. Croats, Slovenes, Muslims, and Mace-donians had a hard time deciding whether they were being liber-ated or occupied. Almost at once they resented Serb dominance and the thought of the Serbs or any "central" government in-terfering in their own states. They did not accept the Yugoslav state wholeheartedly, and constantly promoted local self-govern-ment and decentralization. Later, when they came to believe the Yugoslav experiment had failed, they sought to separate them-selves from it and viewed the Serbian role as oppressive and in-trusive. Their nationalism had a sharper edge to it than the Serbs'; it tended to be more exclusive, bitter, antagonistic, con-frontational, and quite self-conscious; whereas Serb nationalism was by nature more inclusive, absorbing, embracing, and unself-conscious.

For the Serbs Yugoslavia offered them primarily, and continues to this day to offer them the possibility of exercising political

---

3. Andrija Krešić is a Croat from Bosnia-Herzegovina, a former *partizan*, who con-tinues to live in Belgrade, where he once headed an important historical institute during the Communist period. He wrote two papers addressing the present crisis, both in Serbo-Croatian: "Neither Unitary nor Cantonized Bosnia and Herzegovina" and "Why Yugoslavia Failed Twice."

4. Nostalgia for "the good old days" among Slovenes and Croats tends to make them forget the oppression and exploitation they had suffered under the Hapsburgs.

power and a dominance of other southern Slavs. For the Croats and Slovenes, Yugoslavia meant an area where their cultural and economic activity could flourish and expand. These are stark contradictions in objective national interests—two conflicting ideas about Yugoslavism—which could be harmonized in neither of two twentieth-century attempts at creating a common country (1918 and 1945). By the 1990s almost all of the nationalities have been cured of the idea of Yugoslavism, and all of them have returned back to their local nationalisms. They "sobered up," as some of them might say.

From the outset these differences of perception of the state prevented the nationalities from reaching an understanding. The *undemocratic* character of Yugoslavia became visible at once and brought great disenchantment to the Croats and Slovenes. The Serbians, on the other hand, saw themselves as having sacrificed a great deal in order to unite all the Serbs and other southern Slavs into a state structure, and they therefore felt that they had every right to play the decisive role.

THE NATIONAL QUESTION IN THE FIRST YUGOSLAVIA

The state formed in 1918 was called the Kingdom of Serbs, Croats, and Slovenes, who were at the time regarded by many as one people with three names. The former Kingdom of Serbia, with its statehood, dynasty, army, and bureaucracy, dominated the new state. The parliament of the new state, however, reflected the contradictory expectations and styles of the constituent peoples and plunged from one crisis into another. In January 1929, King Alexander established a royal dictatorship, disbanded the parliament, and renamed the country Yugoslavia (meaning "the land of the Southern Slavs").

King Alexander proceeded to create a new hybrid Yugoslav nationality, one that would please those Serbs who believed that the other Slavic nations were crypto-Serbs who would be willing, ultimately, to accept this new identity. The Croat and Slovene alternative ideas of Yugoslavism were now ignored. Accordingly, groups emerged, especially in Croatia and Macedonia, which were totally unreconciled to the notion of being a part of a common state, either because they were not in favor of it in the first place or because they had become disillusioned with it when it became a reality. King Alexander fell victim to a conspiracy of these dissidents when he was assassinated, upon arrival for a state visit to France, at the port of Marseilles in 1934. The assassin's trail went first to a Macedonian revolutionary organization and ended up leading to the Croat *ustashe*, who had their training camps in fascist Italy.

By the late 1930s, larger historical forces were tearing Europe apart. Those Croats who aspired to an independent Croatian state, spearheaded by the pro-fascist *ustashe*, began looking toward the Axis powers as offering them the desired independence; the Allies, to whom Yugoslavia was linked, would likely not. The outcome was that Yugoslavia was attacked by the Axis powers in April 1941 and partitioned. One of those parts was proclaimed as the Independent State of Croatia, which included large sections of Bosnia and Herzegovina, although the new state ceded most of its Dalmatian coast to Italy.

The subsequent war of liberation (1941–45) was simultaneously a civil war, in which Serbs generally were pitted against Croats and Muslims, who for the most part allied themselves with the Nazis. An agonizing war engulfed the country, one in which it is claimed that over a million people were killed. At least half of them were casualties Yugoslavs inflicted upon each other.

THE TITOIST APPROACH TO THE NATIONAL QUESTION

Out of the tragedy of World War II, Tito's Communist-led multi-national guerrilla movement, the *partizans*—in which Serbs were by far the most numerous—emerged victorious. During this war, Tito and his inner circle already opted to restructure Yugoslavia as a federal state of equal nationalities, the king (Peter II) being removed from the picture. He was forbidden to return from exile in London. Already in 1943 at a meeting in Bosnia, the Anti-fascist Council of People's Liberation of Yugoslavia *(AVNOJ)* established the basic principle of national equality in a federal union of sovereign national states. Upon its liberation from the occupying fascist forces and a dreadful retaliation against the "national traitors"—primarily the *ustashe* and *chet-*

niks and the Slovene White Guard—Yugoslavia emerged a Communist-ruled country. The borders between the states were drawn by the Communist Party (some say by Tito personally) and were without discussion or question accepted—some thought forever.

The new federal system seemed to work for the next thirty years. No national conflicts emerged in the legislative, judicial, or executive branches of the government. The reason was simple—no real decisions were made at that level. All the significant decisions were made by the highly centralized Communist Party apparatus, or more accurately, all big issues were finally arbitrated by the head of the Communist Party, Josip Broz-Tito. Tito followed a very careful policy of balancing all national claims and conflicts, sometimes to the point of artificiality and visible injustice. Thus, if a nationalist excess was taking place in Croatia, for instance, he would purge not only Croatians found responsible but at the same time purge an equal number of Serbs and others from the ranks of the government or the party or the university, no matter how innocent these individuals might be of the charges leveled against them. This was done to make sure that no one group could claim that it had been discriminated against.

THE POST-TITO RESURRECTION
OF NATIONAL CONFLICTS

Upon Tito's death in 1980 there was no longer a final arbiter for disputes. None of the other major leaders of the Communist Party could be regarded as supra-national in the way Tito was. The authoritarianism of the Communist Party was better masked in Yugoslavia than in other Communist countries, where it was far more blunt. The deception prevailed that in Yugoslavia issues were being addressed at the local level. This was accomplished by means of the much-advertised "worker's self-management." Self-management was a theoretically interesting device which provided the fiction that all of the most important decisions were made by the direct participation at the local level of all who worked in the respective enterprise or lived in the precinct. But the entire system was subverted by the fact that the Communist Party cell or unit in each enterprise or precinct implemented the decisions that were made by the top party leadership. Although deception created the illusion that problems were being solved in a democratic manner at the local level, the truth was that during Tito's rule the country was a unitary, centrally governed state in which a single charismatic leader monopolized all decisions. As a result, the national question was masked rather than solved.

In the name of the principle of decentralization and democratization the Communist Party's name was changed to the League of Communists of Yugoslavia (LCY). The change was to indicate the loosening of the grip of the party over governance, to become merely a "guiding" force of society. The old and the new names, however, continued to be used interchangeably. Organizationally, the LCY constituted eight branches: one for each of the six republics and one for each of the two autonomous provinces. The leadership of these eight Communist Parties increasingly identified themselves with the national interests of their region.

After Tito's death they were increasingly unable to find effective common solutions to disparate problems. The conflicts and the power struggles increased. The system became increasingly stalemated. In fact, during the later years of Tito's life, the 1960s and 1970s, a transition took place to a federal, and then a *de facto*, confederate system of government in which two forces came into open collision. One was the centralizing unitary orientation espoused by the Army and the Communist-dominated federal government in Belgrade and the other was that of Communist elites of the various republics and provinces, who demanded greater local autonomy. The disintegration of Yugoslavia was not caused initially by a conflict of nationalities, because, after all, in this system the people of all nationalities were *objects* and not *subjects* of decision-making. Rather, the disintegration was caused—and here I agree with the previously mentioned Andrija Krešić—by the political elites of the republics. The federal government of Yugoslavia was a federation of republics and not a federation of peoples, which meant that the state was a matter for politicians and not for citizens.

The end of Yugoslavia took place when the republican Communist elites could no longer agree on how to share power; some wanted to dominate Yugoslavia politically; others, economically.

The division ran along the same lines as it had at the beginning of the union: The Serbian Communists wanted to dominate politically, while the Slovene and Croat Communists opted for economic domination. The leaders of the republican Communist parties adopted nationalistic programs.

Slobodan Milošević made his ruthless but successful bid for leadership of the Serbian Communist Party and thereby the Serbian government. Being the first politician to truly realize that Tito had died (this was five years after Tito's death!) and that there was a power vacuum, he made an equally ruthless bid to become Tito's successor. This became obvious to the other potentates in the various national Communist Parties. Had Milošević belonged to any but the Serbian nation, there might have been less resistance to his bid for power. But he is a Serb and the others saw his grip on power as a confirmation of Serbian hegemonistic tendencies.

Two slogans ran diametrically opposed to one another. The first was "A weak Serbia means a strong Yugoslavia," while the other was "A strong Serbia means a weak Yugoslavia." Milošević and the Serbs showed a contempt for the last Titoist constitution, of 1974, which created a weak federal structure and vested in the two Serbian autonomous provinces of Vojvodina and Kosovo power nearly equal to that accorded the republics. Further, the republics were defined by that constitution as sovereign. This quasi-confederate model was purely a theoretical matter in 1974, because Tito and the Party held all the decision-making power in their hands. The Serbs, however, started complaining that their jurisdiction was restricted to the relatively small territory of Serbia proper and that they had lost control over their own provinces.

By the late 1970s the Kosovo province had become an insurmountable national problem for Serbia. The Kosovo region is in southwest Serbia, bordering on Albania. It was once, of course, the center of the medieval Kingdom of Serbia and the site of the legendary battle of Kosovo Field in 1389. In a strange reversal of concepts the battle has become forever embedded in the Serbian consciousness as a symbol of their people's tenacity—despite their defeat and suffering; a transformation of defeat into victory not unlike that of the Christian perception of Christ's crucifixion. On the other hand, that region was increasingly inhabited by Albanians, a non-Slavic people possibly of Illyrian descent, that is, Balkan aborigines. It is difficult if not impossible to sift out the conflicting claims of just how many Serbs or Albanians inhabited the region at what time. What is clear, however, is that the demographics have not worked in the Serbian interest. The Albanian birthrate skyrocketed while the Serbian dwindled. The process was reinforced by sizeable Serb emigration. Nowadays, Tito and the Communist Party are being blamed by Serbian nationalists for the alleged expulsion of about a quarter-million Serbs and Montenegrins from Kosovo immediately after World War II. This was followed by alleged systematic Albanian brutalities aiming at the expulsion of Serbs. The Albanian Communist elite that ruled Kosovo played hand in hand with those who wanted the ethnic cleansing of Serbs in Kosovo.

Serb migration from Kosovo was not a new phenomenon. In previous centuries, Serbs sought better conditions and protection from Turkish oppression in the lands of the Austrian emperor, and in the post-World War II period Serbs were lured away by much better living conditions and possibilities for advancement in the northern areas of Yugoslavia. Anyone who has been to Kosovo will readily understand why people would wish to leave this poverty-stricken area. Even Albanians had migrated out of the area in goodly numbers. But to understand why Albanians today make up 90 percent of Kosovo, one need only add in the escapees who have arrived from Albania proper. These, and Yugoslav Albanians, have had a burgeoning birthrate, due in part to Muslim traditionalism regarding marriage and family and clan property. Needless to say, the Kosovan Albanians have increasingly made claims for autonomy and self-determination. Some desired the status of a separate republic within Yugoslavia, others annexation to Albania. They have intensely resented the cruel treatment they received at the hands of the secret service, which has always been predominantly Serb in composition. Locked in a bitter struggle, both nationalities have levelled mutual allegations that indignities were perpetrated by the other.

It was Milošević's genius to understand that Kosovo was Serbia's neuralgic problem and that Serbs could be rallied in a battle cry that Kosovo was a nonseparable part of Serbia. And, while the other republics and provinces desired to retain the provisions of the 1974 constitution or even further decentralized decision-making, the Serbians sought to change it and bring greater centralism to Yugoslavia. This desire they punctuated by severely repressing an Albanian revolt in Kosovo and with a unilateral abolishment of the autonomy of both Kosovo and Vojvodina, creating a unified Serbian Milošević-dominated administration for the entire republic.

To do this they used a devilishly clever ploy, called the "Anti-bureaucratic Revolution." Moving from city to city, radicalized Serbs, mostly from Kosovo, appealed for the support of other Serbs against their alleged persecutions by the Albanians and demanded that Serbia restore their rights and regain its own supposedly sharply curtailed state rights. They attacked all those Communists in Serbia who opposed this maneuver, labeling them corrupt, accusing them of wishing only to preserve their privileges at the expense of the impoverished Serbian people.

Indeed, the period of relative well-being of the 1960s and 1970s was over. The time had come, too, to repay the substantial international loans at fairly exorbitant interest rates. These funds were often unwisely invested or even squandered outright. The time came to pay up and the only way to do this in a faltering worldwide recession was by tightening their belts. The population at large was aware that Communist functionaries had, with few exceptions—Milošević allegedly being one of them—enriched themselves enormously, profiting from their privileged position in Yugoslav society. So the theme "Anti-bureaucratic Revolution" had a wide popular support, for the public saw it as a purge of the *"foteljaši"* (the armchair sitters, a word implying a cushiony, nonproductive existence).

What the public did *not* realize was that Milošević and his people had hijacked the "Anti-bureaucratic Revolution." As local government after local government resigned under the pressure of these public street demonstrations and sit-ins, Milošević installed his carefully selected loyal cadres who were at once loyal, without question, to Belgrade and to the larger Serb cause. In Vojvodina, for instance, out went the *"autonomaši"* (pro-autonomy) politicians, giving that word a negative connotation, as if it were unpatriotic or anti-Serbian. In fact, they were depriving the autochthonous Serbian old-timers of all power and bringing into power immigrant Serbs from Herzegovina, Montenegro, Bosnia, or Kosovo. The immigrants generally did not have the traditional tolerance for the multi-ethnic makeup of Vojvodina or the tradition of good relationships with neighbors. The old-timers regard these newcomers, rightly or wrongly, as "primitive." Serbia was now consolidated in the hands of Milošević as he became the hero and the unrivaled boss, having eliminated all liberal-minded alternatives within the Communist Party of Serbia. He could now make his bid to grab power in the rest of the country.

NATIONALISM BREAKS UP THE COMMUNIST PARTY OF YUGOSLAVIA

Two major trends within the Party collided in the 1980s with the conflict escalating by the end of the decade. One trend, seeking central control from Belgrade and led by Milošević, collided with the one that sought even greater flexibility and decentralization and was spearheaded by the Slovenian Communist Party. The fiction of Communist unity was, in fact, shattered by the ever more clear realization that there were eight Communist parties rather than one.

The death blow to the fiction of Communist unity came in 1989. Under relentless pressure by the Serbian Party to homogenize the Communist movement, the Slovenian Communists walked out of the Congress of the LCY. It is said that at least one Slovenian Communist had tears in her eyes saying, "They just killed Yugoslavia." Indeed, the walkout brought the congress to an abrupt end. The Communists were now in total disarray. This proved to be the last meeting of the Yugoslav Communists.

To add to the multiplicity of Communist voices, the Army generals formed still a ninth Communist Party: the so-called Party for the Renewal of Yugoslavia. On the other hand, all, but the Communists of Montenegro quickly changed their parties' names in anticipation of the elections that were to be held in the near-future, because it became apparent to them that under the traditional name they had no chances whatever, while under the somewhat altered names they might succeed. As it happened, only in Montenegro did the Communist Party win. In Serbia the renamed Party, under the title Serbian Socialist Party and led by Milošević, also won a resounding victory. The non-Serbian republics voted non-Communists into power (though many former Communists retained their positions under new party labels) and became postsocialist. The Serbians and Montenegrins claimed that their republics were still socialist—by choice of the people. Thus, one more division occurred between the non-Serbian and Serbian nations.

When the worldwide collapse of the Communist system took place in the late 1980s it became apparent, according to Milan Kučan, the President of Slovenia and one of the major players in the demise of the united Communist movement, that the Yugoslav federal system was unable to adapt itself to the new conditions that prevailed in Europe after the fall of the Berlin Wall.

The acceptance of the multi-party system during the twilight of the Communist period provided the evidence that Tito and the Communist Party had not solved the national question of Yugoslavia. Instead, most Communists quickly embraced a nationalistic agenda hoping to retain power in forthcoming elections. The bug of ethnic nationalism infected the ex-Communists just as surely as it did most of the newly created political parties.

ETHNIC NATIONALISM AS THE NEW ORDER

The vast majority of the political parties formed in the late 1980s and early 1990s operated only within the scope of a single nationality and more often than not carried the prefix of the national identification, such as The Macedonian Internal Revolutionary Organization/The Democratic Party for Macedonian National Unity; or The Croatian Democratic Union; or The Serbian Radical Party; or The Slovene Christian Democrats; and so forth. Each of them addressed themselves only to their own ethnic/national group. They were not interested in building a civil society either in their own republic or throughout Yugoslavia. Rather, they sought to defend only their own political and economic interests and that of their own ethnic group. The federal states, which were now rapidly moving toward breaking away from the center, were now ruled by *ethnocracies*, each competing as to who had the most articulated ethnic nationalist or ethnoreligious credentials. Ethnic nationalism had become the firmly entrenched principle of political discourse and action, and politicians rushed headlong into the blazing inferno of war. This process was generally encouraged and welcomed by the main church or religious group of the respective nations (see Chapter

7). However, few observers outside the country took any notice of these disintegrating processes.

The political transition from a Communist to the post-Communist period had the most disruptive impact upon Yugoslavia's numerous fragile multi-ethnic communities. The basic question in multi-ethnic societies is whether governing is shared or is wielded by one ethnicity. When the Communists were in power, the ethnicity of those wielding power was not a burning question. Of course, even then there was a vague awareness and a resentment among the population that members of one or another ethnic group dominated the government.

During the Communist period, power did not emanate directly from ethnocultural communities. Rather, the discriminatory practices by an ethnic group were carried out by the Communists. In the multi-ethnic communities of Croatia and Bosnia-Herzegovina the most privileged were the Serbs, then the Muslims, and finally the Croats. In communities where Serbs and Croats or Serbs and Muslims lived intermingled the power was held by the Serbs; in those where Muslims and Croats lived side by side the power was held by Muslims. When multi-party elections took place from 1990 onward, they generally swept into power on the local level an ethnic group that was previously underrepresented in the structures of power. No longer was it possible to impose and administer power effectively from a distant center. On the one hand, ethnic groups that had previously held power and were now being displaced were unwilling to relinquish power. On the other hand, the newly elected parties, ethnic in composition as previously noted, were eager to *rapidly* replace the former rulers. Frequently these replacements were not based on merit but along new, purely ethnic lines, seeking revenge for real or imagined harm inflicted by the previous rulers. Therefore, instead of the establishment of a pluralistic democratic civil society the elections only switched ethnocracies in the multi-ethnic communities. Conflict became inevitable.

THE IMPACT OF ETHNIC NATIONALISM

To conclude, the main historical force determining Balkan events in the nineteenth and twentieth centuries has been ethnic nationalism. The various nationalities have, on the whole, been unable to harmonize their divergent national aspirations. Twice in the twentieth century it seemed that these interests intersected. The first time was at the end of World War I, when it seemed that being for the first time bound in a common state structure the southern Slavs would be protected from the hegemonistic aspirations of some of their more powerful neighbors. Unified, they could more easily defend themselves and create a more viable economic and political life. The first attempt ended in failure by the time of the outbreak of World War II.

When Tito created the New Yugoslavia, another chance came to live together. This time the advantage was that the federal system appeared to give the member republics greater equality and that the Communist Party guaranteed a unified political structure that was, initially, committed to keeping the country together. The dictatorial nature of Tito's reign was both an asset and a liability. The asset was that he was able to clamp down on the separatists and those who wanted to sow discord and hatred among the nationalities. The liability was that many of the problems were not really solved but "swept under the rug" and postponed. To use another metaphor, a pressure-cooker effect was created in which the pressures built up but were not visible to the naked eye. What is clear today is that Tito's authoritarianism—and, even more, the totalitarian structure of Communism itself—did not help the political leaders and the citizens to learn skills of negotiating and compromising. Real problems could not be addressed because it was alleged that there *were* no more real problems or divergent aspirations!

Claims have been made that the creation of Yugoslavia was a total disaster, and that the nationalities would have fared better had it never been created. Some claim that, at least in regard to their diverse national aspirations, the experiment was an uninterrupted failure. Such claims are exaggerated. Many, perhaps the majority, and perhaps even the overwhelming majority of Yugoslavs, at one time believed in the greater nation and were proud to be citizens of it. There were as many valid reasons for the creation of a Yugoslavia as there were many false reasons for breaking it up. While there is no point in shedding tears for something that has gone by the wayside of history, tears should be shed for the tremendous harm that has been done in the process of breaking up the nation. There is even room for nostalgia about the loss of an idea that had the potential for creating greater stability than does the present situation. Without knowing whether, in the long run, the situation may change and peace and prosperity may come to the various southern Slavic states, Tito's New Yugoslavia and even the old Yugoslavia were both preferable to the current war-making that has been let loose with such demonic fury.

It is equally true that with the dissolution of Yugoslavia there are many who now experience a tremendous sense of loss, not knowing what to call themselves from a national viewpoint; many of these are products of mixed marriages.[5] For many, nationality had became a matter of *choice* rather than biological destiny. Latent in many people, even those who are in favor of separate national statehoods, is the recognition that they should and could—again—work together with people of other nationalities and that, somehow, ways to do so will need to be found in the future.

However, there can be no talk of creating a "third" Yugoslavia, as was discussed in the late 1980s, harmonizing the divergent nationalist interests in a restructured confederation or union of some other type. After several years of warfare, this has become an utter impossibility. A rump state of Serbia and Montenegro still upholds the illusory name of Yugoslavia. It could be that one or more southern Slavic nations may find a way to enter into some political or economic alliance or union, as has been planned for Croatia and Bosnia-Herzegovina, but never again will all of the former states of the union gather together in a single country. Perhaps someday they can all become a part of a United Europe in which borders are largely inconsequential, but even that seems to be another illusion, given the divisive events of the 1990s.

The chaotic conditions that accompanied the fall of Yugoslavia were suitable for the vigorous dissemination of nationalist propaganda on the part of those who either authentically held strong ethnic loyalties or quickly jumped on the bandwagon seeing ad-

---

5. A powerful portrayal of this situation can be seen in the film *Romeo and Juliette of Sarajevo* portraying the real-life love of a Muslim young woman and a Serbian young man: it ends in their death in "no-man's-land," where they lay for a week as a mute testimony of how hate can destroy love.

vantages for themselves. Milošević, for instance, seems not to be a Serb nationalist by conviction but manipulates Serb nationalism cleverly to maintain a grip on power. In the short period of only several years, nationalisms have gripped the great majority of the former Yugoslav people, though it is not clear whether this will be the case for a long or a short period. Nationalistic euphoria reigns supreme in nearly every segment of the population; few are those former Yugoslavs who are not affected by it. It has always been the true opiate for the masses in times of extreme social crises (when it frequently also takes on fascist characteristics).[6]

Nationalism is, according to Eugen Pusić,[7] a monomaniacal fascination that encompasses both the manipulated and the manipulators. National conflicts accelerate national solidarity, the latter of which envelops not only nationalists but a much wider group of people. The conflict increasingly slips out of control as people who recall both the *ustasha* terror of 1941 and the *chetnik* terror of 1991 say, "I am not a nationalist, but this is really too much." Such people are foolishly ready to make the effort to change a multi-ethnic, multi-cultural, multi-lingual, and multi-religious environment into an impossibly homogeneous territory by means of "ethnic cleansing."

There is currently no ideology in the Balkans which matches nationalism's profound effect upon individuals and groups.[8] This accursed land was always prone to tectonic collisions (both literally and symbolically), and those who have reignited the ethnoreligious hatreds have hurled entire nations into the inferno.

---

6. To quote a truly memorable line by Robert D. Kaplan, "Communism would exit the world stage revealed for what it truly was: fascism, without fascism's ability to make the trains run on time." In *Balkan Ghosts*, p. 76.

7. Eugen Pusić is professor emeritus of law at Zagreb University. His insights are from *Erasmus*, No. 5 (Zagreb, February 1994), p. 74.

8. It is still the issue that needs to be addressed not only in the Balkans but throughout Eastern Europe and even more widely. It will probably remain the main problem for several decades. The challenge of grappling with nationalism's negative effects as well as strengthening its positive effects deserves the utmost attention of politicians, diplomats, scholars, intellectuals, and citizens in the countries of the southern Slavs and elsewhere.

CHAPTER 6

CIVIL WAR OR WAR BETWEEN COUNTRIES?

ALTERNATE PERCEPTIONS OF THE CONFLICT

One of the most hotly debated issues is the nature of the war which is being waged on the territory of the former Yugoslavia. What is to be done about the conflict domestically and internationally hinges upon the way one perceives it. No wonder that the debate about the nature of the war is not merely an academic exercise but is the subject of propaganda on the part of the combating sides. Practically all of the answers serve the self-interests of one or another of the contending parties. This is not to say that there is not a considerable dose of truth in the variant interpretations. Although all seem credible, I believe that the real answer is more complex than what one usually encounters.

The first claim is that this is a civil war between unionists and secessionists within the border of an internationally recognized country, and not unlike the American Civil War of the 1860s. The second claim is that it is a war in which three new and recently internationally recognized countries namely Slovenia, Croatia, and Bosnia-Herzegovina were attacked by an aggressor state, nominally Yugoslavia but *de facto* Serbia; given the collapse of Yugoslavia, the Serbs hope to establish a "Great Serbia," or at least a Serbia greater than its borders within the old Yugoslavian federation. A third contention is held, by some, that the war is a continuation of ancient unresolved tribal animosities resurrected under contemporary circumstances. This theory holds that there is a worldwide strain between globalism and particularism and that in the Balkans divisiveness (i.e., Balkanization) prevails. Yet another interpretation maintains that the war was brought on by former Communist bureaucrats attempting to hang on to their power after the collapse of the socialist system; seeing that the Communist ideology had lost its power, and perceiving an ideological vacuum, they resorted to the dormant but very much alive nationalist ideologies, based on the myths of ancestral land and blood kinships. Finally, the conflict can be seen as the cleaving of great civilizational conglomerates along the fault lines of their historic encounters; in this case, it would be the collision of three civilizations—Eastern European Orthodoxy, Western European Roman Catholicism, and Asiatic Islam.

The answer as to whether this is a civil war or a war of aggression by one country upon others depends largely on the way one defines the character of the conflict. Some or all of the above portrayals are attractive in that they sound plausible and are theoretically streamlined. The problem is that they are half-truths. Overly simplified theoretical frameworks foster what appear to be clarity and easy working out of solutions. Knowledge based on half-true premises is always faulty, however.

The character of the present violence is so complex that it is far more accurate to define it as several intertwined wars rather than a single war. These wars do not merely succeed one another; they overlap and are frequently intrinsically linked in the sense that the heat of one conflict ignites the fire of another. The entanglement of both the peoples and their aspirations is labyrinthine.

This is not only a theoretical debate but one which impacts on their own perceptions and the way they are viewed by other countries or the United Nations. An accurate assessment will make a difference in how international law is to be applied, public opinion formed, or governmental decisions made to intervene or to remain uninvolved.

If it is a civil war—and that variant interpretation has been most frequently advanced by Serbs—what is at hand is a tragic, fratricidal conflict which is primarily an internal matter for the southern Slavs themselves to settle. Some proponents of this interpretation blame foreign countries, primarily Germany (along with Austria and Hungary), the Vatican, the Islamic states, and the United States, for having sown seeds of discord and promoted in Yugoslavia the idea of an unconstitutional secession in order to advance some of their economic and political interests in the Balkans. This variant on the civil war theory, also usually proposed by Serb writers and journalists, argues that Germans, by virtue of their traditional friendship with Croats and Slovenes and because of their newfound prosperity and power following German unification, are now implementing their ages-old aspiration to control the Adriatic Sea and the Balkans. Another slight variant of the same theory is that Hapsburg imperial ideas are being resurrected; the idea is that ever since the Serbs stood in the way of their eastward expansion *(Drang nach Osten)*, the Austrians have harbored a grudge and have used their stooges, Slovenia and Croatia, to foment the breakup of Yugoslavia. The memory of the World War II alliances between Nazi Germany and fascist Italy on the one side and fascist Croats and Slovenes on the other is cited to give credence to this theory. It is claimed that this fascist alliance was interrupted by the creation of the "new" Yugoslavia at the end of the war but that it is now being resurrected, along with fascism throughout Europe. The same theorists, by the way, say that this civil war is so complex that one does not have merely two sides fighting each other but a chaotic multifarious conflict in which sometimes units of the same ethnic group may fight each other. They point out that sometimes members of one ethnic group may fight in the armed forces of another ethnic group against their own (e.g., Muslims fighting in Serb military formations against the Bosnian Army, which is made up in large part of Muslims; or, vice versa, Serbs fighting as members of the predominantly Muslim Bosnian Army against Serbian units). Thus the war may have started as a civil war between those who favored secession and those who favored union and it ended as a war of delineating new borders between the southern Slavic states, now that Yugoslavia has essentially disintegrated.

A variant of this model is the interpretation of Mihailo Marković,[1] a former humanistic Marxist philosopher from Belgrade University who now plays a leading role in the Serbian Socialist Party of Slobodan Milošević. He contends that the war is a conflict of nation-building by various ethnic units. The Serbs had

---

1. Mihailo Marković, "Yugoslavia Under Siege" and "Serbs Under Siege" (typescripts, no date, the latter presumably dated May 1993).

satisfied their urge for independence and sovereignty already in the nineteenth century. They were ready to limit their aspirations in the formation of Yugoslavia, having satisfied their desire to unite all their own nationals within the borders of one state structure. But the other nationalities went straight into Yugoslavia from being subjects of either the Hapsburg or Ottoman empires and were, hence, deprived of any interlude of independent nationhood. Belatedly now, says Marković, they are exercising that aspiration but at the cost of the unity of the Serbian nation. This, as he sees it, justifies Serbian actions to protect and gather all the Serbs' nationals and make border corrections. These borders were previously unimportant when all southern Slavs lived within Yugoslavia, but now that the separatists have prevailed elsewhere, Serbia must affirm its own right for Serbs to live in a single nation state, which Marković assures, will be both socialist and democratic.

All the proponents of this theory argue that it is unwise for other nations to get involved in a civil war they barely understand. Additionally, there is no international law which provides a rationale for foreign states to meddle in the internal political power struggles of another country, even if such a struggle is violent. The Serbs claim that foreign intervention is basically a Western "imperialist" endeavor and they seek assistance primarily from other Orthodox nations, such as Russia, Greece, and Romania.

A second argument is that this is a war of aggression by Serbs against clearly defined, internationally recognized countries for which the sole reason is Serbian imperialism. This argument is advanced generally by Slovenes, Croats, and Bosnian Muslims. The argument states that when the Serbs lost their ability to dominate the other republics within the framework of Yugoslavia, and when Yugoslavia simply fell apart under its own weight, the Serbs decided to conquer as much land as they could grab. Serbian hegemonists continued their age-long aspiration for expansion and opted to deny violently the ages-old aspirations for sovereign and independent nationhood of Slovenes, Croats, and in short order Bosnians-Herzegovinians and Macedonians, which peoples were internationally recognized by many countries. Unwilling to grant greater regional autonomies or accept the offer of the type of confederacy which the voters in these republics approved in a referendum, the Belgrade government, it has been argued, engineered the intervention of the Yugoslav People's Army, aided by Serbian paramilitary forces (the *chet-niks*) in a clear case of foreign aggression. In this light, the newly formed states needed to seek the protection of the international community; and indeed, the activity of the rump Yugoslav state has been repeatedly condemned by many international agencies. Furthermore, the reaction by the international community led to the expulsion of Yugoslavia from membership in the United Nations and to a subsequent embargo, as well as threats of NATO and UN military intervention against the Serbs. Proponents of this interpretation frequently seek such military intervention, as well as argue for war-crime trials, insisting that genocide against Croats and Muslims is being carried out in the name of Great Serbia. They frequently criticize the indecisiveness of the international community and accuse it of not living up to the UN charter, its conventions and declarations, and Security Council decisions. Many of the proponents conclude sarcastically that if there were oil deposits in the Balkans, the United States and its allies would have long ago intervened as decisively as they did against Iraq. They contend that the very credibility of NATO and the UN are at stake when, despite all threats, little has been done and political indecision had been characteristic of the Western powers.

A third alternative interpretation is that this is a war of resurrected ancient ethnic animosities. The contention is these are perennial Balkan characteristics. After a millennium of fighting each other for territory, thriving on revenge and mutual hatred, the Balkan tribes' animosities toward each other culminated in the civil war that took place during World War II upon the destruction of the first Yugoslav state. This theory holds that it was a mistake to have incorporated such ancient rivals into a single state of Yugoslavia in 1918 and again in 1945. We are witnessing the demise of the state structure as conceived by the French Revolution, based on compromise, because the Balkan peoples are uncomfortable with the very notion of compromise.[2] Rather, they should have each been left alone to evolve their tribes into small independent nations. The argument is that nation-making is best left alone by great powers, since getting involved can create a Viet Nam-like quagmire. Outsiders are un-

2. Frank Viviano, "The Balkan Tribe," *Mother Jones*, Jan./Feb. 1993, pp. 30–33.

likely to disentangle, in months, what local peoples were unable to do for decades or centuries. Great empires of the past could not digest the hot stew that was the Balkans. What should make us believe that the UN or the European Community can do any better?

A fourth alternative is to point out that the civilizational and cultural fault lines of East, West, and South meet in the Balkans. Here is where the Byzantine-inspired Eastern Orthodox culture and religion confronted the Roman Catholic and its Western European cultural and religious patterns. Each tried to subdue the other, thereby moving the collision line back and forth but never far from Bosnia. The Orthodox and Catholic interests coincided only when Islamic culture and religion spilled over the Balkans into Central Europe. Again, over the centuries the encounter line between Islam and Christianity moved to and fro but never ranged far away from their central meeting point in the heart of the former Yugoslavia—namely, Bosnia. And so this unfortunate region, Bosnia, as the microcosm of the former Yugoslavia—and, indeed, the Balkans—was to experience the clash of civilizations similar to great continental shelves crashing into each other and permanently causing seismic tremors and earthquakes. This interpretation is advanced by writers from nearly every ethnic group and has recently been brought into the American mainstream by the Harvard professor Samuel Huntington.[3]

Still another claim is that the war is the result of the worldwide collapse of Communism and the attempt by former Communists to maintain their societal privileges. This has been, in fact, the case in all former Communist countries. Indeed, most of the political players who instigated the conflict in Yugoslavia were former Communist functionaries eager to hold on to their positions of power. When they could no longer win power over the entire country, they settled for holding on to power in a part of it. This is especially true of Slobodan Milošević, but it applies also to many others.

The Bosnian ambassador to the UN, Mohammed Sacirbey, espouses a version of this theory.[4] According to him, Muslims,

---

3. "The Clash of Civilizations?" *Foreign Affairs,* Summer 1993, pp. 22–29.

4. These views were expressed during a joint lecture with the author at Rider College in New Jersey on October 6, 1993.

Serbs, and Croats lived fairly harmoniously alongside each other for centuries, creating an identifiable Bosnian culture. They lived, intermingled, in the same cities, towns, villages, and apartment houses, frequently not even cognizant of the specific religious identity of each other. Recently, even a fairly large number of intermarriages took place. The former Communists, in order to cling to power, promoted an ethnic ideology in order to fan hatred and discord between ethnic groups and retake possession of at least some of the territories. Most aggressive among these ex-Communists were Serb politicians, especially Milošević and Karadžić, who, along with other war criminals, did not hesitate to attempt to carry out genocide. According to Sacirbey, Bosnian Muslims need the protection of the international community if genocide is to be halted. At a minimum, the United Nations should lift the arms embargo so that Muslims can more effectively defend themselves and drive out the aggressor.

This interpretation is conceptually clear-cut because it names the aggressor both individually and collectively, and it asks for the punishment of people who have perpetrated revolting massacres of genocidal proportion. The assumption is made that once the aggressor is repelled, Bosnia would return to its previous pattern of harmonious coexistence of the three ethnic and religious groups and make progress as a Western-oriented, democratic, pluralistic society. Muslim fundamentalism is seen as a marginal phenomenon—unless Europe and the United States utterly fail to protect Bosnia, in which case there may be no other alternative but to receive aid from Muslim fundamentalist nations.

Quite apart from the accuracy of each interpretation above, it is obvious that each of these arguments about the nature of the Yugoslav conflict is clearly useful to one or more of the contending sides. It is in the interests of Serbia-Montenegro, which have been militarily more successful than the others, that no international intervention should take place since such intervention would most likely be directed solely against them. They believe that international military intervention is least likely to take place if the world community accepts the interpretation that a civil war is taking place and that only after the civil war ends will it become clear what geographic and political shape the successor states will take. On the other hand Slovenia, Croatia, Bosnia-Herzegovina, and Macedonia prefer the other alternatives, because they see themselves as the aggrieved parties, to whom sympathy and humanitarian aid, and perhaps even military aid and intervention, should be accorded.

It is, therefore of considerable importance to establish which of the interpretations of the war is the correct one. As the reader may have concluded by now, however, this armed conflict has characteristics of *both* a civil war and a war of aggression of one nation upon another.

OVERVIEW OF THE PROCESS OF WAR-MAKING

Milan Kučan, the President of Slovenia,[5] is a man well informed about the aspects of a war in which his state took part and had to make an accurate assessment of the situation in order to lead his nation out of danger. He participated personally in many of the meetings with politicians, diplomats, military leaders, and scholars in which fateful decisions were made regarding the outbreak and the waging of that war. From my interview with him I have come to the conclusion that the Yugoslav conflict is really not a single war but, rather, a series of different wars intermingled within a larger context. Even within a particular war there were sometimes phases which clearly changed its character. One may use the singular noun "war" for the violence in Yugoslavia in the same sense as it is appropriate to use the term "Second World War," though it is clear that quite a few related though quite distinct wars are being summed up together for the sake of convenience.

A succinct overview of the flow of events is offered here, and will be followed by a detailed description. The present conflicts can be traced to two low-intensity wars of the early 1980s, one in the Kosovo province of Serbia and the other slightly later in Croatia. Then followed a war in Slovenia in 1991 which was a war of the Yugoslav federal government against that republic. The intense war in Croatia started on May 2, 1991, before formal secession, and flared up with great intensity in July just as the war in Slovenia wound down. It was a war with only the Serbs,

---

5. Interview with Milan Kučan in Ljubljana in the Office of the President of Slovenia on September 1, 1993.

supported by the Yugoslav Army, who did not want to permit the secession of Croatia from Yugoslavia. The war in Bosnia and Herzegovina started in April 1992 as a war of the Yugoslav People's Army against the newly independent country, but changed its character and became a civil war initially between Serbs on one side and allied Muslims and Croats on the other; then it changed into a three-way war of each against the others. The danger is that the war in Bosnia and Herzegovina may ignite the adjacent regions of Sandžak and Kosovo in Serbia and perhaps even a civil war within Serbia between different factions over Serbia's war-making. Such a war could easily overflow into Macedonia and Albania, and perhaps then into Greece, Turkey, and Bulgaria, making it into a major regional war.

PRELIMINARY SKIRMISHES IN KOSOVO AND CROATIA

While Kučan's analysis (for this writer) started with the war in Slovenia, mine starts earlier, with a low-intensity war that began as early as 1980, first in Kosovo between Serbs and Albanians and then, as if by ripple effect, in Croatia. In retrospect these were preparatory skirmishes for greater wars to follow.

The low-intensity war in Kosovo and in Croatia were more or less unnoticed by the international community, although some foreign parliamentary delegations did go to Kosovo on fact-finding missions. They discovered that they really were not able to gather any additional facts beyond those they had been given prior to their arrival in Yugoslavia. However, the Serbian and Albanian versions of the situation were radically different. Neither side was able to move beyond its own version of the past and the bitter recriminations about how it was being victimized by the other. The international community was therefore unable to do anything about the Kosovan conflict. On the whole, it was scarcely reported internationally and was not perceived as war by the public.

In both Kosovo and Croatia the minority Serb population felt that its survival was severely jeopardized. The Serbs claimed that the threat to them was of genocidal proportions and that they would no longer tolerate it. In Kosovo from the late 1970s on (and in Croatia a decade later), numerous violent incidents took place which included property damage, loss of jobs, harassment, rapes, fights, and killings. In Kosovo by the middle 1980s, these events led to mass demonstrations by *both* nationalities which were usually broken up by the police. It was there that Milošević catapulted himself into the position of champion of the Serbs as he shouted, in response to seeing police beat up Serb demonstrators, "No one will be allowed to beat you in your own land." Thereupon, police beatings and torturing were shifted to Albanians almost exclusively. Several times martial law was clamped down upon Kosovo and very repressive measures were introduced to curb the local Albanians' desire for self-rule. Since then, Kosovo has become a police state, and the Albanians have been so severely repressed by the Serb police and army units that they are loath to give anything but passive resistance, perhaps figuring that, given demographic trends, time if nothing else is on their side.

The Croatian conflict was nearly unrelated to the one in Kosovo because it focused on resurrected Croat-Serb antagonisms. Occasional terrorist attacks by right-wing extremist Croat groups against the Yugoslav People's Army sharply increased tensions. Serbs in Croatia, fearing a revival of the *ustasha* right-wing extremism among Croats and the massacre of Serbs, began making preparations to defend themselves. In the Krajina region around the town of Knin, Serb rebels erected barricades (it was hence called the "log rebellion") on roads and railways crucial to Croatian traffic between Zagreb and Dalmatia. They also took over some police stations, threatening secession from Croatia should Croatia secede from Yugoslavia. In other regions the Croatian government initiated personnel changes in certain police units, firing the once-dominant Serbs and replacing them with Croats. Each side blamed the other for initiating the violence and each side claimed that the other dominated and terrorized them. Answering her own question why such violence should not be called war, a Croatian journalist said that it was not a war as long as the names of the victims were known and as long as regular burials of the victims took place. It was in ways like this that, at that time, most Yugoslavs denied to themselves and to the world that a war was already being waged.

WAR IN SLOVENIA: A FIZZLED *"BLITZKRIEG"*

Open war began in Slovenia on June 25, 1991, the day after the declaration of independence. This was a war of the Yugoslav federal authorities against Slovenia, the purpose of which was to affirm the territorial extent of the federation, deny Slovenia the right to secede, and bring it back into the federal fold. The Slovenes pushed relentlessly (and, one might say, recklessly) to break away from Yugoslavia. While, formally, they used the term *razdruživanje*—a word that indicates gradual disentanglement and disuniting—to describe their secession from Yugoslavia, in fact they unilaterally exited the federation. Their prime minister, Lojze Peterle, representing DEMOS, an alliance of opposition parties that had defeated the Communists in the previous election, proclaimed that Slovenia was no longer a part of Yugoslavia. But he added that by this act the country of Yugoslavia itself no longer existed. Presumably he meant that when a country is created through the free association of states and a single state exits it, that country is simply dissolved. This is a specious argument, one that would not stand unchallenged if, say, Pennsylvania were to declare that it wanted to leave the Union and that by its own proclamation of independence the United States of America no longer existed. Still, in reality the secession of Slovenia did indeed spell the end of Yugoslavia. The leadership of Slovenia bears a good share of the responsibility for the subsequent years of bloodshed, a fate which Slovenia mercifully escaped.

The federal response to Slovenia's secession lacked decisiveness. The eight-member Federal Presidency, which was constitutionally the supreme commander of the armed forces, was at the moment in disarray over the election of its next president. By the principle of rotation, the presidency's member from Croatia, Stipe Mesić, was to become the next President. Nevertheless, the four Serbs who were members of the Presidency blocked his election, claiming that Mesić had compromised himself by stating that he would be "the last President of Yugoslavia."

With the Presidency at such an impasse, the Yugoslav Army bypassed the federal premier, Ante Marković, also a Croat, who had promised to negotiate with the Slovenes despite the clear Slovene attack on the sovereignty and inviolability of the borders of a recognized state and a founding member of the United Nations. Without his knowledge the army started rolling its personnel and equipment to retake control of Yugoslavia's border with Italy and Austria which the Slovenes had unilaterally taken. Slovenia, however, proclaimed these to be its international borders with those two countries and rushed to create an international border with Croatia, which until then had been merely a state line. In a puzzling twist, the army's order to move troops to the border also contained an order not to shoot.

The war was short in duration (a week to ten days) and the federal army, which at that time still included Slovenian soldiers and commanders in its ranks (including Admiral Stanko Brovet, the former federal Minister of Defense), experienced an embarrassing defeat (as described in Chapter 10). The immediate cause for the war was the decision of the Slovene government to place at its borders with Italy and Austria markers bearing the words "Republic of Slovenia"—a change from the "Federal Socialist Republic of Yugoslavia" signs. The Slovenians also replaced Yugoslav customs officers with Slovenian officials. Federal troops, without the premier's knowledge, were then commanded into a quick-response action, assuming that in a matter of hours or days the rebellious provocation would be stopped and Slovenia brought back into line. Much to the surprise of the Yugoslav People's Army (which consisted mostly of young, inexperienced recruits), the Slovene National Guard (experienced reserve units of the Yugoslav Army, but consisting strictly of Slovenian units) had secretly obtained information of the movement of the Yugoslav Army units and had enticed them to penetrate into the mountainous regions. There they were trapped in mountain passes and immobilized. A majority of the soldiers surrendered. There were fairly light casualties on both sides, as well as some civilian casualties as hapless truck drivers found themselves in the crossfire.

The Slovenes drew close together to resist the army's incursion, having been heavily propagandized during the previous few years against staying in the union. Almost comic was the desperate attempt of individual citizens to shoot down army helicopters and airplanes with hunting guns. In the second-largest city, Maribor, others courageously surrounded the tanks which emerged from the army barracks and blocked them with their bodies. The soldiers were unprepared to fire into the civilian population and were not given ammunition to do so. With the exception of the blustering of a few Serb officers the intended federal *Blitzkrieg* fizzled out ingloriously.

European Community negotiators quickly brought together all the major players in the crisis to a meeting on the Island of Brioni (Tito's former residence), asking for a cease-fire in the war in Slovenia, a moratorium on the Slovenian and Croatian declarations of independence, and negotiations between all of the republics. However, the EC leadership did not understand the depth of the crisis—and committed no resources to solving it. Almost all of the signers of the Brioni Declaration eventually violated it, without international reprobation. This established a precedent that is still true today: that international mediators may counsel peace and harmony to combatants but have no clout to enforce agreements once the parties go home and the antagonists brazenly continue their belligerent behavior.

When one might have expected at least protracted negotiations about the manner in which Slovenia was permitted to extricate itself from Yugoslavia, the federal army surprised everyone by cutting its losses (again, without a legal approval of the federal government) and deciding to withdraw and recognize Slovenia's independence. The Serbian government and army brass assented to the secession with the explanation that Slovenia was ethnically homogeneous and that no significant ethnic minority in Slovenia opposed the secession. The Slovene state was at once internationally recognized and assumed its sovereignty unhampered by a further Yugoslav intervention. A precedent was now established, however, that made other secessions likely.

When a larger (second) war broke out in Croatia in August 1991, Slovenes watched it with wary eyes. They recognized that if the Croats succumbed, Yugoslavia may decide to reclaim Slovenia too. Thus the Slovenians aided Croatia in many ways, including the sale of arms, but they supplied no military personnel on the assumption that it was better to defend Slovenia's independence in the war that was taking place in Croatia than to have to fight another war on Slovenia's territory.

WAR IN CROATIA: THE FIRST SERB-CROAT WAR

Croatia had, in fact, declared independence on the same day as Slovenia. Despite their rivalry and friction, Serbs and Croats had not waged real war against each other prior to the twentieth century, making this the first true Croat-Serb war. It started as a war by the Serb minority in Croatia (numbering approximately 10 to 15 percent of the total population) against the new Croatian government. To the aid of Serbs quickly came the Yugoslav Army, first ostensibly inserting itself between the battle lines but very quickly actively aiding the Serb population both by arming them and then fighting their battles. The Belgrade government actively supported the Serbs in Croatia, and it is most likely that the entire conflict was fomented and engineered by Milošević and his supporters in the Belgrade government and within the army. What is not contested is that many Serb irregular paramilitary formations crossed the border from Serbia into Croatia and greatly increased the ferocity and complexity of the conflict. The Serbs commenced taking power into their own hands primarily in Krajina around Knin and in eastern Slavonia. From local skirmishes the war escalated into a furious one-year war and claimed at least 10,000 dead.

The Serbian minority in Croatia only argued, initially, against Croatia's secession from Yugoslavia. Once the secession occurred, they told the Croats, "*You* may secede but *without us,* for we are seceding from you!" They argued that if one unit of a federation has the right to secede, other units may likewise decide to secede from the secessionists. The result was the establishment of a self-proclaimed "*Srpska Republika Krajina*" (Serb Republic of Krajina), which as yet has no international status but is effectively outside the domain of the Croatian government. The leaders of Srpska Krajina have declared that they will never again become a part of Croatia, although the leaders of Croatia have not relinquished their right to regain their governmental authority over the Krajina.

The Yugoslav Army played first a problematic and then a destructive role. Army units proclaimed they would act as mediators, and interjected themselves between warring Serbs and Croats in areas where these confronted each other but almost without exception the military sided with the Serbs—and surreptitiously handed out large amounts of weapons to the local Serb populations. The reason for this is clear. Their command personnel was overwhelmingly Serb and so were the soldiers (since the Serbs outnumbered others and military service was universal, in the army they naturally outnumbered other nationals). And since the earlier low-intensity war in Croatia up to 1991 had already indicated that the two sides were unreconcilable, many Croats and other non-Serbs had already defected from the Yugoslav Army in large numbers, making it even more Serb in character.

An explanation is in order, here, of why Serbs were present in such large numbers not only in the government and Communist Party bureaucracy but also in the police and army. During World War II, when Croatia was a Nazi puppet state, the Communist-led *partizans* of Tito were overwhelmingly Serb. Fewer Croats joined. According to the principle that the victors share the spoil, Tito, an ethnic Croat but Yugoslav in orientation, rewarded his wartime supporters, whom he could trust in suppressing the opposition, with the choicest jobs. Those holding jobs later tended to favor their own kind when it came to additional job opportunities.[6]

The predominance of Serbs in the government and other enforcement agencies irked non-Serbs, who resented not only the oppressive nature of a dictatorial regime's use of force but also the fact that the enforcers were of a different ethnicity. When the Croats declared their independence they were afraid that the Serb bureaucrats and policemen might be disloyal to the newly elected Croatian Democratic Union government and they consequently started firing many Serb policemen and replacing them with mostly young, inexperienced Croats. One should note that while there is a certain logic to this Croatian move, it was too rapid and too rude. Amidst a Croatian nationalistic euphoria, President Franjo Tudjman's dangerous declaration "Croatia is for Croats" (rather than Croatia is for citizens of Croatia) sent an ominous message to the Serb minority who had already suddenly begun losing employment in many places. Hearing the demands

---

6. Even Tito's last wife, Jovanka, a Serb, fell into disgrace when it was disclosed that she was guilty of nepotism as well as of taking part in conspiracy to bypass the aging ruler in decision-making.

by extremist Croats that *Serbs* should go to *Serbia*, the Serbian population feared that this was but the first step in eliminating them from the land where they had lived for centuries. This was reminiscent of the Croat's "ethnic cleansing" carried out by *ustasha* policies during World War II.

Seeing that the army turned against Croatians, the Croatian government as well as the people turned against the army. Nevertheless, despite having secretly secured some weapons from abroad, the Croats were massively outgunned, although they had by now formed their own police and army out of the Croatian National Guard. They then decided to get some arms from the Yugoslav Army, and besieged most of the army barracks and bases on their territory, except in those areas where Serbs had already established their control. In a relatively short time the Serbs held between one-fourth to one-third of Croatia, a size of territory disproportionate to their numerical strength. Lengthy standoffs took place in which the soldiers in the army barracks, most of which were in the cities, were isolated. Many soldiers and officers did not know what was going on with their families, who lived off-base. The soldiers were also denied electricity, water, and food and were surrounded by Croat forces. Eventually the Yugoslav Army withdrew completely from those areas of Croatia where Croat control was complete, often leaving weapons behind. The army withdrew into Bosnia-Herzegovina, where it would later play a fateful role.

In those areas that were ethnically mixed or where Serbs were in the majority, the army lent unqualified support to them. The most symbolic as well as the bloodiest confrontation of the Serbo-Croat war took place between July and November, 1991, in Vukovar, an ethnically mixed town of 45,000 on the Croatian side of the Danube river. Both Serb and Croat villages surround Vukovar. When the Croatian government decided to establish its authority in Vukovar, the Serbs there countered with claims of genocide, later spreading the news that many Serbs had been brutally massacred. This rallied Serb public opinion in Serbia proper, as well as in Croatia, and both Serb *chetnik* and Yugoslav Army regulars of the Novi Sad corpus attacked the area around Vukovar.

Many villages around Vukovar were taken by the Serbs, but the Croats heroically defended Vukovar itself for months while the town was systematically devastated from the Vojvodina shores of the Danube. The city was quite literally destroyed, down to the last dwelling place. Some Croat forces managed to withdraw; those Croats who were captured were allegedly massacred, including the sick and wounded in the hospital. The Serbs, on the other hand, produced documentation alleging an incredible number of massacred Serbs who had been buried in mass graves after being most brutally slaughtered by the Croats. A significant section of Slavonia (especially the eastern part) was captured by the Serbs. Ever since, both sides have claimed that the other side carried out a genocide, pointing out the existence of numerous mass graves, some of which are being explored by the United Nations for evidence of war crimes.

While it is not always possible to trace the genesis of every local combat, many of which were ignited quite spontaneously by one or the other side out of fear and/or hatred, a Serbian Orthodox priest interviewed by the author blames his own people for having initiated the aggression. According to him, on May 2, 1991, two newly appointed young, inexperienced Croat policemen were on their beat near Vukovar when they were killed by three Serbs who had crossed the Danube from Vojvodina for this purpose. Knowing that a search party would come to look for the policemen, the Serbs brought in reinforcements from Vojvodina and set up an ambush. A bus with about twenty Croat policemen did, indeed, arrive, and all were killed in ambush by the reenforced terrorists. Then, suddenly, about twenty to thirty buses came over from Vojvodina, along with a Belgrade TV crew.

The initial terrorist group quickly spread the word that Croat soldiers and *ustashe* would come to avenge the death of the colleagues and would undoubtedly carry out a massacre against the Serbs. Panicking Serbian villagers packed the buses while Serbian TV recorded their fear and grief. This electrified the population in Serbia, which had not been informed of the earlier terrorist action. This was sufficient evidence to convince all in Serbia that Croats were carrying out genocide against the Serb population. At the same time, Croatians had evidence that Serbia was engaging in organized aggression against their state. The priest later recounted the atrocious behavior of the Serb troops, especially the *chetnik* irregulars who destroyed innumerable Croat villages and who especially targeted churches for destruction. The entire

Baranja, large sections of eastern Slavonia, and the entire region of Krajina were thus soon "liberated" by Serbs.

Some villages, for instance Dalj, that had been half Croat and half Serb were ethnically cleansed of Croats, several hundred Croats having been massacred while others fled, some even attempting to swim across the Danube to Vojvodina, where they were frequently killed. A Yugoslav journalist who had visited the Yugoslav Army operating in Slavonia in 1991–92 told me of the practice of Yugoslav soldiers of plundering everything in sight. They also ransomed imprisoned Croatians to their families upon payment of exorbitant sums in foreign currency, and summarily murdered those men whose families were unable to come up with the ransom money by the designated time. He stated that many times a commander or soldier would take a Croat prisoner into the forest, under the pretext of heading to the command center for interrogation, only to return with a story that the prisoner "escaped." In fact, he would have either been exchanged or killed. The journalist recounted stories of fights among Serb soldiers over money that was to be obtained by ransom. In some cases the captured Croat would be killed by a Serb simply to spite another Serb who planned to enrich himself through ransom of the Croat.

Other citizens of Yugoslavia tell stories of returning soldiers and volunteers who brought back with them TVs, VCRs, pigs, cars, jewelry, and other valuables from both Croatia and Bosnia. The pillaging of captured homes seems to be a major feature of these wars, whether it was carried out by Montenegrin troops around Dubrovnik or Muslim soldiers taking over of a Croat village in Bosnia. Serbian news media have openly written about Bosnian Serbs vacationing in Greece who, by the pound, sold jewelry, to which they certainly had not come by means of honest labor. Permits to cross territory captured by one ethnic group invariably have had to be paid for in large sums of foreign currency by would-be refugees who are trying to flee the terror. And continued terror is desirable to the plunderers, for it becomes a constant source of revenue. As people become exceedingly impoverished by the continued war, the plunderers set their aims on whatever commodity is still left—eventually ending in the looting of food distributed by relief agencies.

Parenthetically, it should be mentioned that for most Yugoslavs plundering is seen as a natural occurrence in war, and in some areas, such as Montenegro, it is elevated to a virtue. The forcible taking of significant amounts of property in a very public manner is seen as heroic—a sign of the power of the brigand or warrior. In any case, the economic benefits that the war brings to some—whether by plunder, black marketeering, or war profiteering—are a significant component of the war. Even United Nations relief shipments destined for starving people have been hijacked by thugs who feel entitled to unload from a convoy whatever pleases them as a price for "safe passage."

The war in Croatia was negotiated to a standstill, and a truce took place in 1992 in the form of the Vance-Owen plan. The first Serb-Croat war therefore ended with no peace accords signed but with an agreement to cease hostilities along the line of combat, with only the slightest modifications. UN peacekeeping troops were brought in to deter further fighting and ultimately some of the exiled population returned to their homes, but tens of thousands of Croats and Serbs became refugees. The cease-fire has been occasionally violated, usually by Croats attempting to retake some of their lost territory—especially where the Serbs have cut strategic transportation lines. On the other hand, Serbs routinely bombard Croatian cities like Zadar. And UN troops have been accused, primarily by the Croatian media, of fraternizing with Serb soldiers and turning a blind eye to Serbian violations of the truce.

The two sides have very different interpretations of the present lines of demarcation. The Croats believe them temporary and the Serbs consider them permanent. Croats do not hide their aspirations to return the borders of their republic to those delineated in 1945, and they maintain that this will be accomplished either by negotiation or war. Since the Serbs hold the upper hand and are satisfied with the amount of captured territory, it is not likely that Croat aspirations can be satisfied short of another round of war between them. Thus a second Croat-Serb war is a distinct possibility, if it is not prevented by international restraint and negotiations.

So far, nothing has been settled in open negotiation, although there are rumors that Tudjman and Milošević may have a secret agreement both in regard to Croatia and Bosnia. And yet it is quite possible that once the war in Bosnia settles down, the

Croat-Serb war may continue. In Bosnia there are at least attempts at negotiations; in Croatia there are none. Many Croats and probably Serbs, who consider another round of warfare quite likely, are willing to engage in it, although they imagine that it will be a greater war than the first. For the time being, international public opinion seems to have all but forgotten the war in Croatia, except for faint memories of the bombardment of Dubrovnik and the inconvenience of not being able to vacation on the Adriatic Sea or use the much-traveled transportation lines that lead via Croatia and Serbia. Transportation between Croatia and Serbia is completely halted. Some of the murderous hatred has, of course, subsided in parts of both populations, and it is possible that the necessities of economic cooperation may yet force both sides to work out a manageable settlement.

Essentially the war in Croatia has been a war for territory, for economic advantage, and for power between the two most similar ethnic groups in the former Yugoslavia; but since ethnic identity is wedded to religious identity, the population frequently perceives it as a war between Catholics and Orthodox. Consequently, troops of one side habitually desecrate the holy places of the other in the conviction that they are thereby inflicting mortal wounds on the psyche of the enemy. The consensus of reputable scholars is that Serb extremists bear the major responsibility for the outbreak and unfolding of this war.[7]

WAR IN BOSNIA AND HERZEGOVINA: THE BOSNIAN POT BOILS OVER

There is a popular dish in Bosnia called "Bosnian Pot." It is made of a variety of vegetables with meat and it is greatly spiced with red-hot paprika. It is slowly baked in a ceramic pot. It is quite tasty, but for some unaccustomed stomachs it can create considerable indigestion. This dish is analogous to the war in Bosnia and Herzegovina. The variety of nations there are as mixed as the vegetables in the pot. Hatred has made them fiery-hot, both in spice and in heat. They have simmered for a long time, but now the pot has boiled over and has brought quite an

7. E.g., Denitch, *Ethnic Nationalism*, p. 180.

indigestion to the international community. The pot has broken, too, and the ingredients are scattered all over the place, bringing a tragedy to the inhabitants which is, thus far, the greatest in Europe since the termination of World War II.

The Yugoslav Army had withdrawn a great number of soldiers and weapons from Slovenia and Croatia to Bosnia and Herzegovina. Some say that the war in Bosnia and Herzegovina (hereafter abbreviated to B & H) started because the war in Croatia came to an end or because Western powers gave B & H international recognition too quickly. Actually, the war in Croatia made it almost inevitable, despite some hopes to the contrary, that it would spread to B & H because the same problems existed there as in Croatia—in a more severe form. When the newly elected government of B & H was formed by an alliance of Bosnian Muslims (about 40 percent of the population) and Croats (about 17 percent of the population) who voted in favor of separating themselves from Yugoslavia, the Serbs (about 30 percent of the population) boycotted this election. Several months earlier the Serb population almost unanimously expressed their preference in a referendum to remain a part of Yugoslavia. Hence, they now promptly seceded from the newly elected Bosnian government and formed *Republika Srpska* (another grammatically atrocious concoction, it literally means Republic Serbian).

The war in Bosnia-Herzegovina, a war that people in other parts of Yugoslavia knew would be much more bloody than elsewhere because of the tradition of animosity and memories of past massacres, began on April 6, 1992. The first stage was a war by the Yugoslav Army against the government of B & H. The government of B & H insisted on the unity and territorial integrity of its state. The Yugoslav Army first wanted to prevent the secession, and then, when it became clear that it was unable to do so because of international recognition of B & H, it threw its support behind the Serbian separatists, who claimed that their ultimate aim was only to stay in union with other Serbs.

The official story was that the Yugoslav Army withdrew its own forces from B & H and that only those segments of the army which consisted of Bosnian and Herzegovinian Serbs remained there, due to their justified desire to save their homes and land from hostile takeover by Muslims and Croats. The army units left there were commanded by General Ratko Mladić, who had previously been in charge of army operations in Krajina and who was a dedicated Serb nationalist known for his uncompromising attitude toward non-Serbs. The Belgrade government now threw its unqualified support behind the Bosnian Serbs and left them the superior arms and arsenals of the Yugoslav Army. In addition, many Serbian volunteers, some of them seasoned warriors and war criminals from the battles in Croatia, crossed the Drina River from Serbia into Bosnia to fight along with the Bosnian Serbs; or, more appropriately, as in the Serbian Krajina in Croatia, to spearhead the fighting against Croats and Muslims. Also present were many involuntary recruits from Serbia proper, who were sent to fight in Bosnia, despite official denials by the Belgrade government. Significant financial, medical, transportation, diplomatic, and other assistance was also given to Bosnian Serbs by Serbia and Montenegro. Soon nearly 70 percent of B & H was in Serbian hands, enormous casualties having been inflicted upon both the (allied) Muslims and the Croats.

News of Serb extremist war crimes soon reached the outside world, evidencing not only the merciless bombardment of nearly defenseless cities, many of which fell into Serb hands, but massacres, desecration of holy places, the torture and killing of captured soldiers and civilians, the establishment of concentration camps, innumerable rapes of captured women, and other abominations—all these in the name of "ethnic cleansing." The Serb leader Radovan Karadžić (a psychiatrist by profession and a Montenegrin emigrant rather than native Bosnian) declared that after what happened to Serbs it was impossible for them ever to live again in union with Muslims and Croats and that therefore B & H simply had to be partitioned. This means that Serbs also claimed that they were victims of the same kind of treatment as have been alleged against them. In a propaganda war the charges are always followed by counter-charges, often using the very same evidence (even the same video documentation). Hence, the real truth is hard to come by.

The war in B & H started as a war of aggression by the Yugoslav Army against the Sarajevan government, despite official Belgrade disavowals. Their denial was a farce as evidenced by the return of many Serbs from Serbia and Vojvodina in body bags or with wounds inflicted at the Bosnian front. Incidentally, it must be acknowledged that quite a large number of B & H Serbs opted to support the Sarajevo government with the expectation that such backing provided the best chance for a unified, multi-ethnic B & H, and they fought against fellow-Serbs. Gradually, however, the conflict became concurrently a civil war between Serbs, Croats, and Muslims. To some degree it even became a religious war, because at least in B & H these three groups were distinguished more by religious differences than by linguistic, historic, or cultural ones.

The first stage of the civil dimension of the war was the aggressive attack by the better-organized and better-armed Serbs against the allied Muslims and Croats. By late 1992, however, it became obvious that the Muslim-Croat alliance was also under great strain. By 1993, the alliance ruptured and the second stage ensued, namely savage and protracted fighting between Muslims and Croats, sometimes even between Muslims and Muslims. Only in March of 1994 in Washington, DC, did American and German pressure succeed to bring a cease-fire between Bosnian Croats and Muslims. They were urged to create a loose federation with each other in B & H, which then, in turn, would enter into a confederation with Croatia itself.

The situation in B & H became chaotic because it was difficult to figure out who was in command over the many military forces operating in the territory. There is much evidence of noncooperation and arbitrary decisions by local commanders, although Radovan Karadžić, the leader of Bosnian Serbs, claimed a unified structural command among the Serbs.

The leadership of the three ethnic communities crystallized. Alija Izetbegović became the President of the central government of B & H, and from a *de jure* position, was the only legal and duly elected leader of that unified country. But, *de facto,* his government's influence has been gradually reduced only to about 10 to 20 percent of the entire territory; the government as well as the army has become increasingly Muslim-dominated and identified as a Muslim state.[8] It should be noted that though Muslim

---

8. Some of the Muslims prefer the term "*Boshnyatsi,*" which is a variant of the term "*Bosantsi.*" Both refer to Bosnians, but the latter is equally applicable to Serbs and Croats of that state, while the former is being used for Bosnians of the Muslim tradition. In any case, it is erroneous to use the English term "Bosnians" as if it applied solely to the Muslim inhabitants of that state. Slavic Muslims, Serbs, and Croats have identical rights to be regarded authentic Bosnians and Herzegovinians.

territory is small it consists of most of the cities,[9] industry, and natural resources.

In 1993, Mate Boban, who became the leader of the Herzegovinian Croats declared the territory which the Croats controlled to be a separate state, called *Herzeg Bosnia*. Most of Herzeg-Bosnia is in Herzegovina and Mostar is considered the capital of that region. From the summer of 1993 on, a vicious war between Croats and Muslims for the control of Mostar has led to the near-total destruction of that city. The ultimate aim of Mate Boban, prior to being sidelined in an internal power struggle, had been to eventually annex Herzeg-Bosnia to Croatia.

Radovan Karadžić, of course, became the leader of *Republika Srpska*. Originally, Karadžić accepted the notion of a confederate structure for B & H (which is ironic, since Serbs had rejected a confederate structure for Yugoslavia itself because they felt this was only an excuse for later secession). He offered the notion that B & H should have a government consisting of an equal number of representatives of the three ethnic units, with great autonomy for each of the ethnic territories. Later, even the minimal confederate structure became unacceptable as *Republika Srpska* became a self-proclaimed state with its own parliament and had trappings of sovereignty. It is clear, however, that Karadžić has aims to bring *Republika Srpska* into ultimate union with Serbia and *Srpska Krajina*, forming a greater Serbian state. A good deal of the fighting is for the strategic goal of establishing corridors and contiguous territories to link the three Serb-ruled areas.

When atrocities were committed by troops of any ethnic group, the respective leaders denied these or pleaded ignorance. When confronted with evidence of atrocities, they have claimed that these were acts of renegades in their ranks. The fact is, an enormous number of armed people roam B & H and inflict untold abominations not only against armed enemies but unarmed civilians. The Serbs were the main culprits as they overpowered the other nationalities. According to Vladimir Matović, an advi-

---

9. Muslims were preponderately an urban population because of their dominant status under the Turkish Ottoman Empire, while the Christians (Serbs and Croats) were then mostly rural and inhabited the less congenial and less fertile terrain of this mountain state.

sor on Bosnia to the former President of Yugoslavia, Dobrica Ćosić,[10] Serbs killed five Muslims and three Croats for every Serb. Matović attributed the disparity in the number of dead to the superior armament of the Serbs and said the Muslims were frequently reduced to making guns out of lead plumbing pipes and then in desperation attacking Serbian bunkers yelling, *"Allahu Akbar"* (God is Great) with their guns held high above their heads while the Serbian machine guns mowed them down.

The largest damage in B & H has been done by the systematic bombardment of cities like Sarajevo, encircled by Serbian heavy artillery and armor. Continuous bombardment has indiscriminately destroyed municipal buildings, disrupted services, not to mention killing hundreds of civilians, many of them fellow Serbs. For unclear reasons, the Serb forces seemed reluctant to attempt to take over this city which they wish to be the capital of *Republika Srpska*, perhaps out of fear of failure and a cost too great to themselves.

Often in the B & H war, the destructive urge has prevailed over the urge to occupy. A village or town has been utterly destroyed, as if there was no desire to eventually possess the land; and yet in negotiations that territory would be insisted upon, even though it was no longer fit for habitation. Hatred seems stronger than the desire for gain, though fundamentally the war in B & H is a war over territory.

An insight into the reasons for the indiscriminate destruction of cities, particularly those in which a significant degree of interethnic and interreligious cooperation once took place, is provided by Andrija Krešić. He has suggested the presence of a destructive mingling of ethnic chauvinism with anti-urban chauvinism—something that applies not only to Bosnia but to the other mountainous regions of the country as well. While this is not the only, or even the major, reason for exorbitant destructiveness, the rivalry between rural and urban populations does account for much of the random devastation of the cities. Two facts have to be taken into account. One is that the mountain villages, though sparsely inhabited, extend over expanses that are larger than many cities. The densely populated cities, on the other hand, are in valleys.

---

10. Conversation with Matović in Belgrade on August 19, 1993.

A second factor—a remnant from feudal days—is that the cities in Bosnia were predominantly inhabited by Muslims and the villages by Christians, namely, Serbs and Croats. A memory persists among the villagers that most of their afflictions and indignities were caused by urban dwellers. This memory has been reawakened during the present conflict despite the fact that, in the meantime, a good deal of integration has taken place in the cities. Relatively little mixing of the population took place in the villages. Urban settlers perceive themselves as superior to rural dwellers and maintain a condescending attitude toward the villagers. The villagers resent this disdain and envy the material advantages of the urbanites. War gives those greatly frustrated village bullies, who suffer from an inferiority complex, a chance to settle old scores. War also provides the opportunity to rip away the constraints of the nationalistic-rural mentality, which then allows the carrying out of aggression upon urban centers. And having been given modern armaments, the mountaineers unleash their rage upon "those down there" by destroying everything, in order to show "them" who is the boss. No distinction is made between civil and military targets. Not even members of their own ethnic group who live in the city are spared, because these have been willing to live harmoniously together with "them." The mountaineers can survive great scarcity and adversity and they are a difficult target because they have an intimate knowledge of the terrain where they can hide. However, rapid urbanization in the post-World War II period brought many rural folk to the cities where they still retain the old mentality and are ready to strike back as fiercely and haphazardly as they are being bombarded.

After the collapse of the Athens conference in the spring of 1993, a failure stemming from the formal rejection of the Conference's provisions by the self-proclaimed parliament of *Republika Srpska* at Pale, a suburb of Sarajevo, President Clinton threatened the use of NATO forces later that summer. Milošević and other Serbian officials went to Pale to plead unsuccessfully with the Bosnian Serbs to accept the Athens plan. Milošević, in stark contradiction to his previous claims of Serbia's non-involvement, declared that from this time onward no more military assistance would be provided to Bosnian Serbs. But that threat was never implemented. Karadžić ordered the withdrawal of Serbian forces from the mountains surrounding Sarajevo, but after the fear of American bombardment of Serbian military positions waned, the Serb troops returned to their positions above Sarajevo—from which they continued their pitiless devastation of what lay below.

Serbian commentators maintain that the entire war could have been avoided had not the West made the catastrophic error on April 5 and 6, 1992, of giving recognition to B & H as a sovereign state. Just prior to that, in March 1992 in Lisbon, the leaders of the three parties had agreed to a map dividing the republic into cantons. As soon as recognition was granted, however, Alija Izetbegović, the chief Muslim leader, reneged on the agreement, eliciting a Serbian reaction. Presumably, Izetbegović expected that the West would support his presidency over a unitary B & H.

The subsequent Vance-Owen Plan to divide Bosnia into ten cantons in a united Bosnia, but with different cantons under different ethnic rule, received no solid support of anyone except the Croats. In 1993, under the Vance-Owen Plan the Croats (who number roughly 17 percent of the population) would have received about 20 percent of the territory, mostly in Herzegovina, where they had showed aspirations to establish the Croat state of Herzeg-Bosnia with Mostar as the main city. By this time the Muslims had been reduced to holding only about 10 percent of B & H and were generally considered the losers. The plan offered them nearly 30 percent of the territory but they were unhappy that the plan did not promise the indivisibility of B & H. The Serbs resisted the Vance-Owen Plan as it would have forced them to yield too much territory and would have denied them a corridor which they had already established south of the Sava River connecting Serbia with the two Serbian Krajinas in Bosnia and Croatia.

By this time the tensions between the Croats and the Muslims broke out in open warfare—a conflict of great benefit to the Serbian side. It relieved the pressure on the Serbian forces and it painted both Croats and Muslims as ferocious fighters who committed atrocities on civilians just as the Serbs had been accused of doing earlier. It destroyed much of the propaganda advantage the Muslims and Croats had in the West, where they had been portrayed exclusively as victims.

The immediate reason for the fighting between Muslims and

Croats was that it became evident that the best the mediators could do was make minor adjustments to the territory already won on the battlefield. Units of Bosnia's Army, which by now consisted of mostly Muslims (including many refugees from areas where Serbs had effected "ethnic cleansing") poured into areas not only promised to Muslims but also to Croats. This Muslim migration threatened the Croat majority in the sections awarded to Croatians by the Vance-Owen Plan and the two sides entered into a horrible ethnic war.

Lord David Owen and Cyrus Vance's replacement, the Dane Thorvald Stoltenberg, seeing that the Vance-Owen Plan was unworkable, brought to the negotiation table in Geneva late August and early September, 1993, a plan to divide Bosnia simply into three ethnic states; this was a *de facto* partitioning of Bosnia. It was a plan that Serbs were ready to accept in principle although they were not ready to make the territorial concessions required by it. The Croats were to get about the same as under the Vance-Owen Plan and the Izetbegović government would have its share sweetened by giving it 30 percent of some of the choicest real estate in Bosnia and Herzegovina, while Sarajevo and possibly Mostar were to be placed under a direct UN protectorate for two years.

The Geneva Conference held out the promise that, with solid pressure from the West, the three main groups[11] would sign a peace accord. This precipitated the need for up to 50,000 UN troops to police the negotiated settlement. But the conference dissolved unceremoniously when Izetbegović demanded access to the Adriatic Sea and the Sava River, two territories which neither the Croats nor the Serbs were willing to give up. With no plan left on the negotiation table, the three sides limped back to war. Now the battling between Muslims and Croats for Mostar became ferocious, reporters claiming the small city was more thoroughly destroyed than Sarajevo.

The Serbs, in the meantime, encircled Sarajevo and continued to bombard the city on a daily basis throughout the bitter winter 1993–94. The results were more mutilated and blown-apart schoolchildren and adults. In Mostar even the 427-year-old "Stari

---

11. All the main players had gathered: Izetbegović, Boban, Karadžić, Tudjman, and Milošević.

Most" (Old Bridge), a great cultural monument from the Turkish times that gave the city its name, was blown up by Croatian artillery, thus proving that despite earlier protestations during the Serb bombardment of Dubrovnik, the Croats had no more consideration for cultural monuments than did the Serbs. The war became, indeed, a perplexing ethnoreligious civil war. Cease-fires and separate negotiations between Muslims and Croats would sporadically take place throughout the remainder of 1993 and early 1994, but with no great territorial changes.

Evidence that the war had been transformed into a total civil war was provided when Muslims began fighting Muslims. Around the city of Bihač (a small enclave of Muslims surrounded by Serbs and yet closer to Zagreb than to Sarajevo) a Muslim leader, Fikret Abdić, a former Communist who ran a very successful commercial enterprise in the style of a feudal lord, maintained good relationships with both Serbs and Croats in order to keep the local economy afloat. Abdić became ever more disillusioned with the inflexible policies of Izetbegović, who appeared to be holding out for an American intervention which would be to the Bosnian Muslim-led government's advantage.

Izetbegović has feared, it seems, that history will judge him harshly if he settles for a nonviable Muslim state. Abdić favored making concessions in order to obtain peace and had not followed all orders from Sarajevo. Thus he became Izetbegović's rival as to how negotiations should proceed. Izetbegović's regular army attacked Abdić's renegade Muslim troops in order to bring them in line with the Sarajevan vision, but the people in Bihač could see no advantage in the Sarajevan version. The two Muslim forces eventually stalemated themselves. It would appear that Abdić's vision is for Muslims to incorporate themselves into their neighboring Serb and Croat territories, making the best of coexistence, whereas Izetbegovic ´yearns for a separate unified Bosnian state regardless of whether it is multi-ethnic or totally Muslim in composition.

Frequently, it seems that the Muslims are indecisive and that they are the last to offer a proposal. This is an outgrowth of an age-old practice. According to professor Esad Ćimić[12] it is not

---

12. Interview with Esad Ćimić in Zagreb on September 5, 1993. Ćimić was one of the most creative and prolific Marxist sociologists of religion in the country. He

due to some moral failure or inability to be decisive, but rather that historically there was an equal distance from Sarajevo to both Belgrade and Zagreb and history had taught the Muslims to wait to be last in making a decision so that they could select to stand with the winner. Thus, the Muslim vacillation is not ethical but is an outgrowth of their need for self-preservation. At times, their rivals have taken advantage of this cautious stance. Ćimić has affirmed that before the outbreak of the war the generals of the Yugoslav Army stated that they were going to surround Sarajevo as part of a military maneuver to defend it. This sounded good to Izetbegović and he approved the maneuvers, not realizing at the time that later these weapons would be used to destroy the city.

An Orthodox priest, Rev. Peran Bošković[13] from Bijeljina in northeastern Bosnia, has given the following account of how the war started in the town of Bijeljina in 1992: Bijeljina used to be the epitome of a quiet blue-collar town. Then came post-Communist multi-party freedom and immediately ethnic political parties emerged. Young people who had not previously been nationalistic or religious joined these nationalist parties. A group of young Muslims gathered around a new Muslim tavern named, provocatively, "Istanbul," while local Serb youngsters gathered a short distance from there in a tavern named, equally provocatively, "Great Serbia." Up till then they had all drunk together in a third tavern and no one had really known what this "nationalism" meant. But now the situation was charged with tension. A Serb had a quarrel with a Muslim in "Istanbul," which led to an altercation; then Serb young people threw a grenade into "Istanbul." The Muslim youth answered with a rocket hurled

---

taught at the universities of Sarajevo, Zadar, and Belgrade, and is currently working for an institute for applied social sciences in Zagreb. Like most of his colleagues, he is no longer a Marxist. In his life he embodies the title of one of his books, *Politika kao sudbina* (Politics as Destiny), as he has been forced to move first from Sarajevo and then from Belgrade for his outspoken criticism of exploitative institutions. He explains that he considers himself a Croat Muslim while his brother thinks of himself as a Serb Muslim. He approvingly recalls his grandmother saying that the Turks should have converted either all or none of the Bosnians to Islam; likewise, she had the wisdom to know that Muslims have a chance to survive as long as the battle between the two crosses (Orthodox and Catholic) goes on.

13. Interview with Bošković in Ljubljana on September 2, 1993. Bošković, a native of Bosnia, was the main Orthodox priest in Slovenia at the time of the interview.

into "Great Serbia." Now the old historical animosities were re-suscitated.

The Serbs always thought that the Muslims were not just an ethnic but also a religious unit and felt that there was a danger that the Muslims might want to Islamicize everyone. Muslims, to a lesser degree, also feared conversion to Christianity. Their fears spread with the speed of lightning. The Muslims, who were predominantly a settled urban population, quickly took control of Bijeljina. The Serbs came mostly from the surrounding mountains and were rather mobile; also, they had a nearly pathological fear of all that was "Asiatic." They started bombarding the town, having good positions from the mountaintops.

Fear gripped the town's inhabitants and most citizens stayed indoors. At first, only about 20 were killed, for the most part civilians. The Yugoslav Army nearby decided to stay in its barracks, not knowing what to do, and the troops initially considered withdrawing. But the Serbs blocked the path of the army, fearing the army would destroy the town. A fateful decision was then made by the local Serbs: knowing they could not win alone, they invited extremist Serbians who had gained murderous experience in Croatia, and the notorious war criminal Željko Ražnjatović-Arkan came with about 40 *chetniks*. These took the town and quickly massacred about 200 Muslims. Upon that, about half the Muslim population ran away; the others dared not emerge from their homes. There are claims that thousands of Muslims were massacred later. The war in Bosnia, according to Rev. Bošković, is not a war of armies but a war of neighbors who want to destroy, eliminate, partition, and grab whatever they can grab from the former Yugoslavia.

I believe that it is more accurate to say that the war in Bosnia is a complex war in which regular armed forces from Serbia and Croatia operate in collaboration with paramilitary troops who are either of their own Bosnian ethnic group or volunteers who come from Serbia or Croatia. Occasionally, foreign mercenaries or volunteers participate on all three sides. Most of those Bosnians who were brutally victimized, however, tell that they recognized their torturers as being former classmates or neighbors rather than total strangers. This makes the victims' bewilderment and bitterness even more profound.

From time to time Karadžić, Boban, or Izetbegović have

claimed that the armed forces of their respective ethnic groups are under their control. That is debatable. Control is not always in the hands of those who have begun the war, but is in those of the local commander or in those of the famous warriors (perhaps more accurately called "war criminals") who have come to the region with the purpose of tipping the balance of power. When an individual like "Captain Dragan" (another legendary warrior) arrives in a town, he can quickly turn the tide of war to his advantage by using extremist tactics that lead to "ethnic cleansing."

The frequently inebriated local forces do not exhibit soldierly discipline but impose their own will as they see fit at a given moment, sometimes going against the will of their superiors. Since the atrocities and destruction in B & H have been systematic and on a wide scale, and because disciplinary measures are rarely taken against perpetrators of "ethnic cleansing," it is obvious that the leaders not only condone but promote the practice of "ethnic cleansing." Many Serbs and Croats have become convinced by their propaganda machines that Europe wants them to prevent the reestablishment of a Muslim state and that therefore there is tacit approval of the policy of such "cleansing."

WAR IN SERBIA? BLOODIEST YET?

The war in B & H could spread to Serbia, either through Sandžak (the southwest corner of Serbia adjacent to Montenegro, Bosnia, and Kosovo) and Kosovo, where Serbs are outnumbered by Muslims, or by the toppling of the regime in Belgrade as the army attempts to wrest control from politicians who want to replace Milošević.

The tensions between Serbs and Kosovan Albanians and the tensions between Serbs and Slavic Muslims from Sandžak are such that one can describe both situations as *de facto* wars. Only the harshest repressive measures by the Serbian Army and police have kept revolts from flaring up. Under martial-law conditions nearly all civil rights have been taken away from the Kosovan Albanians, including locking them out of employment and educational opportunities. Tortures and murder by the police are frequent and are supported by the Serbian population. During the so called "Anti-bureaucratic Revolution" in 1988, Milošević had supported the abolition of the autonomous status of the provinces of Kosovo and Vojvodina and achieved their total subjection to Belgrade as the first step toward creation of a Great Serbia. In the minds of the more extremist-oriented Serbs, the "Anti-bureaucratic Revolution" had wider ramifications, namely, the chance of remaking a multi-ethnic Serbia (in which Serbs were only a 60 percent majority) into a nationalist Serbian state from which most non-Serbs would somehow be expelled. If that were accomplished it would perhaps be a harbinger of things to come in other parts of Europe.

The pressures on non-Serb nationalities have increased in many ways, but mostly by informal harassment that is not deterred by the Serbian police or government. Very moderate, pro-Yugoslav Slovaks, Hungarians, and non-nationalist Serbs have spoken of a wave of threats, intimidations, and other pressures aimed at causing them to emigrate. A Serbian journalist has recounted the attack by about twenty Serbian youths on a Muslim family in Bačka Palanka (Vojvodina) who had lived there for an extended period: After midnight, the youths pounded on the door and finally broke it down with an axe. They slashed the man's elderly mother in order to get her out of the way, and then shot him dead. His brothers, who heard the scuffle came to help, but they were chased away by the youths, who wielded axes. Later, the local police carried out a nonchalant investigation and deliberately arrested a juvenile who was clearly not guilty. Nor did the police permit the details of the ethnic nature of the killing to be printed in the newspapers.

On the surface in Serbia itself it looks as if there is tolerance. Yet the population, especially the minorities, is quite aware of frequent incidents of bigotry. These incidents include the firing of shots into churches worship, the destroying or defacing of such churches, and the making of anonymous calls to Muslims, Hungarians, and others, telling them to emigrate or else. This has promoted a considerable exodus of minorities from Serbia; on the other hand, many Serbs from other regions of Yugoslavia having fled to Serbia, there has been a *de facto* exchange of population. Graffiti insulting to minorities have been written on the walls of minority churches and institutions, making the lot of the minorities even harder as they share in the general misery that the economic collapse brought to the population at large. With 60 percent unemployment and the rest semi-employed, it is clear that the few remaining jobs in Serbia are likely to be filled by Serbs.

The other possibility for Serbia is a political civil war. That option is not so obvious, because Milošević and his Serbian Socialist Party have won three elections. The threat to his rule does not come from the moderate wing of the political spectrum but from the right-wing opposition. Milošević has used the right wing deftly, creating short-range alliances with it when this has been useful, only to turn against the right wing and marginalize it at the next turn. The major political parties vie as to who is more patriotically Serbian. The politicians who favor the democratic option and a civil society are in the minority.

It appears that Milošević also has the support of the army; therefore, one of the possible scenarios is that, should a political takeover somehow take place, the army is likely to support Milošević. Despite an increased distancing from his policies by the Serbian Orthodox Church, the mood for rebelling against Milošević is insignificant simply because no politician of reputation rivals him in popularity. Right-wing crazies such as Vojislav Šešelj and Željko Ražnjatović-Arkan are too vulnerable to pressures and too extreme to receive popular support. In fact, in November 1993 Milošević succeeded in discrediting Šešelj by arresting about twenty of the bloodiest *chetniks* and detailing war crimes by them that have indicated Šešelj himself was a murderer. In December of the same year Arkan's and Šešelj's parties were soundly trounced at the elections, thereby eliminating their groups as political rivals, though not eliminating the two leaders from public life.

The novelist-turned-politician, Vuk Drašković, and his wife Danica, were severely beaten by the Belgrade police and his party, Serbian Movement for Renewal, a pro-monarchist group, is, despite sympathy by Orthodox Church hierarchs, not strong enough to capture the support of the majority of Serbians. The members of the Karadjordjević dynasty are attractive to a portion of the population, especially the Orthodox clergy, because this segment of the population has come to believe that only an untainted outsider can restore Serbian dignity. The monarchy could become a viable option should Milošević's popularity be jeopardized. The rest of the political spectrum is too splintered to mount a successful opposition movement. The genuinely democratic parties that promote the creation of a civil society have had little success at the ballot box, but they represent Serbia's only true long-range hope.

The gravest threat to Milošević's government is a twelve digit inflation. The official annual rate of inflation recorded on December 20, 1993, was 197.7 billion percent. A billion Yugoslav dinars toward the end of 1993 was worth about eight cents—and losing value by the hour. The rate of inflation exceeded that of Germany in 1923, as well as Latin American hyperinflations, making it the worst in world history. Normally such a disastrous economy would topple a regime, but Milošević has skillfully blamed the UN sanctions for his country's economic woes. The Serbians and Montenegrins bemoan their situation but stoically vote for their leader as though they are unable to fathom any other savior—and if their situation is ever to reverse itself, they will indeed need a savior! But this is a prospect that is not likely for the near future.

A WIDER BALKAN WAR?

A fearsome prospect is that the entire Balkan region may become embroiled in a war. If, for instance Serbs and Albanians initiate a war in Kosovo, it is hard to imagine how Albanians from Macedonia (between 25 and 40 percent of the population) and from Albania (many of whom are close relatives of the Kosovans) can remain mere observers. If Macedonia thereby becomes embroiled (and Serb extremists may use this as the pretext to annex Macedonia to Serbia), Greece may get involved, because it maintains bad relations with Macedonia.

If Greece comes in, there is no way Turkey can stay out. Turkey has already responded to Greek hysteria over Macedonia by being the first nation to recognize Macedonia and send aid to it. Many Turks maintain strong positive feelings toward their fellow Muslims in the Balkans, but the only way they could become militarily involved is if they entered the conflict by way of Bulgaria or Greece. The West considers Turkey to be a regional power and they may well wish to show their ability to exercise that role—a role that is most distasteful to Turkey's former Balkan colonies.

Relationships today between Bulgaria and Turkey, Macedonia and Albania, Albania and Greece, and Macedonia and Greece, are notoriously bad. Only Macedonia's relationship with Bulgaria and Serbia's relationship with Greece are good. Feelings between Macedonia and Serbia are, surprisingly, neither good nor bad but acceptable. All of this regional instability, coupled with economic conditions—which in the region can be described as ranging from bad to disastrous—indicate that the imagery of the Balkan "powder keg" is apt. It is not surprising that the Clinton administration wanted to send clear signals that it would try to do everything to prevent the spreading of the war throughout the Balkans. Over three hundred American soldiers, along with a greater number of Scandinavian troops, have been placed on the border between Serbia and Macedonia as a symbolic guarantee that the United Nations and the United States mean business when they say that they want to prevent a war in the region. Their and NATO's credibility have, nevertheless, been seriously doubted when their actions have frequently gone barely beyond the humanitarian and symbolic. Thus, it is unclear whether warnings to them about the possibility of a wider war would have any restraining impact.

The involvement of Hungary, Romania, Austria, and Italy in a wider war is much less likely. The situation in Romania is unstable, while Hungary only worries about its large ethnic minorities in Slovakia, Romania, and Yugoslavia. In Yugoslavia, until recently the Hungarian minority did not fare badly; in fact, they have had it better than their compatriots in Hungary. But all this has changed with the wars in the former Yugoslavia, whereby the situation of the Hungarian minority in Vojvodina is becoming dramatically worse. Not surprisingly, this raises the concern of the Hungarian government. Many Hungarians are migrating to Hungary. Still, should most of the half-million Hungarians decide to leave Vojvodina, along with many thousands of other refugees from the former Yugoslavia who have fled to Hungary, this would place a great burden on that small nation and might increase its hostility toward Serbia.

Although not inevitable, the prospect of a regional spread of the war is not negligible.

CONCLUSION

$\mathbf{T}$he analyses of the nature of the war(s) offered above, may affect—as every interpretation does—the manner of dealing with the conflict. Certain simplistic solutions have to be rejected: One of these is that the conflict is so ancient that no one will ever have any impact on it because it will inevitably continue in the future as it has in the past. Let it simply burn itself out, this time around. This is unacceptable. There is neither an inevitability about such war(s), nor can human beings be so callous as to continue forever to be bystanders to massive, documented violence, which, additionally, has the potential to spread.

Another is that the war(s) is/are a simple aggression by the Serb dictator Milošević upon democratic Bosnian and Croatian nations which can be eliminated by forcing him out of office or by a military defeat of Serbia by NATO troops. Milošević might not be sorely missed even by his own people, but one injustice cannot be solved by committing another.

The series of wars which are entangled with each other are not all based on ancient ethnoreligious animosities, for Slovenes and Serbs have not harbored such animosity previously and even Croats and Serbs have not waged war against each other prior to this century. Some of the current wars contain characteristics of civil conflicts which outsiders could never easily resolve by a military intervention. The former Communists do play a very large role in these wars—Alija Izetbegović being the only head of state who was not part of the Communist bureaucracy.

Slobodan Milošević and the generals of the Yugoslav Army have been the major aggravating factor in their awkward attempts to save Yugoslavia by overpowering it. The collapse of the Communist idea and the reemergence of rabid ethnoreligious nationalism pushed the republics to the brink. Politicians, journalists, clergy, immigrants, business people, generals, and hoodlums did the rest (see Chapter 8). The international community responded awkwardly to the crisis in the Balkans, aggravating the situation. The civilizational, cultural, and religious differences have been blown up out of proportion, giving former Yugoslavs a pretext for saying that they can no longer live within the same structure. Tribal passions have been ignited and group solidarity activated. Extremist nationalist slaughterers have brutalized the war beyond even the inhumanity of typical wars, and flames of hatred built on personal and group losses now make the end of some of these wars out of sight. The suffering of individuals and the genocidal dimensions are so real that the situation can hardly be much more bleak. Pessimists may say the situation cannot get any worse; optimists may contend that worse is possible. Whether the peoples and their governments in the land of the southern Slavs may be able to resolve their conflicts by themselves is doubtful. International mediation is crucial, forms of which will be discussed in Chapter 12.

CHAPTER 7

THE RELIGIOUS COMPONENT
IN THE WARS

The leaders of all three major religious communities in Bosnia issued a statement in the summer of 1994 claiming that the war is not a religious war. This is in line with claims of other clergy in other parts of the former Yugoslavia. Such claims are based on a too narrow interpretation of the social role of religion. Evidence to the contrary will be presented here.

The warfare in former Yugoslavia, indeed, did not begin as an explicitly religious war, nor is the current character of the war primarily a religious one. These conflicts, however, do have distinct ethnoreligious characteristics because ethnicity and religion have become so enmeshed that they cannot be separated. The fundamental causes of war are ethno-national yet many nationalists take on a religious label as a way of expressing their identity and many religious institutions and leaders did not discourage this process. Bogdan Denitch corroborates these claims, saying:

> Both the churches and the nationalists have labored mightily to get close to a 100 percent fit between religion and ethnic identity among Serbo-Croatian speakers and have tended to reinforce nationalism rather than any sort of "catholic" universalism. The churches are indeed both militant and national in former Yugoslav lands. The two identities thus reinforce each other.[1]

If religions were viewed only from the perspective of their proclaimed ideals, then these wars are not religious. But, then, reli-

---

1. Denitch, *Ethnic Nationalism*, p. 30.

gions epitomize far more than their original cores and inspirations. In practice, religion is often the very antithesis or perversion of its authentic ideals. Religions are historically mediated, and greater or lesser discrepancies exist between their original ideals and their present-day embodiments.

My thesis is that the concrete historical embodiments of religions in the Balkans did contribute religious traits to the present warfare, usually in combination with ethnic and other aspects. While not every religious person or leader there is implicated in barbaric behavior, the regretful fact is that many individuals and groups have sanctioned and "sanctified" these wars. My thesis has been corroborated by two unlikely sources. One was the Roman Catholic Bishop Joakim Herbut of Skopje, who stated, "It is hard to tell whether these are ethnic or religious conflicts, but ethnic conflicts can be conducted under the aegis of churches, so they take the appearance of religious wars." The other was the Roman Catholic Archbishop of Ljubljana, Alojzije Šuštar, according to whom both the Serbian Orthodox Church and the Croatian Roman Catholic Church are nationalist entities.[2]

The fusion or overlapping of ethnicity [3] and religion is a well-known phenomenon in much of Eastern Europe, especially in the Balkans. For centuries the church was the people and the people were the church (Muslim as well as Christian religious organizations are meant here; the term "church" is used for the sake of convenience). The church envisioned its role so broadly that it contributed not only to the awakening of national consciousness but also to feelings of nationalism. The result was sometimes positive, sometimes negative. For both good and bad reasons, the Communist regime in Yugoslavia tried to rupture this close identification. A generation or two grew up under Tito believing

---

2. Interview with Bishop Herbut in Skopje on August 23, 1993, and with Archbishop Šuštar in Ljubljana on September 1, 1993.

3. I prefer the use of the word "ethnicity" over "nationality" because some ethnic groups in the former Yugoslavia do not have a state of their own yet possess a distinct sense of identity, a feeling of distinction from others, and a yearning for self-determination and sovereignty. The nation-states of the former Yugoslavia display, simultaneously, nationhood in the modern sense and tribal traits. Serb or Croat ethnic identity resembles more the tribal loyalties of a Yoruba or an Ibo or a Tutsi and a Hutu than the national self-awareness of a Swede or a Norwegian. Another acceptable alternative is to use Bogdan Denitch's term "ethnic nationalism," as in his book *Ethnic Nationalism: The Tragic Death of Yugoslavia.*

that ethnic and religious differences were not unbridgeable and that virulent ethnic nationalism had been laid to rest at the end of World War II. We now know that this was not so; the coalescence of ethnic and religious identification returned with such a vengeance that it is mandatory to use the single word *"ethnoreligious."* Casual observers may have discovered this only after the "Great Transformation" in 1989, but it was discernible much earlier.

Political scientists had already noticed that the phenomenon of "national Communism" was a powerfully disruptive factor in the international Communist movement, and it was nurtured in Yugoslavia with the hope that it would erode Soviet hegemony. This it did—but one wonders whether the results have not been somewhat akin to nurturing Islamic fundamentalism as an antidote to Arab socialism or Saddam Hussain as an antidote to the Ayatollah Khomeini's Islamic revolution! In any case, Communists were able to dispose neither of nationalism nor of religion despite their efforts in each directions. As the Communist *pterodactyl* perished and left the nest empty, the eggs hatched an entire flock of birds of prey who are now viciously pecking at each other in the fight to dominate the nest or at least a segment of the nest.

The large religious communities played a divisive role during the pre-Communist, the Communist, and the post-Communist periods. Conventionally it was said that Yugoslavia was the meeting place of three great religions: Eastern Orthodoxy, Roman Catholicism, and Islam. However, religiously Yugoslavia was in reality divided not merely into these three communities but into smaller, ethnoreligious units. The Roman Catholic Church of Slovenia reinforced Slovenian nationalism, Roman Catholic Church *u Hrvata* (an awkward linguistic term even in Croatian which transliterates even more awkwardly into English: "in Croats," but should be more freely translated "of Croats" or "among Croats") supported Croatian nationalism, the Serbian Orthodox Church supported the idea of Serbdom among Serbs and Montenegrins and tried even to incorporate the Macedonians. And the "schismatic" autonomous Macedonian Orthodox Church contributed to the strengthening of Macedonian national awareness. Islam contributed to the affirmations of Slavic Muslims in Bosnia and Herzegovina and adjacent areas (e.g. Sandžak) as well as those of Albanians in Kosovo, Macedonia, and Montenegro. This I know from personal experience as I interviewed prominent Roman Catholic theologians in Slovenia and Croatia who were members of the same Bishops' Conference but did not know even rudimentary data about each other's life although they were able to provide detailed analysis of the situation of their church among their nationals, even those in the diaspora. Another illustration of the ethnoreligious separatisms is the case of a village which belonged to the Zagreb Archdiocese but which had an overwhelmingly Slovene population and was served by a Croat priest. This priest caused great distress among the villagers because only one of about twenty masses celebrated per week was in the Slovene language despite the repeated petitions of his parishioners. They finally requested the transfer of their village into the Ljubljana Archdiocese. This took place as recently as 1991–92.

Orthodox ecclesiology provides for the formation of national churches whereas Catholic and Islamic ecclesiology eschews such an approach. So, for theological, political, and national reasons, religious leaders would frequently use the vague term "our" church when a closer examination would reveal that "our" was quite limited to their own national unit. Likewise, Bosnian and Albanian Muslims had little interaction with one another. (I found in 1969 that leaders in the Supreme Islamic Headquarters in Sarajevo were quite uninformed and uninterested in Islam among Albanians.) The Roman Catholics of Slovenia perceive themselves as having a quite separate religious dynamic of interaction with their nation than does the Catholic Church among Croats, and vice versa. If Roman Catholic ecclesiology allowed it, these churches would in no time call themselves Slovenian Catholic Church and Croatian Catholic Church. Illustrative of this nationalistic character of religion is the unhappiness among Croats over the decision of the Vatican to separate the Bishops' Conference of Croatia from the Bishops' Conference of Bosnia and Herzegovina—both of whom are composed largely of Croats—although no regret was shown over the split with the Slovenian Bishops' Conference.

To put it bluntly, the leaders of each religious community justify their enthusiastic and uncritical support of rising nationalism among their peoples. Yet they condemn rival religious leaders for an "unholy" support of nationalism, which, they believe, contributed to the outbreak of the war. This is analogous to a blind person calling a deaf-mute handicapped!

Most of the religious communities contribute to the sacralizing of their respective nationalities, religion thereby playing the role of a political ideology. As Ivan Cvitković remarked, "The greater the participation in religious activities in a region, the greater the tendency toward national homogenisation and separatism."[4] Let us now look at several specific cases.

CONTRIBUTION OF THE RELIGIOUS COMMUNITIES TOWARD HATRED AND WAR

1. The Roman Catholic Contribution to Nationalism[5]

Recently, several authors[6] have claimed that the Roman Catholic Church, unlike the Serbian Orthodox, does not identify Croat-Catholic and has a more reconciling, ecumenical posture than the Serbian Orthodox. I believe this to be simply an error and, indeed, aim to prove it by the very data that are used in support of their contentions.

Josip Beljan, in *Veritas*[7] writing about the role of the Pope and the Holy See, declares that these, in an unprecedented act, be-

---

4. Ivan Cvitković, "God is Dead," in *Breakdown: War and Reconstruction in Yugoslavia* (London: Yugofax, 1992), p. 52.

5. I will zero in on the Roman Catholic Church among Croats (*Katolička crkva u Hrvata*, or frequently simply *Crkva u Hrvata*) because I have more data on it and because there is a war in Croatia.

6. Geert van Dartel, "The Nations and the Churches in Yugoslavia," *Religion, State, and Society*, Vol. XX, Nos. 3 & 4 (1992), pp. 275–88. Van Dartel is a Roman Catholic lay theologian from Holland who studied in Zagreb under the late Josip Turčinović, one of the most liberal Catholic priests, rather exceptional in his ecumenical stance; and Van Dartel mistakenly ascribes this attitude to the entire Roman Catholic Church in Croatia. See also his article "Nikolaj Velimirović (1880–1956)," *Glaube in der 2. Welt*, Vol. XXI, No. 4 (April 1993), pp. 20–26, which is fundamentally sound yet does display an anti-Serbian Orthodox bias because he tends to ascribe ethnoreligious bonding uniquely to Serbian theologians, when in fact this characteristic was discernible among all ethnic groups, especially among emigre theologians. Also Jure Krišto, O.P., "The Catholic Church in Times of Crisis" and "Diverse Functions of Catholicism and Orthodoxy in Social Upheavals (1989–1992)," unpublished manuscripts; and Anne Herbst, "Tod und Verklärung: Die Orthodoxe und die Katholische Kirche im südslawischen Konflikt," *Glaube in der 2. Welt*, Vol. XXI, No. 4 (April 1993), pp. 14–18.

came the amplifier of Croatian independence and sovereignty as a reward to the Croatian people for thirteen centuries of loyalty to Rome.

> God has, by way of his Church, by way of the Holy Father, looked at his faithful people, spoke out on their behalf, directly inter-vened in history, in the struggle, warring together with his people for their liberation . . . With this war God also returned to his people, in its heart and home. [God] returned to the entire mass media, political, social, and state life of Croatia, from where He was driven out forty-five years earlier. The cross of Christ stands next to the Croatian flag, Croatian bishop next to Croatian minis-ter of state. Croatian priest and teacher are again together in the schools. Present at masses in churches are officers and Croatian soldiers. Guardsmen wear rosaries around their necks. . . . This was truly again a real war for "the honored cross and golden lib-erty," for the return of Christ and liberty to Croatia.
>
> The Church is glad for the return of its people "from the two-fold" slavery—Serbian and Communist. This is a great "kairos" of God's grace for the entire Croatian people.

He continues:

> Here was not a battle for a piece of Croatian or Serbian land but a war between good and evil, Christianity and Communism, cul-ture and barbarity, civilization and primitivism, democracy and dictatorship, love and hatred. . . . Thank God, it all ended well, due to the Pope and Croatian politics.

Another example was an interview carried out with Franjo Cardinal Kuharić by a journalist of the now defunct *Danas* about a gun-toting Franciscan friar accompanying Croatian troops in battle. To the question of whether he condemned such activity, Cardinal Kuharić wove a lengthy answer saying that ideally chaplains ought not to go into battle but that "when Pater Duka wears a uniform and carries a revolver, he is not doing this as a representative of the Church, but it is his private matter."[8] Since the head of the Franciscan order, in whose jurisdiction this friar

---

7. Josip Beljan, "Priznata vjernost" (Recognition of Faithfulness), *Veritas*, Nos. 9–10 (Zagreb, Sept.-Oct., 1992), pp. 24–25. *Veritas* is a popular Catholic magazine. Translated from the Croatian by P. Mojzes.

8. Darko Pavičić, "Svećenik nije komesar" (A Priest Is Not a Commissar), *Danas*, Vol. X, No. 503 (Oct. 8, 1991), p. 28.

belonged, did not condemn him, neither would the Cardinal—though he would prefer to see him out of uniform. The conclusion that can be drawn from the Cardinal's response is that such action is permissible. And, indeed, many priests and seminarians *have* fought in some of the battles.

Cardinal Kuharić's leadership has been characterized as skillfully steering the Croatian people to sovereignty. In the late 1980s,

> [u]nlike his communist compatriots, the Cardinal was not timid about the defense of national sovereignty. Catholic bishops were convinced that by defending Croatian sovereignty they were doing something good. Hence, they used every opportunity to stand in defense of Croat national interests. One such opportunity was the debate about constitutional amendments concerning the name of the official language in the Socialist Republic of Croatia.[9]

They pressed the exclusive use of the Croatian language rather than Croato-Serbian or Serbo-Croatian. Apparently the bishops and other Catholic leaders did not have the foresight that this would be threatening to the Serb population of Croatia, who would interpret it as a denial of their cultural rights. (This would later be aggravated after the victory of the Croatian Democratic Union by the immediate removal of signs that were both in the Latinic and Cyrillic script. This could only be interpreted by the Serbs as a decision to obliterate evidence of Serb presence from Croatia. One should note that in Serbia to this day signs and newspapers appear in both alphabets). Did not the Catholic bishops have enough wisdom to promote the rights of the Croatian people in such a way as not to threaten local minority populations? Did they not act anti-constitutionally in their advocacy of a move that would tear apart the federal structure? Surely they knew of many cases in which civil wars broke out for the preservation of a federation.

Other unconstitutional initiatives of the Catholic bishops took place. For example, as soon as they succeeded in their aim of unseating the Communist Party of Croatia and replacing it with the Croatian Democratic Union (*Hrvatska Demokratska Zajed-*

---

9. Jure Krišto, "Diverse Functions of Catholicism and Orthodoxy in Social Upheavals (1989–1992)," pp. 7–8.

nica or HDZ), they switched attention to Bosnia and Herzegovina and supported the political activity of the HDZ among
Croats there in blatant contradiction of the existing law that for-
bade the creation of political parties based on exclusively national or religious bases. The Catholic Church suggested that
this legal provision be eliminated. Catholics were encouraged by
the Church to form political parties along national and religious
lines.

Indeed, they—and other—nationalists prevailed. Exclusively
national-religious parties were created by all: Croats, Muslims,
and Serbs. They became the three major parties of Bosnia and
Herzegovina. Those who know the national and religious problems of that state realize how fragile the balance of ingredients
there was and that the *only* nonviolent alternative was for a government that could somehow keep all three national-religious
groups working together in a secular context. The Roman Catholic bishops initiated the process of ethnoreligious confrontation.
The outcome of that political move was nothing short of catastrophic, and the Roman Catholic leadership bears a considerable
responsibility for the ensuing tragedy. It does not take great wisdom to see that Catholic initiatives in this complex region could
only lead to war. The Communists, it appears, were far more
realistic about the ethnoreligious threat than were the Roman
Catholic and Croatian leadership.

Another manner in which the Roman Catholic leadership contributed to the tension in Yugoslavia was its support of the Albanian cause in Kosovo. This the Catholics did ostensibly in the
name of protecting human rights. It is true that the human rights
of Albanians in Kosovo were severely curtailed by the bloody
politics of repression on the part of Milošević's regime, and that
no decent human being could have been totally silent on this
issue, but the leadership of the Roman Catholic Church was not
evenhanded; it did not speak out on behalf of *other* repressed
minorities—especially those on Croatian territory! Their speaking out about the Kosovo situation was bound to aggravate the
Serbians, who have some legitimate grievances about the fate of
Serbians in Kosovo, though they have pressed their interests in a
very brutal and unacceptable manner. The Serbs would naturally
interpret these appeals as both an anti-Serb and anti-Orthodox
move by the Roman Catholic Church.

When the first free elections in Croatia yielded the victory of the Croatian Democratic Union and the Roman Catholic Church was finally publicly rehabilitated after years of oppression, the Catholic Church at first displayed nearly unlimited support of the new regime's superpatriotic Croatianism. The church leadership was present at the opening of the *Sabor* (Parliament) sessions, politicians and clergy did not fail to use photo opportunities in order to be seen together in the media, and much was done to reinforce the notion of the unity of the church, nation, and state. The Catholic leadership erroneously regarded the HDZ as a national movement rather than a political party—which, indeed, is how the HDZ wishes to be represented in order to obtain a near-monopoly over Croatia. Since 1993, Cardinal Kuharić felt the need to explain that he was keeping a distance between the Church and the government despite apparent linkages and efforts on part of the HDZ to present itself as pro-Catholic.

Also the church leadership vigorously promoted the cult of Alojzije Cardinal Stepinac, a controversial figure, whom the Communists had accused of complicity in forcible conversions and in the genocide of Serbs in Croatia during World War II. Insofar as the Catholic leadership rejected the labeling of the entire Croatian people (by some Serb extremists) as genocidal, and indicated that Stepinac was badly treated by the Communists, they were, of course, right. But they showed too little willingness to express regret for the massacres against Serbians in World War II, in which a number of Catholic clergy were directly involved and for which Stepinac had been held culpable. Bishop Pihler in 1963 did issue an apology asking Serbs for forgiveness, but it appears to be the single apology by a lone Croat bishop in 1963 for the massacre of anywhere from 50,000 to 700,000 Serbs! This is not the place to discuss the numbers of massacred, which the Croats tend to diminish and the Serbs tend to exaggerate. Even if it were only a thousand massacred Serbs, would it not be appropriate for the entire Bishops' Conference to issue a statement of regret? After all, there were numerous attempts of forcible conversion of Orthodox to Catholicism and such an act is ecclesiastical and repentance would be in order. During the tense times prior to the outbreak of the current war, Serbian bishops have often pleaded with their Roman Catholic colleagues to issue a more emphatic statement of regret and condemnation of the Croat war crimes in World War II. More often than not, however, Catholic bishops have reacted by minimizing the casualties and responding that many Croats were killed after the war by the *partizans*.[10] This too, of course, could have been interpreted by the Serbs as a threat, wondering as they did whether the Croats were again planning a World War II-type "ethnic cleansing."

So, did the Roman Catholic Church of Croatia contribute to the outbreak of the war? I would answer this with an emphatic Yes. The Church leadership (some representatives more than others), together with President Franjo Tudjman, made provocative and imprudent moves. They pushed their agenda too speedily and with no regard for the consequences of their behavior. Certainly they have to be seen as being among the culprits for the current conflict.

Živko Kustić, who was for thirty years editor of the main Catholic weekly paper *Glas Koncila* (Voice of the Council), has pointed out that unfortunately there has come about a rebirth of the *ustasha* fascist movement, indicating that it occurred spontaneously, under the conditions of today's rapid social changes. For instance, someone's grandfather may have been an *ustasha*, the father went to Germany as a migrant worker, and the unemployed son (who did not attend church) and lacked other meaningful identification commenced rebelliously boasting with Ante Pavelić and Catholicism.

Resuscitated religious and national values have mutated into false divinities. Idols of Nazism and fundamentalism have escaped control like an evil genie, and now the Church is indeed confronted with this idolatry. The reintroduction of religious liberty induced a state of euphoria in the Church, which the Croatian Democratic Union has used to claim Church support. Instead, stated Kustić, the Church should withhold its blessing of political and military events.[11]

However, priests continue to be used by politicians. Church

---

10. An Austrian Catholic theologian, Dr. Philipp Harnoncourt, provided information in January 1993 to this author that he obtained at a meeting in Vienna convened by Cardinal König to work on reconciling the two churches: a plea by the Orthodox Bishop Irinej Bulović of Novi Sad and Bačka that the Roman Catholic bishops could do much to allay Serbian fears by condemning the destruction of 500,000 Serbs during World War II. However, the Catholic Bishop Djuro Kokša responded that the charge was exaggerated—there were only 50,000 killed, he claimed—and then did not proceed to apologize even for that number. This author, likewise, never heard a Croatian Roman Catholic priest make any statement that could be considered as a condemnation of the atrocities of the past war.

11. Interview with Živko Kustić in Zagreb, September 4, 1993.

publications continue to disseminate ethnoreligious messages. *Glas Koncila*, for instance, published in 1993 a picture and text about hundreds of Croatian soldiers from the front being paraded on a pilgrimage to the shrine of the Holy Virgin in Krasno, a shrine that claims to be the first and foremost shrine of the Croatian Army for all eternity! Another article reported a Croat military pilgrimage to the French shrine at Lourdes.

With the onset of Croat-Muslim warfare, the tone of Catholic articles about Muslims became strident, the tendentious identification being that all Muslim combatants are *mujahedins.* The proclamation of the Croat Republic of Herzeg-Bosnia was at first greeted by Catholic Church leaders. Later, they distanced themselves, seemingly for the sole reason of saving the Catholic presence in other parts of Bosnia. And while the Catholic bishops in Bosnia began to depart from the official policy of the Tudjman government toward prospective partitioning of Bosnia, their statements were a veritable test case of the ethnoreligious formula of fusing Catholic with Croat.[12] Little concern for the fate of non-Croat Catholics is evident, much less for non-Catholics. The Catholic theologian Vjekoslav Bajsić has remarked that the Catholic clergy of Herzegovina in particular do not know how to work with others; they always perceive others as dangerous and unfit for cooperation.

It would be erroneous not to report that most of the articles in *Glas Koncila* proclaim genuinely Christian charity and forgiveness. But this intermingling creates a feeling of considerable ambiguity. It is questionable which of these messages make the greater impact on the average Catholic. The future of the Church, ecumenism, and peace depend on that fateful choice.

2. The Serbian Orthodox Role in the Disintegration of Yugoslavia

Since the Serbs had far more vested interests in keeping Yugoslavia together than the other nationalities, it may seem odd that the Serbian Orthodox Church contributed to the outbreak of hostilities, but they did so decisively. The Orthodox Church did so

---

12. This is also confirmed by Gerald Shenk, who wrote, ". . .the actions of the Vatican, the Croatian Cardinal [Kuharić], and the other Catholic bishops clearly served to strengthen even more the view that identity as a Croat necessarily means identity as a Roman Catholic." In *God with Us?: The Role of Religion in Conflicts in the Former Yugoslavia* (Uppsala: Life and Peace Institute, 1993), p. 42.

first by its role in the Kosovo conflict, whipping up claims of the uniqueness of Serbian victimization by others, and later by its uncritical support of Serbian nationalist aspirations.

Already in the late 1970s, the Serbian Orthodox Church was warning about the Albanian "menace" in Kosovo. The Albanian population explosion there and the exodus of Serbs was labeled as genocide of Serbs. Before too long the claim would be generalized that Serbs were threatened on all sides by conspiracies. As the Yugoslav government cracked down on Albanian demonstrations and repeatedly repressed dissent—evoking concerns by non-Serbs about violations of Albanians' and their own rights—the Serbian Orthodox Church went on a propaganda counter-attack by issuing appeals regarding alleged rapes, murders, expulsions, and the destruction of Serbian cultural monuments and sacred sites—in other words "ethnic cleansing" of Serbs—by Albanians. One such appeal is "The Declaration of the Bishops of the Serbian Orthodox Church Against the Genocide Inflicted by the Albanians on the Indigenous Serbian Population, Together with the Sacrilege of Their Cultural Monuments in Their own Country,"[13] This strengthened the Serb resolve not to give up Kosovo and produced a powerful anti-Albanian feeling among Serbs.

Another nationalist conflict was fanned by the Serbian Orthodox Church in its strenuous opposition to the separation of the Macedonian Orthodox Church. The Patriarch of Belgrade claimed jurisdiction over nearly all Orthodox churches in Yugoslavia, namely in Serbia, Montenegro, and Macedonia. Already at that point it became obvious that Serbian Orthodox leaders and Serbian Communist leaders saw eye-to-eye on the Macedonian questions, just as the Macedonian Orthodox Church hierarchy saw eye-to-eye with the Macedonian Communists. Tension also arose in the Montenegrin Orthodox Church, where a pro-Serbian branch negated the separateness of the Montenegrins. A pro-Montenegrin branch asserted that the Montenegrins ought to insist on the autocephaly of their church, which they claimed they had obtained in the past. These two groups occasionally came to literal blows and a church schism took place in 1993. Neither the Macedonian nor the Montenegrin conflict is yet resolved.

---

13. Photocopied typescript signed by five Serbian Orthodox bishops of Western countries, September 14, 1988.

The Serbian Orthodox Church vigorously joined the Memorandum of the Serbian Academy of Sciences and Arts in voicing Serbian grievances (see Chapter 8); The Orthodox were particularly incensed by what they regarded as the lack of Croatian Catholic willingness to atone for their wartime crimes against the Serbian Orthodox population in Croatia and Bosnia. Prominent Serbian Orthodox bishops and theologians began speaking up on behalf of what they considered threatened Serbdom in areas where, in World War II, massacres of Serbs took place, especially the concentration camp of Jasenovac in Croatia. It was lamented that no Roman Catholic official came to the commemorations to the victims of Croatian fascist "ethnic cleansing" during the dedication of the Serbian Orthodox Church in Jasenovac in 1984. Cries of "Never again!" could be heard from both Serbian nationalist and church circles.[14] The Orthodox Church kept reiterating its age-old claim that the Church always was, is, and will be—even when all others fail—the defender of Serbian national interests. The gravest threats to Serbdom and Orthodoxy, they pointed out, were Muslims and Catholics. Two years prior to the commencement of warfare, the Serbian Orthodox publication *Pravoslavje* (Orthodoxy) clamored for the defense of Serbs and Orthodoxy—if necessary, militarily. The crimes of the Independent State of Croatia and the *ustashe* were frequently linked to the Roman Catholic Church and its leadership, and were seen as a continuation of the ages-old Catholic aspiration to convert and absorb the Orthodox into the Roman Catholic fold.[15] The Serbian Orthodox have staunchly sided with other Serb nationalists, who saw in the Croatian independence movement many "ustashoid" elements.

---

14. The real aim of Pavelić's regime was to have a pure Croatian "Great Croatia." I am stressing this in order to point out that the Serb attempts at "ethnic cleansing," which I under no circumstances support, are in fact retribution for what happened in World War II. Namely, we are witnessing the ending of that war on the Balkans as well as the beginning of the next round of warfare. The Serbs are carrying out what is popularly known as *"milo za drago,"* or tit for tat.

15. Interview with Bishop Danilo Krstić in Kecskemét, Hungary, on August 26, 1993. It should be noted that the Serbian Orthodox claim of unrelenting Catholic hegemonistic aspiration is the exact opposite of the claim of two centuries of sustained, planned Serbian expansionism at the expense of Croats and Catholics reflected in the special issue "Rat protiv Hrvatske" (War Against Croatia), *Društvena istraživanja*, Nos. 4–5 (Zagreb, 1993).

By the late 1980s the anti-Albanian, anti-Slovene, and anti-Croat feelings were conflated, and the Serbian Orthodox Church saw initially in Milošević's "Anti-bureaucratic Revolution" the salvation and liberation of the Serbian people. Only in 1992 did some Orthodox leaders, especially Patriarch Paul I, see Milošević's populism as a threat to the well-being of the Serbian people. The Patriarch and several other prelates openly criticized his government at anti-government demonstrations in Belgrade and elsewhere, and have charged that the government is harming the interests of the Serbian people.

Some authors demonize the role of the Serbian Orthodox Church for allegedly always supporting the state, this in contrast to what they perceive as the much more independent role of the Catholic Church among Croatians. This author does not see any significant difference in the relationship of these two churches toward the nation which they represent. It is true that the Serbian Orthodox hierarchy was more servile to the former Yugoslav government than was the Roman Catholic hierarchy, but there are a host of plausible explanations for that. In the rise of national chauvinism, both churches have contributed heavily. It is symptomatic that running parallel to the notion *Crkva u Hrvata* is its match, *Srpska crkva*, a synonym for the Orthodox Church. The term *"Serbian"* seems to carry more weight than the term *"Orthodox."* (It is yet to be seen which will win the soul of the Croats, the Catholic or the Croat identity; different Croats have made different choices, just as have the Serbs.)

An interesting editorial in an Orthodox journal has indicated that there are those who mistakenly emphasize only the Serbian national identity as a measure of their adherence to the Christian church. During the decline of Communism some observers blamed the Orthodox Church for the errors of government policies—having identified the church with the state—and claimed that this entanglement brought about God's wrath upon both the Serbian church and state. Such equations of church and state are to be rejected. Yet in typical Orthodox fashion these authors rejected a sharp division of the worldly (political) and spiritual (ecclesiastic) domains. Even the official documents of the Holy Assembly of Bishops uses terms such as "the Christian Serbian nation" and "the Serbian Church, truly indigenous and encompassing of all the people" and thereby constantly contribute to the *terminological* ethnoreligious identification.

The Metropolitan of Sarajevo, Nikolaj Mrdja, was the first Serb leader to point out that organized rapes were being carried out by Serb extremists. However, at Christmastime in 1992 the Orthodox hierarchy issued a sharp statement categorically denying that Serbs have organized rapes and challenging anyone to name a single concentration camp where such rapes occurred; it simultaneously charged that many Serb women had been raped by Muslims and Croats. All this indicates the delicate position of the Serbian Orthodox Church, namely to truthfully point out events that it cannot conceivably condone and its need to be the protector of the Serbs' national reputation when the entire nation is demonized by the outside world.

When the United Nations and NATO issued an ultimatum that all the heavy weapons be withdrawn to a distance of twelve miles from Sarajevo or else they would be destroyed by air bombardment, the Holy Synod of the Serbian Orthodox Church, through its spokesman, Bishop Irinej Bulović, issued a sharply worded statement on February 21, 1994, condemning what they considered the moral misuse of the Sarajevo shelling (which they blamed on the Muslims) for a one-sided attack upon Serbs. They warned that such an action by NATO could spread the war to other parts of the Balkans or Europe. A parallel is drawn between the threat of NATO to the Serbs and Goliath's threat to David. The Russian peace initiative, however, was welcomed. The Serbian Orthodox Church will always defend the Serb people from unjust attacks, pointed out Bishop Irinej. He does not believe that it is the Church's first mission to be a national institution but to assemble the people of God. However, the present national prominence of the Church is a necessary by-product of the crisis situation. He felt that the leaders of the Roman Catholic Church in Croatia made and continue to make mistakes in not recognizing the embittered memory of Serbs who suffered under the Croats.[16] Bishop Bulović is considered as the gray eminence of his church, apparently representing the moderate wing of the Church.

Like the Roman Catholic Church in Croatia, the Serbian Or-

---

16. Interview in Novi Sad, August 18, 1993.

thodox Church favors obligatory religious education in schools. But unlike the Croatian *Sabor*, the Assembly *(Skupština)* of the rump Yugoslavia defeated the motion with a large majority. In contrast the *Republika Srpska Krajina* in Croatia and *Republika Srpska* in B & H introduced Orthodox catechism into the schools, an action praised by the Orthodox hierarchy hoping to pressure the Yugoslav parliament to introduce religious education in Serbia and Montenegro. The Orthodox Church worried about Serb children being catechized by Roman Catholic teachers in Croatian schools but seemed unconcerned about the fate of non-Orthodox children in the event of mandatory Orthodox catechism in schools of Serbia. Serb theologians also undertook the defense of Serbs and attacked Croats (and others) when Croat views critical of Serbs appeared in foreign journals.

Neither Orthodox ecclesiology nor Serb nationalism is at ease with a theology of repentance and a sharp criticism of one's own nation. The same failings can be found in Catholic ecclesiology and Croat nationalism, which likewise has difficulty admitting wrongdoing by their own people. The immense transforming power of internal criticism is left unutilized by both of these Christian communities.

Individual Orthodox prelates and priests have excelled in contributing to the warfare. Bishops Atanasije Jeftić of Herzegovina and Amfilohije Radović of Montenegro set the pace for promoting Great Serbian nationalist interests by engaging in public controversies with those Serb politicians who favored less violent alternatives. A number of priests voluntarily joined the *chetniks* (who embody the ethnoreligious fusion and who frequently employ Orthodox symbols on their uniforms and weapons) not merely as chaplains but as combatants, justifying their participation by saying that they are doing this in order to prevent a Muslim domination of their people ten years hence.[17] Other hierarchs contribute to the war propaganda by deliberately issuing false reports of destructions of Orthodox churches or murdered Serbs, knowing full well that any such claims may easily disrupt the fragile stalemate in Croatia. And finally, rather than have a calming effect, the communiqués of the entire Assembly of Or-

---

17. In the documentary film *Romeo and Juliette of Sarajevo* an Orthodox priest uses this justification for taking part in combat.

thodox Bishops tend to exacerbate the warfare by their exaggerated claims and alarmist tone all in the name of protecting Orthodoxy and Serbdom.

3. Bosnian Muslims: Ethnoreligious Ambiguity

The Bosnian Muslims are in the unique and somewhat awkward position of being the only group of Muslim believers in the world who are considered Muslim both by religion and by *nationality*. Some claim that national consciousness among the Slavic Muslims of Bosnia and Herzegovina came late. Others maintain that the Muslims were the mainstream of Bosnian life, having come peacefully to Bosnia in the ninth century and created a Muslim civilization, culture, language, script, and so forth. However, most scholars contend that Christians of the former Bosnian Church (along with some Catholics and Orthodox), underwent a mass conversion to Islam from 1436 onward.

One thing is sure: Most contemporary Slavic Muslims do not remember their pre-Islamic religious or ethnic origin. Since they were the ruling class during the rule of the Ottomans, they were detested by their neighboring Slavic Christians, Orthodox and Catholic. When the Turks withdrew from the Balkan peninsula, it was expected that the Slavic Muslims (the so-called *poturice* or Turkicized people) would return to their Christian origins, thereby swelling the ranks of the Orthodox and/or Catholics. When this courting of the Muslims turned out to be unsuccessful, the surrounding Christian populations continued in their resentment and eventually began to subjugate them in order to forestall any possibility of Muslims' lording over them ever again. The Muslims who, heretofore, had had a fairly nebulous identity now had to work on a clearer one. Some preferred to call themselves Yugoslavs, some *Bošnjaks*, others Muslims. The Croats and the Serbs vigorously continued to claim that all the Muslims had been converts from the two respective religions and nationalities. It is in fact most likely that both Serbian Orthodox and Croatian Catholics, as well as Bogumils of the Bosnian Church, converted and in any case repressed their previous identities so effectively that most of them do not care to regard themselves as one or the other.

Islam became more a cultural than a religious identity for most Muslims in Yugoslavia. They may well be one of the most secularized Muslim communities in the world, gravitating toward Europe rather than the Muslim East. The current President of the Bosnian government, Alija Izetbegović, wrote a pamphlet at the time when he was a Communist prisoner that some describe as "Islamic fundamentalist" because, allegedly, he aimed to establish Bosnia as an Islamic state in which the Muslim majority would take over totally and rule with the help of the *shariyat* (traditional Islamic) law. Parts of that pamphlet do have troublesome implications for non-Muslims. However, since he was elected President of B & H, he has consistently pledged himself to a secular, multi-national and multi-religious state in which everyone's rights would be respected (though some observers still think that he says this is in order to placate the West.) Izetbegović does believe, nevertheless, that the Muslims are the *cardinal* people of B & H; i.e., if it were not for them, B & H would long since have been divided between Serbia and Croatia.

To bypass the unfruitful discussion of what Izetbegović meant or did not mean to say in his "Islamic Declaration"—which people tend to interpret according to their Islamic sympathies or antipathies—one can still see that Izetbegović's Islamic convictions contributed to the outbreak of the war. Namely, he created the Party for Democratic Action, which was almost exclusively Muslim and clearly religion-identified, and he championed the homogenization of a Muslim ethnoreligious identity. He is, thereby, along with the Serb and Croat nationalists, coresponsible for the deterioration of the political situation.

Since the Western World has not given any effective assistance to the Muslims—who became the major losers in the ensuing war—Bosnian Muslims may eventually be driven into the arms of Islamic fundamentalists, who seem more eager to assist them than do others. Some observers have already noticed—in addition to the presence of a limited number of *mujahedin* from Islamic fundamentalist countries—a growing *jihad* mentality. When predominantly Muslim military units of the Bosnian Army are addressed by Muslim leaders, the speeches become religious in character. If Islamic radicalization therefore takes place, it will be less a conscious and free decision of the Bosnian Muslims and more an act of a desperate people on the verge of extermination. Under this pressure they will simply be forced to create a totally Muslim state or face genocide.

The battles between Muslim and Croat forces from late 1992 to early 1994 are an evidence that the earlier Muslim-Croat alliance was temporary, driven only by a common hatred of the Serbs. For strategic reasons the two peoples may agree to work together, but it is not a relationship based on respect and shared interests. Whether the American maneuver to create a Bosnian Muslim-Croat federation, which would then enter into a confederation with Croatia itself—a plan based on political interests rather than national—will be workable is yet to be seen. It is not clear what this plan has to offer to Bosnian Serbs. If it fails to include the Serbs, then the plan will inevitably fail to stop the war.

Muris Baščaušević[18] points out the failure of the previous Communist regime to deal with nationalism because of its avoidance of recognizing the spiritual dimension of human existence. Because of the crisis of morality under Communism it was evident that people of the former Yugoslavia were not ready for the transition toward democracy in the post-Communist period. Rather they slipped back into primitivism. The only way the people could come to grips with conflict situations was to turn to violence. Savages and criminals came to the surface after the death of Tito. Of course, this did not happen all at once, but was the result of a long neglect of the spiritual dimension. Had people been educated in a moral atmosphere they would not have turned to killing so heinously. The worst is yet to come if these terrorists finally assume power, for they will both subjugate people and falsify history. This will only be fodder for a new round of ethnoreligious warfare in a not-too-distant future.

4. Macedonian Orthodox Separatism

It is general knowledge that the Macedonian Orthodox Church was supported in its schism (dating from 1967) from the Serbian Orthodox Church by Tito's government in order to make a more determined effort to prove the separateness and identity of the Macedonian nationality. Since in Eastern Europe one cannot imagine a nationality without its own religion, it was important to establish an autocephalous, or at least autonomous,

---

18. Baščaušević is a Bosnian Muslim who is the leader of the Muslim community in Slovenia, most of them exiles. From an interview in Ljubljana on August 31, 1993.

Macedonian church. This was done to deter the Bulgarian, Greek, and Serbian claims that Macedonians were not separate but were parts of their respective nations. Though Macedonia was one of the last nations in Europe to become free of Turkish overlordship (1913), and one of the last ethnic groups to proclaim its own national consciousness, some of the Macedonian leaders in turn have made some outrageous claims about uniting Greek, Bulgarian, and Yugoslav Macedonia into a Great Macedonia—a move which has cost them, especially, Greek recognition as an independent, sovereign state upon the fall of Yugoslavia. Maps had even been distributed showing the claims of a Great Macedonia.

Macedonian Orthodox higher clergy have dutifully carried out the task of promoting Macedonian sovereignty and been fairly effective ambassadors abroad. It is interesting that the Macedonian Orthodox hierarchs have nurtured fairly good relationships with the Vatican and the Croatian Catholics—one presumes, on the old European principle of being friends with the enemies of your enemy. A minor reconciliation with the Serbian Orthodox Church was recently in the offing since no Orthodox church in the world was willing to grant autocephaly to the Macedonian Orthodox Church, but no accommodation was worked out with the Serbian Orthodox Church and the Macedonians accuse the Serbian Patriarchate of wanting to Serbianize the Macedonians.

The Macedonian Orthodox hierarchs have a perception of being treated by other Orthodox churches even worse than Muslims. They claim that, prior to the introduction of the multiparty electoral system, the Macedonian Orthodox Church had a good relationship with the Albanian Muslims of Macedonia—so much so that the latter were willing to support the proposed election of Metropolitan Mikhail Gogov to the presidency; but since then, the good relationship has deteriorated.[19] On March 11, 1994, two mosques, one in Veles and the other near Kavadarci, were burned to the ground, indicating increasing tensions.

Some Macedonian Orthodox politicians advocate church-state union in order to promote the domination of ethnic Macedonians, revealing their dissatisfaction with the constitutional separation of church and state (see Chapter 10). The Macedonian

---

19. Interview with Metropolitan Mikhail in Skopje, August 23, 1993. On December 4, 1993, Mikhail was chosen to be the primate of that church.

Orthodox Church is not in doctrinal conflict with any Orthodox church, but ethnically it is in conflict with them all and this has resulted in a canonical schism that leaves the Macedonians without Orthodox backing in their efforts to maintain independent nationhood, particularly against Serbian and Greek pressure. In response to these animosities, Bishop Kiril claimed in a press interview that Macedonia was a holy land. From such a claim one can surmise that if a war were to break out here it would be a holy war—another proof of the ethnoreligious grounding of the present conflicts in the Balkans.

5. Protestants: Inability to Withstand War Propaganda

The Protestants, making up less than 1 percent of the population of the former Yugoslavia, are quite marginalized. Generally, the larger churches have tended to be churches of national minorities (those of Hungarians, Slovaks, Germans). Among the larger Yugoslav nationalities the number of Protestants was quite insignificant and played only a marginal role.

In the past, the Free Church Protestants—e.g., Baptists, Pentecostals, Seventh-Day Adventists, Methodists—tended to attract membership from a variety of national groups nurturing exemplary harmonious relationships between the members of various nationalities, and there was hope that these good relationships could survive the war. They were also outspoken in maintaining that God is not a nationalist and that religion ought to reconcile rather than divide people.

But that would have been too good to be true. For one, these formerly unified churches that acted wherever they had members on the territory of Yugoslavia now found themselves in separate countries and had to break up along the new nation-state principles.

Then, many of the Protestant leaders in Croatia became so morally outraged at what they perceived, along with the rest of the Croatian people, as Serbian aggression that they condemned this aggression and urged foreign military intervention against Serbians, often criticizing foreigners, especially Americans, for their inaction. This incensed their fellow-religionists in Serbia, and formerly close colleagues now regard the Croatian Protestants no longer as peacemakers but as supporters of the war effort.

On the whole, the Protestant communities have tended to accept the official propaganda of their respective new states, and they often interpret events the way this propaganda channels them. This does not mean that they uncritically support all the policies of their governments, but it does show that even *they* are unable to bridge the enormous abyss that now separates Croats and Serbs, Serbs and Macedonians, etc.

THE RECONCILING ROLE OF RELIGIOUS COMMUNITIES

We have already noted that the reconciling role of the religious communities is undeveloped in comparison to the divisive role. Calls for peace and reconciliation are not lacking, but many of these do not go beyond platitudes and claims that this or that religion has always stood for peace. Frequently the call for peace has been tempered by strong defensive language, rejecting the culpability of one's own side and directing the blame toward the other. Very few *positive* statements have been uttered about other religions and nationalities during these times—which is not surprising, given the cruel treatment that has been dished out to each. It is clear that religious leaders are concerned about the biological and religious survival of their peoples, fearing that as a result of these wars their peoples and their institutions will be expelled from lands in which they have lived and worked for centuries. It is that fear that propels most of the ecclesiastical pronouncements and actions.

Of course, like most others the churches regret the war— though not many mourn the disintegration of Yugoslavia. Few members of the religious communities can give a sound assessment of the situation that is not merely a reflection of what they hear from their mass media. Any dissenting assessments rarely receive wide circulation. And even fewer are those who decide to become activists on behalf of peace. Most religious organizations and their members see themselves as being victims of forces far too great for their modest abilities. Survival in tumultuous times is the overwhelming desire—active peacemaking is neither a tradition, nor do individuals have enough psychic energy left for conflict resolution. Most are too shell-shocked by the brutality of the war and the troubled times for their communities and themselves to be able to stem the confrontational mood throughout the region. Many feel that exaggerated expectations exist abroad about the influence of the churches on political and military decisions; as one theologian said, in despair, "They think that all the Cardinal needs to do is to whistle and say 'Stop the war' and they will immediately carry it out."

Several remarkable statements have been made, however, by leaders of religious communities, both by themselves and in meeting with others. The most significant such occasions were the meetings between Patriarch Paul I of the Serbian Orthodox Church with the head of the Roman Catholic Bishops' Conference, Franjo Cardinal Kuharić. Their first meeting was in Sremski Karlovci (Serbia) in May 1991, the second in Slavonski Brod (Croatia) in August 1991, the third in spring 1992 in St. Gallen, (Switzerland), and the fourth in Geneva in September 1992; the fifth was a meeting which the *Reis-ul-ulema* of the Islamic Community, Jakub Selimovski, also was able to be present at, a meeting that was convened by the Conference of European Churches and the European Catholic Bishops' Conference in Switzerland in early 1993.

The most powerful text emerged out of the 1992 Geneva meeting partially reproduced here as follows:

> Following our prayers and conversations, we appeal with one mind and voice to the faithful of our churches, to the responsible organs of the state, to military commanders and troops, to all peoples and men and women of our common geographical and spiritual area, as well as to all international forums and institutions engaged in the search for a solution or in the provision of aid to our region and in our states; and we do not only appeal but demand, on the basis of our spiritual position and moral responsibility:
>
> 1. Immediately and without condition to cease all hostilities, all bloodshed and all destruction, in particular to stop the blasphemous and insane destruction of places of prayer and holy places, Christian and Muslim alike; and that negotiations between the warring parties be initiated without delay.
> 2. Immediately and without condition to liberate all prisoners of war and hostages, as well as to close all prison camps and to free all those incarcerated in this evil war.
> 3. Immediately and without condition to cease the inhuman practice of ethnic cleansing, by whomever it is being incited or carried out.

4. To permit all refugees and deportees to return to their homes and to ensure all bishops and priests of our churches as well as Islamic spiritual leaders free access to their flock and undisturbed exercise of their office.
5. That normal communication and unrestricted circulation be re-established, as well as the possibility of free movement and settlement for all people, whatever their religious or national affiliation, and
6. that all suffering people be assured undisturbed and equal access to humanitarian aid.

Equally with one mind and voice we condemn all crimes and distance ourselves from all criminals, irrespective of which people or army they belong to or which church or religious affiliation they claim. We especially express our horror at the perpetration of extremely immoral misdeeds, at the mistreatment of older and younger women and girls, which only monsters can perpetrate, no matter what name they give themselves.

Before God, before humanity and before our own conscience we pledge that we will use all evangelical means and the full influence of our office and responsibility in church and society to work, in our own states and peoples, decisively and openly for peace, justice and the salvation of each and every one, for the dignity and inalienable rights of every individual and every people, for humanity and tolerance, for forgiveness and love.

We ourselves call, individually and together, for repentance before the God of love, for conversation and for service to him, that we can live anew as neighbours, friends and brothers,

Peace to all![20]

Of great importance was the distancing which the prelates took from those who would wage war in the name of their religion, saying that to do so is the greatest crime against one's own religion.

The Christmas message 1992, by all the Orthodox bishops presided over by Patriarch Paul I, is likewise very peace-oriented. In it the bishops give an answer to why such destruction ensued after the proclamation of democracy and multi-party elections. The reason cited was

that the proclaimed principles were accepted only externally, formally, but in the soul matters stayed unchanged due to espousing the notion that one can help oneself and one's people more by

---

20. Full text in *Occasional Papers on Religion in Eastern Europe*, Vol. XII, No. 5 (October 1992), pp. 50–51.

doing evil than by good, and that one can defend oneself and one's people from crimes and criminals by doing the same, namely by means of inhumanity and crimes . . .[21]

The bishops proceeded to point out that these attitudes brought about the unhappiness of all the nations involved in this war, and then invoked love toward all as a mark of Christian discipleship.

The Roman Catholic Archbishop of Belgrade, the Slovene France Perko, also rejected the linkage between war massacres and religion, yet admitted that the coupling was now closer. While urging patriotism instead of nationalism, the Archbishop conceded that many believers saw themselves more as nationalists than as Christians due to the current lack of evangelization.

Examining the leadership of the religious communities, it is difficult to find prelates with a distinct orientation toward peace. The top leadership of the three communities—Orthodox, Catholic, and Islamic—are more conciliatory than some of their colleagues, but no one has emerged with a Christlike, Ghandian, or Martin Luther King, Jr. type of strategy for resisting evil. Minuscule groups of dissenters, of course, oppose the war or look for alternate peaceful ways in Belgrade, Zagreb, Mostar, and Sarajevo.[22] In Sarajevo, for instance, there is a small group of Catholic, Orthodox, and Muslim clergy led by Marko Oršolić, a Franciscan (who founded the International Center for Interreligious Dialogue, Justice, and Peace) who together are working toward converting one of the military barracks into a dialogue center following the war, but these leaders are not only isolated but also despised by their own religious communities. Some have already been assassinated by members of their own groups! Oršolić, a Croat, has been attacked in the Croatian press as a "Communist." Oršolić continues, however, in his efforts to create ecumenical support for peace in Bosnia by planning a conference

21. *Glasnik*, Vol. 73, No. 12 (December 1992), pp. 198–199. Translated from the Serbian by P. Mojzes. It should be noted that the text is not directed at enemies of the Serbs.

22. In Zagreb Gerald Shenk, an American Mennonite theologian and activist, taught pacifism at the gathering of a group of religious citizens convened by the Fellowship of Reconciliation. He also proposed specific actions to peace groups from abroad in his booklet with David Steele, *God with Us?: The Role of Religion in Conflicts in the Former Yugoslavia.*

(probably in 1995) to discuss future ecumenical studies programs and other joint interfaith actions, once Sarajevo becomes accessible again.

An American peace activist who asked to remain anonymous reports that most of the clergy, especially the higher clergy, in former Yugoslavia have been inundated by foreign ecumenical and fact-finding delegations, and that they feel overburdened by high expectations that the churches can be agents of reconciliation whereas, indeed, they do not see themselves as having that much influence. The above-mentioned activist reports that it is fairly difficult to find key middle-level or higher clergy who wish to meet with their opposites from other churches. The most that one can expect at the present moment is relief work by the churches, an effort for which they are neither trained nor particularly well suited. While some of the church centers seem to be able to effectively distribute relief based only on need, there are reports of abuses; certain local churches distribute aid only to regular churchgoers of their own denomination or use aid in order to promote church attendance or even conversion.

While the larger Protestant churches (Lutherans and Reformed) tend to be single-ethnic in compositions, Free Church Protestants have a greater tendency to be of mixed ethnic background and sometimes epitomize the harmony that ought to prevail among people of different nationalities. These latter Protestants are also very willing to work for peace among people of different ethnic origins, but sometimes even this work is flawed in that they see it as a missionizing enterprise to increase the membership of their flock.

All religious bodies have immersed themselves, regardless of size, into relief work. Particularly impressive is that of the Seventh-Day Adventists, who, at considerable personal risks to themselves, deliver mail and packages to war-ravaged areas where no postal system functions any longer.

CONCLUSION

It is difficult to have hope of a better future for the devastated and brutalized people of the former Yugoslavia, including the religious segment and its institutions. Most people expect matters to become worse before they become better. In Dante's *Inferno* there is a sign over Hell: "Abandon hope all those who enter." The people in former Yugoslavia are, indeed, closer to hell than to heaven—at least as regards life here on earth. The religious communities suffer along. Perhaps some of them will learn that inspiring national chauvinism and separatism, rather than tolerance, pluralism, and concern for fellow-human beings regardless of nationality and religion, is a recipe for hell.

CHAPTER 8

WHO OR WHAT IS TO BLAME?

Even the most cursory reading of politicians' statements and media claims in the now independent Yugoslavian states will show that each side has provoked the other. The name-calling was belligerent; speeches and articles were untruthful and incendiary. Without hesitation, one can say they all have lied. Innocent blood has been shed by all parties in the combat. Nationalism quickly turned to chauvinism, with claims such as "Croatia is for Croats"—a clear signal to Serbs living in Croatia that their role there was now, at best, unclear; at worst, unsafe. And "All Serbs everywhere have the right to live in a single state" did not grant the same right to Albanians, Hungarians, and others. Those in power do not appear to realize that the only permanent solution is to grant equal rights to *all citizens* of each state rather than only to its ethnic nationals.

The question of responsibility and blame, however, cannot be avoided. All have sinned but not all are equally guilty. All players shared in preparing this catastrophe. Blame and responsibility belong to all parties, not just for the sake of even-handedness, but because fair interpretation of the data demands that we acknowledge the involvement of nearly all domestic actors and quite a few international. There is an inclination by many in the former Yugoslavia to blame an international conspiracy. Notwithstanding such claims, I am convinced that the culprits have been entirely domestic—at least initially. An international component was present, but made mistakes in *reacting* to the crisis rather than *initiating* it.

A definite hierarchy of culpability can be established. But first, some preliminary remarks: The fear and hatred-induced acts that brought about the war cannot be explained rationally. They were evoked by human destructiveness and self-centeredness. Sinfulness and intransigence are at the motivating core of the war. Some conflict of interests was inevitable in Yugoslavia because of the contradictory self-interests of its divergent groups and individuals. But war was *not* necessary. It resulted from a human degeneracy and a propensity for sinful destructiveness. Having said this, let us identify those who were most actively responsible for the slide into Europe's most dreadful war since World War II.[1]

1. The Unsolved National Question

The *fundamental* reason for the disintegration of Yugoslavia was, without question, the unsolved nationality problem (extensively discussed in Chapter 5). Yugoslavia was an artificial entity created at the intersection of defunct empires. Nations of the area had some common interests in entering this union, but their self-interests were frequently at odds. On the one hand, during 70 years of living together, the southern Slavs drew closer to each other. They not only shared adjacent territory and kindred languages but were able to work together for extended periods of time. Had they lived together for another 50 or 100 years, or even 10, they might have solved their problems peacefully and forged a permanent union.

Yet, no instrument was ever found to effectively forge a common state. Interests were too divergent and intolerance was too great to foster the pluralistic society that the ethnic intermingling demanded. Nor did they have the democratic traditions necessary to "negotiate" their differences. However, long historic intermingling made a *clear break* from each other impossible. Even in the process of disengagement, self-interests would clash. What might be to the advantage of one group often disadvantaged another.

---

1. One of the most detailed accounts of the fall of Yugoslavia and the allocation of blame particularly to politicians and the media is the recently self-published book by Predrag Tašić, *Kako je ubijena druga Jugoslavija* (How Second Yugoslavia Was Killed) (Skopje, 1994), p. 240. The book arrived after this manuscript was finished, making it too late for some insights to be included. However, it is evident that Tašić's views to a large extent corroborate my own, and I only regret that I did not know of him or his work when I visited Skopje in the summer of 1993.

War would solve nothing, of course. On the contrary. The southern Slavs are destined for, and someday must accommodate to, life next to each other. Although some hotheads opt for genocide, catastrophic damage to one group or another is possible, but actual extermination is not. Each group is too numerous for that.

2. Politicians

The politicians—mostly former Communists who realized that that ideology was unable to keep them in power—quickly latched onto nationalism as a substitute. Some former anti-Communists did likewise to achieve power. Both groups manipulated and exploited nationalism to the point where they could no longer control it, and this has played the most destructive role in the breakup of the Yugoslav state.

Tito, the man who ruled Yugoslavia from 1945 to 1980, did a great deal to control the nationalities issue during his tenure in power, but paradoxically he contributed to the post-Titoist national conflicts. He did so by essentially sweeping national problems under the rug, where they festered for years. Thus, national conflicts were muted rather than resolved and, like an infection that cannot break out to the surface, they moved ever more deeply inside, until the entire organism was contaminated. Also, Tito created a climate in which the greatest virtue was obedience rather than capability. Obedience was the earmark of Communist cadres; public opinion was characterized by gullibility. Tito's regime was able to convince most people to believe what they read in the newspapers or saw on television. The vast majority of the Yugoslavs had no mind of their own. They were therefore no more able, later, to resist the tide of national chauvinism than they were able to resist Titoist socialism (which, of course, had become discredited with the disintegration of Communism).

As the old Communist leadership died out, new leadership rose, primarily from the ranks of second-generation Communist managers groomed in the party organizations of their respective Yugoslav republics. These, naturally, more closely identified themselves with the national interests of their own republics than with interests of the federation. Further, a new group of anti-Communist nationalists, suddenly and with little experience, was swept into the highest offices of the state in a wave of popular enthusiasm for multi-party "democracy."

Multi-party elections became a reality as Marxist ideology lost its attraction among the electorate. With a few regional exceptions, people were no longer intimidated to vote Communist. In effect, therefore, the only ideology left to politicians was nationalism, and they began vying to be considered most ardent in that regard. Former Communists (some still clung to the doctrine after formally rejecting the designation) had an advantage of governing experience. They also knew how to use strong-arm tactics. For this reason, many of the new nationalists were "cut out of Tito's cloth." They of course did all that was in their power to preserve the considerable privileges that were part of the former power structure. One difference was that whereas the Communist elite had once been monolithic, the new nationalist elites were pitted one against another in a desperate struggle over frequently contradictory interests. The situation was aggravated most of all by the quality of the politicians who emerged at the top. Most of them were second- and even third-rate in ability, in fact were incapable of rising to the task of dealing with complex inter-republic negotiations.

Within this amorphous and largely incapable group, one politician seized the initiative and made the boldest, most ruthless moves. Others were forced to react. His name was Milošević, and we turn first to his role; then we turn to theirs.

Slobodan Milošević and the Serbian Socialist Party

Slobodan Milošević's rise to power was the turning point in the rising tension among Yugoslavia's nationalities. In 1987, Milošević boldly outmaneuvered his reformist patron Alexander Stambolić for leadership of the Central Committee of the Serbian Socialist Party (the renamed Communists). Milošević's approach to rule has been dogmatic Bolshevik dictatorship. He is a hardliner regarding goals, albeit pragmatic in selecting a path to reach them. He is a complex personality with a strong streak of privacy, one that enhances a sense of mystery which has served him well in the process of accumulating all power in his hands. Even his enemies concede that he is a very able politician—who can "play a card" even when he does not believe in it, if he thinks it can gain him the victory.

In his personal life, Milošević is rather puritanical, and has not shown evidence that he longs for the perquisites of his office (although he has been accused of amassing wealth and stowing it in a Cyprus bank which he allegedly owns). His is an image of incorruptibility and cool calculation, of a man with a penchant for making clear-cut decisions—implemented with an iron hand—and all this makes him a darling of much of the Serb population. After decisively taking the Serbian side in the conflict with Albanians in Kosovo, contrary to the hedging that was typical of other Serbian officials, Milošević became an instant hit with the Serbs, even a figure of legendary proportions, of whom epic songs have been composed. One might say that after the charismatic Tito disappeared from the scene, the simple people of the largest ethnic population in the country, the Serbs, felt a need for another leader with charisma and found it in "Slobo" (Slobodan means "free" in English). Milošević promised the Serbs throughout Yugoslavia that he would free them from acts of oppression by non-Serbs. Seeing chaos looming, his people saw his firm hand saving them, while in fact it led them into chaos!

While Milošević is personally *not* a nationalist, he plays that tune. He has dictatorial attitudes and knows how to show these even in the new system of multi-party elections. Upon taking over as the chief Communist of Serbia, he began espousing themes expounded by the Memorandum of SANU (see below) and disparaging the *alleged* threat to the Serbian nation under Tito's 1974 constitution, demanding that it be amended to give Serbia equal rights. He masterminded and skillfully led the "Anti-bureaucratic Revolution," the alleged aim of which was to rid Serbia of corruption, but which served as a pretext to abolish the autonomous status of Serbia's two provinces, Kosovo and Vojvodina, and nearly annex Montenegro. This was done by inciting so-called "spontaneous" mass demonstrations by transporting a large number of his followers from one location to another, sweeping out of office the local politicians who resisted Milošević's monopoly. In a matter of weeks, the "mass movement" changed anti-constitutionally not only the intra-Serbian governments; the newly installed Milošević leaders actually abolished the status of the autonomous provinces and homogenized Serbia. Doing all of this without consultation with the other republics, Milošević attacked the integrity of Yugoslavia's system of consultations between states and nationalities.

After becoming the unchallenged leader of Serbia, Milošević moved to remake Yugoslavia according to his notion of what were the best interests of Serbia (i.e., of Serbia's ruling elite). In doing so, he showed himself unwilling to make any substantial concessions to the other republics. He wanted to form a unitary Yugoslavia centralized in Belgrade, where the government would be under his control. To achieve this, he sought to replace the 1974 Constitution—which the other republics by and large favored. When proposals were made by other states, to whom the Serbian domination of Yugoslavia was unacceptable, Milošević would yield not an inch. One proposal then made was for an asymmetric federation in which each state would have equal influence regardless of the size of its population; another was for a confederation. None were for partition, not at the time of Milošević's rise to power between 1987 and 1990. Milošević, however, favored a constitution according to which the influence of the most populous nation would be determinative. The real issue, however, was whether Yugoslavia would remain a state dominated by the Communist party or whether it would evolve into a law state.

Ultimately realizing that his ideas could not be implemented against the will of the other nationalities, Milošević opted for a "truncated" Yugoslavia in which all Serbs and their allies would be gathered, while those like Slovenia which "wanted out" would be allowed to break away. But a problem of course arose in those large areas with mixed populations. These Milošević relegated to Yugoslavia, regardless of what their populations wanted. In order to convince all Serbs to support his vision, he spread alarmist news of alleged plots to exterminate them in areas where they lived mixed with Croats and Muslims. The ploy worked with the Serb population, and alienated the others, who, now having seen Milošević's brutal tactics, could not tolerate living under his rule.

Next, Milošević bribed the top brass of the Yugoslav Army to join him in his vision of a reduced Yugoslavia that would be equivalent to a Great Serbia. After the army joined him, he then purged the officers corps of nearly all non-Serbs and took the renamed army (today called the Military of Yugoslavia) under his control. The army was used ruthlessly. No sacrifice in human lives or material was too great if it served Milošević's goal. In pursuit of a Great Serbia, not only did more than 100,000 non-Serbs die, but tens of thousands of Serbs as well. Over two millions Yugoslavs ended up as refugees. Meanwhile, Milošević plunged his state into utter poverty (see Chapter 9).

Numerous attempts have been made to get rid of Milošević, especially after he was singled out by the United Nations as being most responsible for the war, and by the UN's suggestion that his removal from a dictatorial position was a precondition of removing its embargo. Milošević's hold on power is quite tenacious, however. He was twice freely elected with enormous pluralities; in the first election, he and the Serbian Socialist Party received 89 percent of the vote. In some municipalities south of Belgrade he won 98 or 99 percent of the vote. Not depending solely on his somewhat legendary image, he has manipulated public opinion with his near-monopoly of the media, especially TV, and by voting irregularities. But the fact is, the population of Serbia gave him and his program support in three separate elections (1989, 1992, and in December 1993), thereby sharing with him in any guilt for the wars. Milošević and his colleagues have changed the Serb people, otherwise not particularly nationalistic, into the chauvinistic bully of the Balkans.

Challenges of Milošević's rule have been many. Students and workers demonstrated and nearly toppled him, but they were violently repressed. He has faced criticism by leaders of opposition parties and by independent political figures such as Serb-American millionaire Milan Panić (who briefly served as Yugoslavia's Prime Minister), as well as Dobrica Ćosić (the famous novelist who served a short tenure as the President of Yugoslavia), but he routed them within a few days.[2] Segments of the Serbian press criticize him daily. Calls for his removal have been made by leaders of the international community, including U.S. Assistant Secretary of State Warren Zimmermann, a former ambassador to Belgrade. Patriarch Paul I has distanced himself and his Orthodox Church, after an initial support of Milošević's policies, stating

---

2. An insider's view of these processes was provided by Dobrica Ćosić's advisor, the Belgrade philosopher Svetozar Stojanović, in "Political Struggles in Serbia under the Blockade" (translated by Harley Wagler), a typescript dated August 1–15, 1993.

that the rule of the Serbian Socialist Party is not in the best interest of Serbs. Significant numbers of the Serbian population speak critically of him. But none of this matters. Milošević remains undaunted—the spiteful, unyielding, vengeful leader of the Serbs. He may not be remembered by history as he wishes: as founder of the greatest Serb state ever to dominate the Balkans. Instead, he has isolated Serbia from even its most steadfast allies, rendered it a pariah nation, ruined it economically, and may yet pull it down into utter collapse. In the meantime, to his people he justifies all the sacrifices made by Serbs, hoping, somehow, that Serb military victories will be ultimately approved by the international community and that a Great Serbia will be accepted back into that community. Even if Serb territorial expansion wins international acceptance, any expectation of the nation's return into the good graces of the world is an illusion. It is a pity, indeed, that the Serb people as a whole do not realize this.

Milošević, along with Karadžić and Gen. Mladić, has been listed on the UN's list of war criminals. While these three are the worst offenders, the political leaders of other nationalities— e.g., the Croat Mate Boban of Herzeg-Bosnia, and possibly even Tudjman—have also acted like fascists. There is a general feeling that one cannot trust them. International peacemakers such as Vance, Carrington, Owen, and Stoltenberg, who are familiar with the major protagonists, know that many of them lie blatantly and without remorse, making promises without the slightest intention of keeping them (except when they are in their own interests). Long years under foreign occupation and brutal dictatorship, including Communist, have made deviousness a virtue. One finds deliberate distortions of the past and the present not only in the blatant propagandizing of politicians but also in the general media and even in theological journals (frequently presented therein in a scholarly or pastoral guise). No wonder mistrust is nearly as universal as "fear of the other"!

Non-Serb Political Leaders and Parties

The reactive political elites who contributed to the fall of Yugoslavia were leaders in Slovenia and Croatia. Those in other Yugoslav republics were distinctly lagging, taking advantage only later of the momentum created by the big three. The two stellar personalities were the Slovene Milan Kučan and the Croat Franjo Tudjman. Both former Communists were decidedly popular in their respective states for providing leadership toward independence. They were surrounded by a bevy of equally or even more nationalistic politicians and parties. Some of these supported them and some rivaled them, but nearly all were strategically allied in the common aspiration to repudiate Milošević and the increasingly belligerent policies of the Serbian government.

Kučan and Tudjman deserve merit from the perspective of gaining the independence of their countries. From the perspective of the breakup of Yugoslavia and the resultant carnage, their contributions are problematic. Quite unlike each other in most respects, the two men have in common a resolute separatist drive. Both have considered Milošević and Serbia inimical to their own national interests. Kučan and the Slovenes relentlessly spearheaded the separatist drive without regard for ultimate consequences to others. Slovenia was fortunate to extricate itself from ties with Yugoslavia with only minor consequences; other republics did not, however, have such a clear-cut ethnic homogeneity. Yet the Slovene example proved contagious.

Tudjman had been a general in the Yugoslav Army whose Communist convictions were deemed faulty, and he was retired. He used this to become a historian, concluding that the Croat position in the federation was unfair. Turning to politics, he became head of the right-wing Croatian Democratic Union (abbreviated in Croatian as HDZ); it was swept into power by a large majority in the first free election. Since then, the HDZ has consolidated its power and tends to act monopolistically.

Tudjman is an authoritarian who often makes decisions without consulting others. He matches Milošević in stubbornness and inflexibility, although he is considerably more given to bedecking himself in nationalist symbols, pomp, and ceremony. While not fond of each other, Tudjman and Milošević are rumored to have forged a secret agreement following the disastrous Serb-Croat war on how to divide Bosnia and delineate new borders. This in spite of Tudjman's official insistence on the permanency of the previous internal borders of Croatia. Evidence cited is the signing of an agreement in Geneva on January 19, 1994, by the governments of Serbia and Croatia, the two presidents being present. Issues between the two states are still unsettled, but their willingness to partition Bosnia with or without a role for the Muslims is obvious.

Alija Izetbegović, the President of the Bosnian government is a Muslim politician who also contributed to the conflict. In 1970 he wrote an essay entitled "The Islamic Declaration." In it he claimed that there "could be neither peace nor coexistence between the Islamic religion and non-Islamic social and political institutions." He envisioned a great Islamic renewal and the establishment of "a great federation from Morocco to Indonesia, from tropical Africa to central Asia." In typical Muslim fashion he pointed out that Islamic beliefs must be embodied in an Islamic political construct. Once the Muslims make up more than fifty percent of any population, the country should become an Islamic republic. It is somewhat unclear whether he intended the application of these Islamic principles to Bosnia. This essay was written in prison while Izetbegović was a political prisoner for his Islamic activism.

Allegedly Izetbegović no longer holds these views. However, such statements were incendiary and have generated apprehension among non-Muslims even though they did not (likely) contain a genuine threat to Christians unless Izetbegovic intended to create, in the long run, a classical Islamic state in which minority rights would generally not be protected. As the Muslim birthrate exceeded that of the other Yugoslavs, non-Muslims felt endangered, seeing that time worked against them and that they might once again have to live under Muslim rule. Thus Izetbegović's immoderate writings did wave the red cloth to infuriate the Serbian bull. Once in power he became much more moderate, but the damage had already been done and these earlier words have been held up against him in adversarial propaganda.

3. Intellectuals

Intellectuals have been the second most responsible group for the disintegration of Yugoslavia.

The Memorandum

The ideological prop to Milošević's seizing and holding power was the Memorandum of the Serbian Academy of Sciences and Arts, issued in 1986. It is an anachronistic document by a group of eminent Serbian academicians. Some consider Dobrica Ćosić, the novelist later elected first President of the truncated Yugoslavia (June 1992–May 1993), to be the writer of the document. He rejected that attribution, saying that were he the author it would have been better written. If he is not its actual author, he is the spiritual father of the Memorandum and may stand accused of having irresponsibly activated the dormant tradition of Serbian nationalism.

The Memorandum expresses concern lest Yugoslavia fall apart, and urges the Serb people to be the keystone of Yugoslavia. It defends the Serbs from charges of dominating the others by claiming the opposite: that despite their, the greatest, sacrifices on behalf of Yugoslavia, they were the most exploited and victimized during the period under Communism. It indulges in the kinds of charges of economic exploitation by which intellectuals of the other republics also fired the first salvos of this war.

Whether a demagogical document, as its detractors have claimed, or a patriotic analysis of what ailed the country, as its defenders have claimed, the content of the Memorandum was not as important as was its role. It galvanized the Serbs to become militant in demands to remake Yugoslavia and frightened non-Serbs. One doubts that the writer(s) of the Memorandum in 1986 could have foreseen the destructive impact of this document when they prepared it in secrecy. Nevertheless, the impact of a handful of Serbian intellectuals on the rise of Serb national chauvinism was disastrous. It is fair to say that the vast majority of the Serb intelligentsia is now rabidly nationalistic. At first, they used *Milošević*; now, Milošević uses *them*.

Nationalistic Intelligentsia

Most of the intelligentsia of all Yugoslavia's nationalities placed themselves and their prowess at the service of their nations. Albanian intelligentsia headed the Albanian separatist movement in Kosovo. Slovenian, Macedonian, Croatian, Muslim, and Serbian intellectuals became the ideologues of their respective nationalities. They did this in two ways. One was to write nationalist novels, poems, songs, essays, monographs, cartographies, etc., and make films, all of which aimed at supporting nationalist claims. Particularly damaging was the war of maps and statistics of victimization, used to buttress the claims that one's nation had the right to territories which today or centuries ago members of its nation inhabited. The intellectuals of the Balkans may be unique in their competition to exaggerate the number of killed and other losses of their own side, because this can be used to garner public support for the revenge that is going to take place in the next round of fighting.

The second role of the intelligentsia was to serve in elected or appointive political positions based on the respect that the population gave them for their merits. They compete with each other as to who will make more outrageous claims on behalf of their nationality and who will vilify the others more tendentiously.

Contrary to remaining open-minded, some intellectuals deny the legitimacy of changes that have taken place in certain leaders. For instance, although Alija Izetbegović wrote the above-mentioned essay about Bosnia as a Muslim state while he was still imprisoned by Tito, these views continue to be imputed to him—and he repudiated them some time ago. Another example is Vuk Drašković, who as a novelist wrote some Serb nationalistic novels but has matured and moderated his views as a politician, and this change is also being denied.

History is being rewritten today in a nationalist vein. Under Communism many themes had been taboo and history was interpreted in a strictly Marxist manner. All of that has needed correction. But much of what is being written now matches or surpasses the Marxists in perverting data. Relatively small groups of intellectuals bravely oppose the war and criticize their own governments and nations for the misdeeds that have taken place. The majority of the intellectuals, however—particularly those in the humanities—regretfully have lent their talents and efforts to generate hatred.

4. The Yugoslav Army

The Yugoslav Army has played a disastrous role not only as an enforcer of political decisions but as an independent agent. In Tito's time the army had only a subordinate political role, although officers were required to be loyal members of the Communist Party. And it might not come as a surprise that army officers were dogmatic Communists. The Communist Party and the army were the glue that held the country together. When the Communist Party of Yugoslavia broke up into six component parts in January 1990, the army remained the sole power that guaranteed the union. After the secessions, it became an army without a country.

The ethnic composition of top army brass was predominantly Serb. The reasons were that more Serbs took part in the national liberation during World War II, and naturally they became the core of the army. Serbs and Montenegrins, their closest kin, were more numerous and their warrior tradition provided for their decisive influence in the army.

The army was initially a training ground for the Yugoslav idea. The army's policy of integration was deliberate. With time, however, recruits became more nationalistic and the predominantly Serb officers attempted to control them. Then, when the initial violent nationalistic confrontations occurred, large-scale defections took place. Slovene and Croat soldiers refused to fire on their own people and frequently switched sides. Macedonians and Albanians did not want to die in a war that was not theirs, and escaped.

Its ill-fated intervention in Slovenia lowered the army's morale. The self-image of invincibility was shaken. After all, the army had been billed as fourth largest in Europe, equipped with the most modern Western and Eastern-bloc armaments, and supported by a huge domestic arms industry as well. The real reasons for the army's indecisiveness in Slovenia may take years to uncover. Even top government officials were puzzled by it. Some say that it was trained primarily to fight foreign intervention, and therefore was at first reluctant to fight domestically. Others say that the general staff deliberately played Milošević's game of cutting off Slovenia and Macedonia, in order to concentrate on creating a Great Serbia. Still others say that the army was a victim of the indecisiveness of the federal political leaders, and that the general chaos in the country led to delays until it was too late to save the federation.

As war neared in Croatia, the army allegedly interjected itself along the battle lines to separate Croats and Serbs and keep the fighting down. In reality the army's guns were almost always aimed at the Croats and the army busily supplied the Serb fighters with military equipment. Realizing that the pluralistic makeup of the army became a hindrance, the generals decided to Serbianize it. Thus, the army's sympathy came decidedly to the Serb side. In a few weeks, the Yugoslav Army was fighting vigorously against the Croats as co-aggressors with local Serb rebels. This resulted in Serbs taking nearly a third of Croat territory. However, the army did negotiate a complete withdrawal from purely ethnic Croat territory where it was viewed as the enemy.

From Slovenia and Croatia, enormous quantities of personnel and equipment were then withdrawn by the army into Bosnia. By 1992 the army saw itself distinctly as a Serb military force. When Bosnia declared independence, it was the army that struck at the Bosnian government, joining with the separatist Serbs. Bosnia had been the area chosen by Tito to defend against a potential Soviet invasion because of its mountainous terrain, the local people's propensity for fighting, and the storage of an immense arsenal and most of the arms industry. Only about one-third of the stored ammunition had been used by 1994, it has been estimated, whereas additional supplies of everything, including fuel, are purchased from abroad despite the embargo. The borders are porous because the governments want them to be. Where there is a demand for weapons there will be weapons dealers. The economic resources of these countries and monies collected by their compatriots abroad all serve as means of payment. Civilians may starve; armies rarely do.

Officially, Milošević and the rump Yugoslavia maintained the façade that the regular army units withdrew to Serbia when the armed conflict broke out in Bosnia and Herzegovina. It was said that army units comprised of Bosnian Serbs could not be deterred from fighting on behalf of their countrymen. This was only part of the truth. Regular army units fought in Bosnia under the direction of the regular army general Ratko Mladić. (It should be pointed out that generals of various ethnic origins quickly shifted allegiance and joined their respective national armies, thus providing them with experienced leadership.) The Serb fighting force in Bosnia was very large and quite successful, occupying in a short time about 70 percent of Bosnia and Herzegovina. The tactics it used were merciless. Many contend that some of the military leaders deserve to be tried as war criminals for their relentless pounding of civilians.

The Military of Yugoslavia, the army's new name as of 1992, is firmly on the side of Milošević. He seems to be in control of it, having carried out a few purges at the top levels. The military and the police have become privileged segments, while the rest of the country has sunk into extreme poverty. The army is still large and well equipped, despite the embargo. Should Milošević's regime be seriously threatened, some speculate that the army would defend him or take over the government. It surely would be willing to engage in civil war in Serbia, as it has done elsewhere—except in Macedonia. There, after 1992 negotiations between the Macedonian and Yugoslav governments, the army withdrew in an orderly and peaceful manner. Defenders say the same could have been accomplished in the other states had not locals ambushed, surrounded, and attacked the army.

The army's participation is described as defensive. Detractors counter that the army has acted belligerently as a tool of Serb political elite. It is clear that whatever secret agreements might bind Serb politicians and the military, the army was wielded indiscriminately against anyone opposing policies of the governments of Serbia and Montenegro. When Montenegrin soldiers complained that they were endangering themselves without benefiting directly, some say that the army brass permitted both regulars and irregulars from Montenegro to attack the Dubrovnik littoral, to plunder, burn, and bombard the old city of Dubrovnik, destroying many priceless monuments of culture. This was their reward for loyalty. Robbery, after all, is a sign of courage!

5. War Criminals

Along with the army came a great variety of irregular troops whose manner of fighting gravely aggravated the situation. They used such dreadful methods that reconciliation and peacemaking in areas where they have operated is all but impossible. Their scorched-earth tactics decided the outcome in many areas of fighting. Leaders of these bandits resemble warlords, but they are simply war criminals of the crassest sort. They give their units romantic names such as White Eagles, Tsar Dušan the Mighty, and Tigers. (Both Croats and Serbs have Tigers!) Many have criminal records; some are wanted by Interpol. Some are psychotics; most are given to bouts of alcoholism. Until recently, most were "nobodies"; now they are "war heroes," feared by friend and foe alike for lacking even the most rudimentary military ethics. These local commanders (many sport first names or nicknames only) seem unwilling to obey the politicians, although it was the politicians who initially decided to release and use them. To the criminals, cease-fire documents are not worth the paper on which they are signed. No one can be sure of the warlords' total compliance. Or perhaps the command for noncompliance comes from higher up. Most war criminals distinguish themselves by the utterly ruthless slaughter of people of other ethnicities. But that is not all. Many *chetnik* units, as they sweep into a multi-ethnic Bosnian village, first kill those Serbs who favor ethnic integration and then proceed with "ethnic cleansing."

Almost all of the war criminals have become political figures to be reckoned with. They win elections and enjoy congressional immunity. Politicians court them, then back off when they feel threatened by the criminals' popularity. Although the United Nations is laying the groundwork for war crimes trials, it is unlikely these men will allow themselves to be captured. Rather than sacrifice their "heroic" reputations, they will probably rather die than surrender. So they will continue to fight.

There is also an economic incentive for irregulars and war criminals. Many are now rich with war spoils. Jewelry was being sold by the pound in Greece in the summer of 1993 by vacationing Serb war criminals! By the winter of 1993–94, secure sources of food were so sparse that armed bands proceeded to loot even meager UN aid rations.

6. The Press and Media

Inflated rhetoric is the order of the day. Half-truths and outright lies bolster one's own nationality and put down others'. Press and media have fanned the smoldering fires of nationalism, disseminating the ideas of politicians, intellectuals, and army. But communications have not been merely means of transmittal; they have exhibited an independent source of extremism. Reporters might protest that they do not create news but only report it; in fact, they are protagonists and antagonists, acting not only as tools but independently aggravating the situation. Having mastered communications skills, they serve poisoned information to the common person. Newspapers and other media have vied (with some decent exceptions) over which could become the most one-sidedly nationalist. The freedom they obtained after Communist censorship was misused to breed hatred based on fears and misperceptions. Entire newspapers and broadcast stations, once respected, became uncritical supporters of ideology, political party, or person—offering only praise.

No lie was too great. The Yugoslav Army, for example, prepared a video shown on Belgrade TV, purportedly made secretly by army intelligence, of the activities of Croatian defense chief Marjan Špegelj. The Croatian press and government said it had been doctored; someone was lying. In reporting the war, enemy attacks are exaggerated and the battlefield activities of one's own forces are proclaimed as "defensive." Unconfirmed rumors are treated as truth. Propaganda and disinformation is both crude and quite subtle. The press and the media are the most immediate source of the hatred that has sprung up in the hearts of the former Yugoslav people.

The international press has also fallen to waging propaganda, consciously or unconsciously. Most foreign journalists have neither spoken the local language nor understood the issues. They have gotten much of their information from local journalists, who interpreted the situation tendentiously, or from hired interpreters, who told them the truth as they knew it—i.e., partially. Unable to cross battle lines, reporters have been satisfied to write or film what they experienced on one side. A British reporter, for example, shot footage on the Muslim side of Mostar for several weeks and, of course, Croats looked like monsters. What viewers did not see was similar devastation on the Croat side from Muslim shells. Only Muslim casualties and suffering were shown. Similarly, Serbs complained about one-sided Western reporting of Croat and Muslim deaths, rapes, wounded, and refugees while ignoring Serb victims. Serb complaints that Western media cover exclusively their negative behavior are justified; Croats and Muslims have won the first round of the international propaganda war. Only in 1993 did reporting become more balanced, when uncontestable evidence came to light of Muslims starving in Croat concentration camps and looking no better than those in Serb camps. By 1994, Western media returned to vilifying only Serbs.

A hysterical competition has occurred about who could come up with the most raped women. From a relatively few proven cases tens of thousands were extrapolated and reported worldwide. Without question, women were raped both spontaneously and with calculation, but it is doubtful that governments sent instructions in that regard. They can be blamed for not taking measures to halt the rapes when they learned of them, however. As many as 60,000 alleged rapes were reported when critical examinations yielded only several thousand. When it became known that rapes were less frequent than initially reported, and that Serbian women also shared in these atrocities, the international outcry subsided.

Rape stories certainly fit someone's agenda! Propagandists found ammunition to taint entire nations. Some feminists could show the malevolence of an entire gender. Some Jews could manifest concern about another holocaust-in-the-making, this time threatening non-Arab Muslims, and thereby appear not to be anti-Muslim. The Bosnian Muslims, however, while outmaneuvered and overpowered, have not been defenseless. They also knew how to inflict horrible casualties upon others.

These comments are not to be misconstrued as belittling the suffering of victims or the concern of well-meaning people. Rather, readers need to be aware of press and media manipulations and need to heed the victims' needs rather than their own. The same happened with the people of the former Yugoslavia, nearly all of whom, in the post-World War II years, were duped by propaganda.

7. Religious Leadership

The religious leadership of former Yugoslavia also bears responsibility for fanning the fires of ethnoreligious intolerance. As detailed in Chapter 7, the religious leaders had a role both in promoting the process of disintegration and in adding a religious element to the wars. These were not typical religious wars, of course. But given the ethnoreligious entanglements, they automatically have taken on a religious guise. And religious leaders did not do enough to distance themselves from such misuse. Some even actively promoted such developments.

In the context of Yugoslavia, the limits of church and nation ultimately became obscure, and when the nation came under siege the religious leaders came to its defense. The interests of one's nation were perceived as those of one's corresponding religious community. When the interests of the nation, as in the Serbian case, were to expand Serb territory, then the church supported that measure too. As shown previously, not all prelates actively promoted nationalism, but the more recently appointed, younger ones tended to be more militant than the older generation of leaders. There are courageous clergy who admit the painful truth about the atrocities that have been committed by their nation and will reveal that some clergy in their own churches have not acted as peacemakers but as warmongers. Most clergy, however, have been simply passive consumers of official propaganda but are not particularly belligerent.

The population of Yugoslavia had become somewhat irreligious, but the state of war is driving people back to the church or mosque, at least nominally. The more an ethnoreligious group is driven into a corner, the more its members are radicalized. This is especially a danger with the Muslims. It is still true in 1994 (as I contended in 1991) that insofar as this is a "religious" war, it is being fought largely by irreligious people who wear religion as a distinguishing badge but do not know what the badge stands for.

8. Collective Responsibility

Can entire nations be held responsible? On the whole, this is to be answered in the negative. Surely one cannot blame all citizens for what their respective governments are doing, particularly in non-democratic settings where the population has little or no say in policy-making. One cannot lay blame on the entire Serb, Croat, Muslim, Slovene, Albanian, and other peoples for the current wars, no more than one can blame the entire German or Japanese or Soviet nations for inhumanities once caused by their leaders. However, insofar as a population majority gives consent—even enthusiastic support—for the destructive actions their leaders take, then they *do* share responsibility. They also especially bear responsibility for voting massively for those parties which have stressed ethnic nationalism above everything else. And they bear responsibility for allowing themselves to be duped so easily by the manipulators of public opinion, when there are alternate sources of information. The masses act impulsively, uncritically, gullibly, destructively, intolerantly, and vengefully. Their behavior is characterized by rage, anxiety, conservatism, and willingness to follow authoritarian, charismatic leaders. People have been manipulated and propagandized. They feel threatened and they have longings. They may not see too many alternatives to present policies. But in the 1980s and 1990s, the nationalities of former Yugoslavia *did* have options. Yet people voted overwhelmingly for the politicians who later brought them disaster. This was especially true of the Serbs.

Serbs are the most numerous and the best armed. In Yugoslavia they once held the majority of administrative, police, and army positions. They enjoyed the support of the powerful Belgrade political establishment. This former privileged position in the federation, linked to the ongoing belligerence, renders them more culpable. They occupied more land, destroyed more enemies, expelled more non-Serb civilians, bombarded more cities and villages—and, thus far, none of this destructive activity has been on the territory of Serbia proper. In the process, they lost the sympathy of world public opinion, and are now a pariah among nations. As Vesna Pešić, an opposition Belgrade politician, has indicated: Serbians *deserve* UN sanctions because they could have voted differently several times but, instead, gave their confidence to the bellicose Serbian Socialist Party. (For a fuller discussion of sanctions see Chapter 9). Many citizens of Serbia know, at least subconsciously, that ethnic cleansing and territorial conquest have been the goals of the war. Yet they have not summoned the courage to throw out Milošević, despite the great suffering he has inflicted upon them. This renders the nation culpable, though not every person in the nation equally so.

The sad truth is that, based on their past actions, neither the Croats nor Muslims would do better. If more powerful, they would have been carrying out "ethnic cleansing." They, too, of course have concentration camps; Croatian journals and papers even boast how orderly these are kept. They, too, slaughtered civilians while speaking only of their own suffering. They, too, massacred villagers and tried to "ethnically cleanse" territory under their control. Whether in response to Serb aggression or because they did not yet have equally potent weapons, lesser casualties resulted. The Croat and Muslim populations, as well as those of the other republics, continue to give support not to political parties that seek to build civil society but to nationalistic parties that want to build nation-states. And this renders them, too, in some degree culpable.

Moral discernment should compel us to condemn killings, torture, persecutions, and expulsions wherever and by whomever they occur. Serbian nationalist chauvinists deserve our most resolute condemnation because they have been most effective in carrying out the program of slaughter. But we should not demonize the Serbs and regard the Croats and Muslims as true democrats. To this day, all three sides are inclined to fight rather than compromise. It may be decades before the development of civil societies based on rule of law is achieved by them. The basic societal element has become *"ethnos,"* not *"demos."* But so far, none of the ethnic groups is willing to live in a state not its own. Small groups of politicians, intellectuals, religious people, and journalists who do understand democracy and who are struggling to promote it are not given significant support at the polls, but instead are frequently maligned and threatened. It may be that in some hour of utter despair people will see that it is these "weak democrats" who have more to offer for the future than the brutish ethnocrats.

The last point of culpability is the lack of repentance. With extremely few exceptions, no remorse or sense of their own wrongdoing characterizes the ethnoreligious groups. They find blame with everyone and all, except their own group. Such utter lack of moral contrition highlights the collective responsibility of the ethnoreligious groups which so willingly joined in the war dance.

9. International Community

There are those who blame the present calamity on the great powers who remade the map of Europe at the end of World War I. Their contention that the nations comprising Yugoslavia entered unwillingly is simply untrue. The dream of a unified land of liberated southern Slavs was widespread and certainly not doomed from the outset. It is true, of course, that the expectations of Serbs, Croats, Slovenes, Macedonians, Montenegrins, and others of this multi-ethnic unmeltable pot were not equally met. Today it appears that no one was happy with it, and that, hence, there is no longer a Yugoslavia.

Another view is that foreign conspiracies and great-power interests started the bedlam in Yugoslavia. That, too, we have rejected in previous chapters. International political leaders were involved in the Yugoslav crisis, but primarily reactively. CIA and scholarly studies indicated, early on, that civil war loomed, yet little was done to forestall it. As the crisis mounted, the European Community and the United States responded primarily with words urging a peaceful resolution of problems—weak counsel when no peaceful solution could be found to work.

In former Yugoslavia a frequent question heard is: What is the international community doing? The answer is that, regarding Yugoslavia, there is no international community. Europeans cannot agree on what to do. If the United States wanted proof that Europe required American leadership, this has been apparent in the case of Bosnia. Yet no American leadership was forthcoming. Tentative overtures by the Bush and Clinton Administrations toward more decisive intervention were parried by nearly all Europeans, and the U.S. acquiesced into becoming a bystander. Only by rendering humanitarian aid did the Western nations act as a community. A certain consensus developed in NATO after the February 1994 "Saturday Massacre"; an ultimatum was issued to all troops surrounding Sarajevo to pull back twelve miles, but there is less certainty that such a consensus would be applied to end the war. As far as political or military intervention is concerned, this is not the *united* Europe that had been envisioned for 1992. Rather, it is a Europe of political-interest spheres that looks more like 1914 than a dream of European unity. There are now German, French, British, Russian, Turkish, and American interest spheres, and as one country makes its moves, others block them.

The United Nations, the European Community, and NATO have proven themselves helpless to influence the war decisively. They are consistent in applying an arms embargo but inconsistent in punishing aggressive behavior. The UNPROFOR is a laughing stock throughout Yugoslavia despite considerable sacrifice by UN soldiers and commanders. The political will to enforce resolutions is lacking. Perhaps one might believe the UN is farsightedly playing a game of restraining Yugoslavia until the war burns itself out—at which time the main culprits will be brought to justice. A nice scenario, but too much to expect. There is no effective international plan as to how to stop the carnage, except perhaps by mutual extermination or allowing the strongest to emerge victorious. The indecisiveness of other countries, the threats to intervene followed by timidity, only encourage each side to persist in fighting because each is bolstered by its own reading of the confusing signals that emanate out of New York, Washington, Paris, London, Moscow, Bonn, Ankara, and elsewhere. In the case of the Yugoslavian inferno, not to intervene is to permit the ethnoreligious warfare to go on indefinitely.

TO SUM UP

The numerous factors contributing to divisiveness, and the fewer that were supportive of unity, created the Yugoslavian conflict. Those who justify and promote the war have summoned a multitude of historical and politico-economic reasons why the peoples of former Yugoslavia can no longer live in peace. They point to:

- Yugoslavia's formation after World War II, following the breakup of the first Yugoslavia, as well as bitter memories of the war's ethnic extermination that verged on genocide
- the lack of democratic traditions
- the Communist suppression of the many forms of legitimate expression of nationalism
- the ethnic and religious mixing which took place in the context of bigotry
- real, but allegedly unbridgeable, cultural chasms between a Byzantine or Oriental and a Western (predominantly German and Roman) heritage
- patterns of propaganda, such as the Serb claim that all Croats are fascist, genocidal, and instruments of an old/new German *"Drang nach Osten,"* while the Croats claim that Serbs are Byzantine, Communist, and prone to Bolshevik-style central leadership
- claims of exploitation. Slovenes and Croats complain that their financial resources were syphoned off by the central government in Belgrade, which they perceived as Serb-run. Serbs charge that they and the southern republics were economically exploited by the Slovenes and Croats during Tito's rule, which they characterize as keeping Serbia weak in order to make Yugoslavia strong. The southern republics claim they did not receive enough economic development.

All the above factors played a role in the collapse. The guilt in the ensuing war must be shared widely. But there are individuals and smaller groups who directed the course of events with maniacal single-mindedness toward war. They are the most guilty. Their personal pathologies have resulted in the social psychosis called war. If those who are still healthy do not do something to heal this social pathology, then *we*, too, stand indicted as accomplices.

CHAPTER 9

WILL UN SANCTIONS TOPPLE THE REGIME IN YUGOSLAVIA?

I encountered United Nations sanctions against Yugoslavia—a country now consisting of Serbia and Montenegro—long before I arrived there. Since Yugoslav consulates in the United States, with the exception of the embassy in Washington, have been closed, arranging for an entry visa has become more complicated. Transportation to the region also involves roundabout routes, now that service to or from the country is no longer offered by Yugoslav Airlines (JAT) or any other carrier. (Many people who purchased JAT tickets prior to the imposition of sanctions lost their money.) Anyone who wants to travel to the embargoed land has to fly to a country adjacent to Yugoslavia. The most convenient of these is Hungary. From there the only path is overland. Train, bus, and automobile transportation have not been affected by sanctions and are fairly dependable.

As soon as I arrived at the Budapest airport, some enterprising young men offered to transport me to Belgrade or other destinations along the road—to one's home address, for example—for about $30. The driver of the van with whom I struck a deal gassed up in Hungary because gasoline is one of the major targets of sanctions. He also filled several cans with gasoline and placed them in suitcases so that Hungarian and Yugoslav customs would not detect them. Had we been rear-ended we could have become an enormous Molotov cocktail!

Just before we reached the border the driver stopped at a Hungarian supermarket and told me and my fellow passengers to take advantage of a 15-minute shopping break. The others seemed to know what they should buy. I asked the driver what might be needed once we crossed the border. He replied: "Sir, there is nothing that we do not need—the shops in Yugoslavia are empty. Oil, sugar, flour, milk, meat products, pasta, detergent, toothpaste, soap, toilet paper, coffee, fruit . . ." I got the idea. Along with the others, I rushed to purchase whatever I could for those whom I planned to visit.

The line at the border was immense. But the transportation vans such as the one in which I was riding had prearranged permission to drive straight to the border ramp. Our driver, playing chicken with oncoming traffic, passed the six-mile-long column of cars, and we managed to cross the border in less than an hour. We passed over, gasoline and all, without a luggage inspection. Even though border formalities on both sides were minimal, when I later crossed back into Hungary in a passenger car the procedure took five and a half hours.

The shortage of gasoline is evident on all roads and in all cities in Yugoslavia. Gas stations are closed except for a few private ones where gas can be purchased for hard currency (mostly German marks) for the equivalent of about $5 per gallon. Most of the people whom I met had not driven their cars for four to five months. Gasoline is available, however, for public transportation, farm machines, police, medical services—and for the clergy. That the last group should be privileged reflects a sharp departure from the Communist era, when clergy were routinely discriminated against even for minimal services. The new order views clergy as socially important. Nowadays clergy are performing not only burials but other religious and secular rituals (including, in some cases, the blessing of weapons and fighters). Serbian Orthodox liturgies and personalities are frequently featured on television and held up in the public eye.

Public transportation used to be inexpensive and was patronized by the public to a straining point. Now overcrowding is not a problem, except in Belgrade, where crowds waiting for trolleys and buses are so large that who gets on is sometimes determined by fist or gun. Travel in Yugoslavia is still cheap for a foreigner, but for most local people it is too expensive. Incomes for many people have plummeted to about $5 a month and others are not making much more, unless, of course, one is an army officer, policeman, high government employee—or a private entrepreneur willing to walk on the other side of law. There are always people who profit from war.

Travel has also been impeded by the many new borders that have sprung up between the republics. While bus and train traffic used to be heavy between Ljubljana and Zagreb, or Belgrade and Skopje, it has slowed to a trickle because of restrictive border-crossing formalities, customs inspections, and the general interruption of normal business relations. Of course, travel between Zagreb and Sarajevo, and Belgrade and Sarajevo, is inhibited by difficulties greater than bothersome customs procedures. Commerce of all sorts between Belgrade and Zagreb, which until 1990 was one of Europe's busiest international and domestic corridors, has now completely ceased. Those needing to travel between Croatia and Serbia have to do so by way of Hungary. Some fairly enterprising ways have been found to accomplish this formerly simple task.

It is difficult to separate the effects of UN sanctions against Yugoslavia from the effects of socialist mismanagement and the burdens of a war economy. In any case, the combined economic consequences are catastrophic. Unemployment has reached about 60 percent, and the rest of the population are either on forced extended vacation or are holding jobs for which there is little work and little pay. I also heard sarcastic claims that since most of Yugoslavia's industry is standing still and no industrial waste is being released, at least Serbia will soon possess the world's most ecologically pure air, land, and water.

The government copes with these conditions by feverishly printing practically worthless money, issued daily in order to pay the population. Since no real economic production supports the currency, Yugoslavia is gripped by runaway inflation that surpassed the disastrous situation in Germany in the 1920s, when citizens had to carry their grocery money in baskets. Nothing costs less than 1 million dinars—worth only a few pennies. There is no point in my writing what the exchange rate to the German mark (hereafter DM) or the dollar was at a given moment; three times each day, hard foreign currencies bought more dinars. A daily newspaper purchased on August 20, 1993, cost 15 million dinars; one purchased on August 24 cost 20 million. Prices on goods were being adjusted several times a day.

No one used banks to change money; people went instead to

black-market dealers who have, along with the police and army, the steadiest jobs around. Both the government and the banks have their own black-market dealers on the streets in order to obtain precious hard currency, which is the only means of payment for *important* goods. Prices are usually quoted in DM. In order not to have to reprice all the goods on a daily if not hourly basis, some stores have resorted to tagging prices in points that usually correspond to the DM. The price in dinars for the goods were in the billions. In the end, most people did not understand what the prices mean. In the spring of 1994 a monetary reform was instituted creating a "super dinar" that was declared to be on a parity with the DM (allegedly completely convertible for hard currency in any bank); this was done ostensibly to eliminate the black marketeers but had the transparent aim of extracting hard-currency reserves that might still be in the possession of the population and placing it into the government's coffers. Still, as long as the government prints money whenever it needs it, the inflation cannot be stopped.

Most people do not need to know how much things cost because their incomes are so small that they cannot afford to buy things anyway. The insecurity caused by the current economic collapse is difficult to imagine; the struggle for sheer survival overshadows all other concerns. Some retirement pensions are barely sufficient to buy two rolls of toilet paper. At the same time, there are not many goods to be bought. Belgrade is being supplied better than other cities in order to lower the risk of social unrest in the capital. But in Novi Sad, for instance, the center of the agricultural region of Vojvodina, salespeople and cashiers in most stores stand surrounded by empty shelves. A previously well-supplied supermarket in the center of the city, one that used to be crowded with shoppers, had only a dozen or so items to offer. I saw people peek in to gaze at several hundred jars of pickled peppers, some bottles of juice, maybe ten pounds of tomatoes and plums, and one head of cabbage. No bread, milk, cheese, or meat products were available, as was the case with many other customary food supplies. They pushed on to look elsewhere—with little luck, I am afraid. This was in August, when seasonal food was always plentiful.

Even people whose past living standards could have been described as middle class do not have enough food to invite a visitor for a meal. Only those who have hard currency or relatives in the villages who provide them with food are spared the threat of starvation. Hardest hit are the retired, the sick, and the children in urban areas. An alarming number of retired people have committed suicide; many have left notes explaining that on their income they were unable to buy food.

Food is unavailable for a number of reasons, including 1993's devastating summer drought. In addition, the costs of transportation are so high that farmers cannot afford to bring produce to market. Farmers also have no real incentive to sell their goods at market when they are able to buy so few things with dinars, and when saving the profits from their sales makes little sense because the currency loses its value by the hour. Many food stores and market stalls are closed or "on extended vacation" because they would sustain financial losses with every day of operation. The UN embargo was not supposed to affect food, but it does. It even affects the availability of water. Since water in Yugoslavia frequently requires chemical purification, and since those chemicals have been unavailable due to the embargo, citizens suffer frequent water shortages and with them the inevitable danger of contaminations and plagues.

The embargo is also supposed to exempt medicine, but medical supplies have been drastically affected nonetheless. Even aspirin is unavailable. Chemicals used for making medicine have been placed on the embargo list, shipments of medicine from abroad (when the government is able to afford it) wait in trucks at the border for days, and most life-saving medicines are nowhere to be found. Doctors are as desperate as the patients, especially those who require dialysis; and hospitalized children, whose lives could be saved by specific medical supplies, are dying for lack of them.

When a friend of mine needed dental care for a sore tooth, the dentist took out the pliers for tooth extraction and said that it was nearly the only procedure he was still able to perform. His drill bit was worn-out, he had no novocaine, and he had to telephone several other clinics to obtain medicine to treat my friend's infected tooth. My friend was a tough man and was able to endure the ordeal; not everyone can, especially those whose medical problems are far more serious than tooth decay.

The embargo was also not supposed to affect scholarly, artistic, cultural, and scientific exchanges, but it does. I talked to professors from the University of Belgrade who are sharp critics of the Milošević regime. They cannot afford a postage stamp to acknowledge invitations to go abroad, much less pay to attend the meetings. They can only travel if their trip is paid for by the foreign organization. Hence the sanctions isolate and punish them despite their opposition to the dictatorship. These scholars and intellectuals wonder how democracy can grow when potential leaders are being isolated from the rest of the world. In one case, a non-Serb Lutheran bishop complained that the Norwegian Embassy did not issue him a visa to attend a meeting of the Lutheran World Federation because of a broad application of the sanctions. The bishop wondered what lesson was being communicated if those who are against the regime are treated in the same way as those who are its supporters. Sanctions applied indiscriminately affect even those who have absolutely no sympathy for "ethnic cleansing," and, of course, they themselves stand in danger of being "cleansed."

Sanctions are also massively enlarging criminal activity. Ethical and legal standards were never very high in the Balkans, but they are now eroding even further. For many, breaking the law is simply a device to survive. While traveling by train from Belgrade to Skopje (Macedonia) I witnessed a large number of poor peasants who were trying to smuggle several pounds of cheese, pork, and other farm products to the Skopje market in order to smuggle back a few pounds of detergent, soap, or toothpaste, which are not available in Serbia. Customs officers of both Yugoslavia and Macedonia delayed the train for five hours in an unsuccessful effort to deal with the petty smuggling.

In the meantime, real smuggling proceeds apace: ammunition, oil, and other strategic products get in and out of the country with the help of bribes to UN personnel and customs officials. Much money can be made by large-scale violations of the embargo. I saw many petroleum tanker-trucks cross from Bulgaria and Greece into Macedonia that probably ended up in Serbia. UN monitors are stationed at newly established border crossings, but even when they are honest (which they frequently are not; over a dozen Ukrainian UN soldiers have been dishonorably discharged for corruption), numerous ways can be found to move across unpatrolled borders, including simply driving on little-known dirt roads or straight across a field by night. Gasoline purchased abroad for one DM a liter is sold in Vojvodina for 2 DM, then resold to Bosnian Serbs for 4 DM, and then to Bosnian Muslims for 8 DM.

The embargo is often violated by cleverly routing trucks bearing sanctioned goods. A truck may be earmarked for a city in Bosnia which is under Serbian control. Once on Bosnian-Serbian territory, it is redirected to the actual recipient elsewhere in Yugoslavia. Trucks en route from Hungary to Greece are frequently unloaded in Serbia. The governments of Greece, Romania, and Russia are generally sympathetic to the Serbian cause and at least tacitly aid in the violations of the embargo. Consequently the embargo does not completely halt the importation of items that are needed by the government to wage war, but is effective in depleting supplies of food and medicine needed by the population. Even here the government plays a cynical game; in the spring of 1994, with the introduction of the "super dinar," suddenly the stores were stocked with food items that had been withheld when the currency was worthless.

Are the sanctions effective in weakening the government of Slobodan Milošević and handicapping the war effort? The answer is mostly negative. Surely the Milošević government is inconvenienced by the country's impoverishment and the unavailability of some items needed for the conduct of normal civil life. But Yugoslavia does not have a democratic government that feels compelled to resign because it is unable to meet the needs of the population. Dictatorial regimes generally do not make it their highest priority to rule for the good of the people. Primarily, if not exclusively, they pursue their own power interests, and in the case of Yugoslavia these do not appear to be seriously threatened by the embargo. There is no evidence that the Serbian war effort is hampered in the least by attempts to deprive the military of ammunition and fuel. Indeed, all ranks within the army are undergoing a process of professionalization; and since the government pays them salaries at a much higher scale than the rest of the population, it has the unqualified loyalty of the armed forces and the police. There is little doubt that any group aspiring to replace the Milošević government could and would be quickly eliminated by a powerful army—one that boasts it is the fourth-strongest in Europe. On the other hand, the embargo is a godsend for the Milošević regime; it can blame someone else for the country's economic woes and thus not be held accountable by the population for mismanagement.

The embargo, instead of weakening the regime's hold on the population, does exactly the opposite—it rallies public support. The ordinary citizen's thinking is simple, however flawed: "The whole world is against us. We must unite in order to survive. We are not the only ones who are doing wrong. The world community wants us and the Croats to do their dirty work in preventing the establishment of a Muslim beachhead in Europe. On top of that they impose sanctions that target for death innocent children and the elderly of a country that is not formally at war. They are not morally superior and hence have no rights to make demands upon us."

Yugoslavs' revulsion against the embargo and their blaming of Germany, the United States, and other Western as well as Islamic countries for their troubles is nearly unanimous. The view is widespread that the U.S. shows only nominal interest in the Muslims in order to secure a steady supply of Arab oil. Yugoslavs do not expect the U.S. to do anything concrete on the Muslims' behalf.

Only a few small groups seem not to have succumbed to blaming others for the Balkan turmoil. One of them is the Citizen Alliance *(Gradjanski Savez)*, a small democratically oriented political party which truly seems to understand the notion of democracy and civil society. Its leader and spokeswoman, Vesna Pešić, has the courage to say: "We deserve the sanctions." She maintains that the country had the chance in three elections to remove the Milošević regime, but that for nationalist reasons a great coalition consisting of the Serbian Academy of Science and Arts, the Army, and the Serbian Orthodox Church keeps the entrenched government in power. Also, the "Belgrade Circle," a group of about four hundred nonpartisan intellectuals, seeks to create "The Other Serbia"—that is, a democratic, post-Communist society. A bi-monthly newspaper, *Republika* intends to instruct people in civil self-liberation and is promoted as "a paper without hatred and scandals." *Republika* publishes all the antiwar activities that take place in Serbia and Montenegro, which have been numerous though not effective in changing the government's policy.

Milošević's ideologues, such as Mihailo Marković, a former professor at Belgrade University and the University of Pennsylvania, maintain that today Serbia is the only democratic socialist country in the world. The Citizen Alliance and the Belgrade Circle advocate another view, however. Evidence exists that the Serbian Orthodox Church has also become disillusioned with Milošević, but it is not pursuing a Western-type democratic alternative. Rather, most church officials favor restoring the monarchy, which would be both Serbian and Orthodox.

The broader question about sanctions is this: Are they, as a tool of international pressure, capable of bringing down a dictatorial regime? The answer seems to be that they cannot. Instead, they serve to solidify public support of dictators. Perceptive observers maintain that Croatian President Franjo Tudjman, whose popularity is waning somewhat, would benefit were the UN to impose sanctions against Croatia (and were the world community to realize that the Serbs are not alone in having committed atrocities, but that the Croats as well as Muslims are also adept in the art of torture, killing, and ethnic cleansing). Such sanctions would serve to boost Tudjman's own undemocratic hold on power. A glance at Cuba, South Africa, Iraq, Syria, Libya, North Korea, Haiti, and other sundry regimes that have been boycotted in one manner or another show that such measures do not bring down a government.

If sanctions were lifted from Yugoslavia, Milošević's regime would have to bear much more responsibility for the country's economic disaster. Only with the lifting of sanctions will Serbs truly realize the magnitude of their economic crisis. A widely held illusion in Serbia is that the economic situation will improve as soon as sanctions are lifted. But an economy as devastated as Yugoslavia's will not show signs of real recovery in less than a decade. The deeper the country sinks, the harder it will be for the world community (and let us not kid ourselves—that means the United States and the European community) to assist recovery in the future.

Is it wise to facilitate the destruction of a country's economy to the degree that no amount of relief work by religious and other humanitarian agencies will be able to mitigate the subsequent human disaster? This question applies primarily to Serbia, but it is also relevant to Croatia and Macedonia and other Eastern European and former Soviet lands. The imposition of a foreign military settlement in the former Yugoslavia appears to have a better chance than sanctions of stopping the hate-filled carnage that has been so wickedly unleashed by power-hungry leaders. One thing is clear: whether the cause is war or sanctions, the innocent suffer the most.

CHAPTER 10

SLOVENIA AND MACEDONIA: A STUDY IN CONTRASTS

Two states extricated themselves least painfully from the former Yugoslav federation. The two are located at the opposite ends of the former country: Slovenia was in the northwest corner and Macedonia in the southeast. The two of them are a study in contrasts. Slovenia has cool, green, Alpine landscapes. Macedonia has hot, sun-parched, brown, Balkan mountains. Slovenia is industrial, with a relatively high standard of living, and Western. Macedonia is agrarian and shepherding, poor, and Mediterranean. Slovenia has a homogeneous Slovene population which was for centuries under Germanic (Austrian) domination. Macedonia has a heterogeneous population the identity of which is hotly contested, but the country is predominantly Slavic with a very large Albanian minority (which, if present demographic trends continue, could become a majority in the not-too-distant future) and was for centuries under Turkish domination. As a Macedonian parliamentarian, Jordan Boškov, remarked, "We have nothing in common with the Slovenians. We have to orient ourselves to a different interest sphere."

Slovenia spearheaded the drive to sovereignty, independence, and international recognition, with the United States recognizing the small country as early as 1991. Macedonia was the last to sever its relations with Yugoslavia and even now has not completely cut itself off. It is recognized in the United Nations only as "The Former Yugoslav Republic of Macedonia," primarily because of Greek objections to its use of the name "Macedonia." The United States recognized Macedonia only in 1994.

THE SLOVENIAN SECESSION AND WAR

In sports the player who fouls first often goes unnoticed. Those who retaliate may find themselves engaged in an all-out brawl while the initiator walks away relatively unscathed. This is what has happened in the case of Slovenia, one of the former republics of Yugoslavia. Having noticed Slobodan Milošević's surge to power in Serbia in 1987 and fearful that this would impede their own democratic and economic development, the Slovenians spearheaded the drive toward greater autonomy and ultimately to secession. This act led to the fateful eruption of merciless warfare in more central Yugoslavia, though the Slovenians have remained more or less on the sidelines as interested observers.

As the old Yugoslavian order crumbled, Slovenia was the first territory to implement a multi-party system. Following a public referendum, Slovenia's political leaders recognized that the vast majority of the population no longer wished to retain close ties with Belgrade, but instead preferred a confederated relationship. Since the reforms and the confederate arrangement proposed by Slovenia were inflexibly rejected by the pro-Milošević forces in the Yugoslav Communist Party and the federal government, the Slovene Communists walked out of the last congress of the Communist Party of Yugoslavia in 1990. It is said that at least one of the representatives cried, saying that their act spelled the end of Yugoslavia. She was right. The Slovenes subsequently felt justified to make the bold move for secession. They unilaterally declared independence and sovereignty on June 25, 1991.

The Slovene Communist and military leadership (the latter consisting of most of the Slovene high commanders in the Yugoslav People's Army and the commanders of the National Guard) realized that their bid for independence would be challenged by the federal government and its army. In utmost secrecy they trained their own National Guard and placed it in a state of military readiness (in the old Yugoslav federal military system each republic was allowed to maintain a National Guard). The Guard forces were armed with weapons secretly purchased abroad prior to their confrontation with the Yugoslav Army. The Slovene National Guard not only knew the mountainous terrain well; it also penetrated the federal army's communication system and was able to anticipate its tactics.

When the Slovene government decided to replace federal border guards and customs officers with its own, near the end of June 1991, the federal army struck, aiming, at least ostensibly, to reclaim the federal border crossings. The federal air force, tanks, and armored vehicles crossed the newly declared Slovenian borders from Croatia and Bosnia. Initially they encountered no opposition. However, when ground forces reached the most mountainous terrain, they were suddenly pounced upon from mountain heights by the Slovene National Guard, and they were stopped in their tracks. The federal army units—young, inexperienced conscripts in an alien terrain with no clear sense of mission and inadequate ammunition—were no match for the experienced and highly motivated Slovenian Guardsmen. The fighting resulted in about 50 killed and 200 wounded, but many federal army units surrendered. The Slovenes reported that they offered all federal soldiers civilian clothing and 100 German marks, then set them loose to go wherever they wished. Most returned home, some of them—according to Serbian reports—only in pajamas, giving an impression of humiliation to the army, an insult that the Serbs did not take lightly. The remaining federal army barracks in Slovenia were surrounded by civilians and Guardsmen. Instead of surrendering, the federal army unit commanders negotiated for their soldiers to withdraw into Croatia.

When it was still unclear whether, when it came to real shootings, the general population would side with the secession or passively succumb to the federal forces, a student in Slovenia's second-largest city, Maribor, was crushed to death by a federal tank. Although the event may have been an accident, Maribor rose to action and surrounded the army barracks located there. The encircled soldiers were unwilling to shoot unarmed civilians, hence the federal army could only cut its losses and negotiate a withdrawal.

Both the federal government's and the army's behavior are puzzling, given traditional Communism's willingness to use strong measures and even bloodshed to obtain desired goals. It appears that they were so surprised by Slovenian resistance that they were thrown into indecision and ended up conceding the loss of Slovenia—widely regarded as the least militant of the Balkan states. Had the Belgrade government conquered the secessionists by force, further developments in the war might have been very different. In any case, the Slovenians celebrated victory and independence and have been left alone since the summer of 1991. They have actively assisted in the sale and transfer of arms and other supplies to Croatia and Bosnia-Herzegovina in the belief that such assistance contributes to Slovenia's defense; they hoped they would not need to fight directly against the remnants of the federation, which for all practical purposes means the Serbs.

On the political side, the Slovenians created a multi-party coalition government led by Milan Kučan, a former Communist Party leader whose family background happens to be Protestant. (Slovenia contains small pockets of Lutherans—descendants of people who joined the Protestant Reformation in the sixteenth century and who somehow survived the Counter-Reformation that reclaimed practically all of Slovenia for the Catholic Church.) Kučan is a reformist whose skillful leadership is largely responsible for Slovenia's relatively painless separation from the old Yugoslav federation. He has since been elected to office in free elections—and by a considerable majority. When I interviewed him, I found him to be a very bright man who seems more the professor than the politician—although, unlike most professors I know, he is said to put in 18- to 20-hour days.

This Government of National Salvation, however, has been racked by continuous inter- and intraparty fights as politicians allow their ambitions for power to take precedence over their commitment to guide Slovenia into democracy and economic well-being. The nastiest of the conflicts pitted Kučan against Janez Janša, the nationalistic Minister of Defense. Kučan represented the reformist Communists, who, by changing and adapting themselves to new circumstances, succeeded in holding on to power. Janša represented a younger generation of leaders whose bids for power have been propelled in large part by their claim that all who had been involved in the Communist rule should be kicked out.

Some journalists have argued that Kučan represents the politics of the last decade of the twentieth century and that Janša heralds the politics of the next. What is clear is that Janša was in no mood to wait that long. He either seized upon or, some say, manufactured a crisis in July 1993 for his own political gain. Called the Maribor Airport Weapons Affair, the intrigue lacked none of the adventure and mystery of a James Bond movie.

Twelve containers of weapons and ammunition were discovered at the tiny provincial airport of Maribor on the Slovene-Austrian border. They contained some 11,000 Kalashnikov machine guns, plus hand rockets and mortar launchers (with no serial numbers or manufacture identification) as well as ammunition. The containers held enough material to arm the entire Slovenian Army. Further investigation uncovered a truly Byzantine enterprise. The weapons were manufactured in the People's Republic of China and flown to Maribor via Russian helicopters piloted by Ukrainians. The firm that arranged for the transportation is Hungarian but is run by an Austrian. Sudan and Egypt were the original purchasers of the weapons. Not known was the intended recipient of the weapons shipment; also, no one appears to know how the weapons were discovered. Were the arms bound for the Communist hard-liners in Slovenia to help return them to power? Were they intended to reach Muslims in Bosnia but, owing to the onset of Croat-Muslim fighting, blocked from being delivered? Or were they meant to further arm the Croats? And on and on.

Other questions focus on those involved in the planned transaction. Who was the middle man? Did the President of the Republic know about it, as, according to Janša, he should have? Did Janša, who claims to have discovered the containers, actually know about the weapons deal, but impounded the arms because he was not paid by the smugglers? Journalists, politicians, and average citizens have had a field day—the Balkans have long been a breeding ground for intrigue and conspiracy—while the President and Minister of Defense have exchanged public accusations and counter-accusations.

Unfortunately, affairs such as this absorb the energies of politicians and the population while economic problems remain unresolved. In the spring of 1994 Janša was forced to resign after it was divulged that despite his loud accusations against those who had been members of the former regime he himself had been working for UDBA, the Communist State Security. (It should be mentioned that Slovenia has been deeply involved in the region's arms trade, despite the embargo; it has sold some 800 tons of weapons to Croatia, and quantities of obsolete Slovenian weapons were delivered to the Bosnian Muslims—paid for with wheat shipments to Slovenia by Turkey.)

ECONOMIC WORRIES

Economically, Slovenia occupies a place between disaster and hardship. Kučan told me that prior to his country's secession the confederate system proposed by Slovenes and Croats for Yugoslavia could have led to a nonviolent dissolution of the Yugoslav federation as well as the creation of a joint southeastern European market that might have included Bulgaria and other countries as well. But rigid Serb opposition to the idea eliminated this option. According to Djordje Mandrino, an electrotechnical engineer, the national euphoria that accompanied independence still prevents Slovenes from seeing the overarching economic problem that followed: lack of trade. Not only did Slovenia lose its natural market—the rest of Yugoslavia—but it also lost the possibility of sending its products to distant markets. Products which are now, for lack of alternatives, placed on the Western European market have little chance of being profitable. Mandrino told me that when he became an engineer thirty years ago Slovenian technology was seven to eight years behind that of Western Europe; now it is twenty years behind. This means that Slovenian products can compete in the West only if they are cheaper than comparable products. Since productivity is fairly low, however, Slovenian goods end up being sold in the West at a price lower than actual cost. Mandrino pointed out the obvious: this circumstance will lead to economic ruin. Zdenko Roter, a professor of sociology also worried aloud to me about Slovenia's ability to achieve economic self-sufficiency. He expressed concern that the small nation is in danger of becoming a mere transit country for the drug and white-slave trade carried out by the mafias of East and West.

The current situation does not stand out as bleak to the visitor to Slovenia, who sees plenty of well-dressed people and well-arranged consumer products. Not visible to the naked eye, however, is the large number of unemployed and the absence of a stable public-assistance program for those not able to enter the competitive market. Nevertheless, whatever economic troubles Slovenia may confront, it is by far the best positioned of all former Yugoslav states to solve its problems. Moreover, it also has Western neighbors that may be willing to assist it during the transition to a market economy.

THE RELIGIOUS FACTOR IN SLOVENIA

As Slovenia's President Kučan acknowledged to me, religion has played a significant role in Yugoslavia's breakup. In Slovenia's case, the Roman Catholic Church has become a major factor in the new nation's public life. Among churches it has no rivals. Slovenia's Protestant community is small and suffers from a centuries-long inferiority complex that does not allow its members to face the present situation creatively. The Serbian Orthodox Church is active only among small immigrant communities and is currently on the defensive in light of Slovenia's anti-Serb politics. The Orthodox are reduced largely to defensive measures such as trying to justify Serbian actions abroad. The Muslims, mostly Albanian and Bosnian, enjoy official status and even support, but Slovenes can be quite condescending toward them, and sometimes reveal an ostracizing (one might almost say racist) attitude. These cultural biases make it unlikely that Muslims will become a significant factor in public life except when they serve the aims of Slovenia's political system. However, Muslim groups use Slovenia for international meetings and publishing ventures; the country is close, but not too close, to the war.

Despite the Roman Catholic Church's dominance, one might debate how Catholic the country is. Traditionally, all ethnic Slovenes are at least nominal Catholics, but during the Communist period strong currents of secularization served to weaken religiosity. Even though many are now returning to the Catholic fold, empirical studies and opinion polls conducted by scholars such as Niko Toš and Zdenko Roter point to a much more complex situation. Slovenians respect the Catholic Church, but the population is not overwhelmingly churchgoing, and many people reject a strong public or political role for the Church. Many complain that the Church is overplaying its hand. Toš and others have demonstrated that the attitude of Slovenia's population toward it resembles West European patterns in which the Church is culturally marginalized; it does not resemble central European models such as Poland, where, at least until recently, it exercised considerable political clout. Many Slovenes point this out with a certain pride. They see it as an indication that Slovenia is more Western in orientation and thus is removed some distance from struggling post-Communist Central European states like Croatia, Hungary, Slovakia, and Poland.

The Roman Catholic Church is led by the mild-mannered, unpretentious Archbishop Alojzije Šuštar. Forgoing the personal and bureaucratic formality—including the gauntlet of receptionists, secretaries, and assistants that often mark East European curates—the Archbishop not only was willing to receive me on short notice but personally came into the palace yard to meet me. Inside the archbishop's palace I found the same lack of protocol or, for that matter, the same lack of security measures that I had noticed in the President's office. It is both refreshing and strange to be in a country—especially a Balkan country—where hovering police, metal detectors, or secret service protection seem unneeded in public places.

Archbishop Šuštar faces the difficult task of leading his church into the public arena without alienating the bulk of the population. His humility will serve the Church well in allaying public concern about its return to a pre-Communist privileged social and economic position. What does not seem to be seriously contested by either enemies or friends of the Catholic Church is that it has the right to a prominent social position (although the smaller religious denominations worry excessively about the consequences of such a position). The two major issues now facing the Slovene Catholic Church are the question of religious education and the return of former Church properties.

Catholic theologian Janez Juhan believes that under Communism functionaries propagated and accepted the erroneous belief that religion was a private matter; today many former Communists have no understanding of the Church's needs and rights. He also believes, however, that future church-state relationships will be tailored after the Western European rather than the American model. In Austria and Germany certain historic Churches are given special government protection and privileges, including financial support and religious education in public schools. The Catholic Church in Slovenia desires a similar church-state compact.

A mixed government–Catholic Church commission has been established to adjudicate controversial church-state issues; representatives of other churches are not members of this commission. The debate is not over whether to teach or not to teach religion in public schools but who ought to do it. Most Catholic spokespersons claim that a form of catechism ought to be taught in all grades, while the more secularized voices argue that it should be done by people specially trained at the university to teach religious studies.

Regarding the government's return of former Church properties, which were extensive, the Church initially demanded a return of all of these. However, some politicians, journalists, and others oppose total restitution, and the Church has moderated its demands, saying that it does not expect the return of properties that have been given to others, or in cases where others used and improved them. The Church does insist upon the return of its forests and other lands and upon its right to become an economic factor in the new state. Pragmatically, the Catholic religious leaders believe that the Church is more likely to be economically successful than other Slovenian institutions.

Juhan argues that Church members in the past made significant economic sacrifices to assist it under Communism. It is now high time, he says, that such sacrifices cease and that the Church become economically self-supporting. Juhan believes that the Catholic Church can provide for itself economically if the properties it seeks are returned. He says Slovenes trust clergy because they, and the Church in general, remained close to the people under Communism and have, historically, defended national interests. Juhan also maintains that Slovenes believe that the Church has learned how to be socially responsible in its economic and educational enterprises. At the same time, many others in Slovenia, fearing the return of clericalism, oppose allowing the Church to have such wealth and influence. These dissenters say that anti-clericalism has had strong roots in Slovenia for good reason. According to their perceptions, the Church, as recently as World War II, collaborated with Slovenia's enemies and, contrary to Juhan's contention, remained aloof from the average believer.

In terms of social teaching, Slovenian Catholic theologians and leaders by and large reject not only Marxism but also political liberalism and the Enlightenment that engendered it. Classical liberalism, they argue, is an invention of Protestant individualism that, because it grants so much freedom, can easily be turned against the interests of others. Instead, these theologians are looking toward a religiously or spiritually inspired national community. To them, individuals should not be granted unbridled freedoms in the face of other people's rights. Only a renewed faith, they contend, can cope with excessive nationalism or excessive individualism, both of which they see as the products of liberalism and Communism.

All Yugoslavs agreed that Slovenia is the most economically developed and most standoffish of the republics. If *it* does not succeed in making the transition to a modern industrial democracy that protects human rights, then none of the other states of former Yugoslavia stand a chance of doing so. Provincialism and nationalist isolationism stand in the way of this development, but Slovenians' industriousness and culture, which emphasizes work and responsibility, provide reasons to think they will succeed.

THE MACEDONIAN NEGOTIATED SECESSION

Not everyone agrees that there is a nation called Macedonia. Detractors say it is an entirely artificial amalgam of people elevated to nationhood, like the Bosnian Muslims, by the policies of Yugoslavia's longtime strongman Marshal Tito. Some Bulgarians claim that Macedonians are simply western Bulgarians; some Serbs similarly claim that they are southern Serbs; some Greeks insist that Macedonians are either northern Greeks or Slavic impostors who mischievously named themselves after a Greek province. Greeks strenuously oppose the use of the word "Macedonia" by Slavs in almost any form, though they seem to have consented to its use when the term referred simply to a federal state within Yugoslavia.

Macedonian Communist politicians did not spearhead the drive for their region's secession from Yugoslavia. First they were fence-sitting, and then slowly, during the troubled years of Yugoslavia's collective presidency—between 1989 and 1991—they gravitated toward the decentralized and then confederate model proposed by Slovenia and Croatia. Macedonian representatives in the collective presidency, like the Bosnians, tried to play the role of mediators and conciliators. But when Slovenia, Croatia, and Bosnia-Herzegovina opted for independence, so did Macedonia. They had already bitterly complained that Macedonians serving in the federal army were being killed in Slovenia and Croatia in regional wars that had no interest to Macedonians. They today say, indulging in a bit of historical constructionism, that a dream of a sovereign Macedonia long inspired their state—a dream that some of the more rabidly nationalistic Macedonians trace to Alexander the Great. Political parties, such as the Internal Macedonian Revolutionary Organization: The Democratic Party for Macedonian National Unity, ultimately seek to unify all Macedonians, including those who live within the national boundaries of Greece, Bulgaria, Albania, and other disputed territories within the former Yugoslavia. Needless to say, these national dreams trouble their neighbors. Though Macedonians are not pushing for immediate annexation, recently issued maps that trace out a Great Macedonia as well as the political speeches of Macedonians leaders indicate that such concerns appear legitimate. In response to the stated misgivings of other nations, Macedonians marshal evidence that it is high time for a people who, after centuries of partition, now have the right to reunification.

The Yugoslav Army withdrew from Macedonia in 1992 without a single shot being fired. The withdrawal was negotiated, which provides Serbs with a handy—though not necessarily accurate—argument that other republics could have seceded from Yugoslavia in an equally orderly fashion had they not opted for violence. During my visit to Macedonia I was struck by the relatively few indications of anti-Serbian or anti-Yugoslav feelings among Macedonians. Many automobiles still bear the "YU" tag on them, and some enterprises still retain the word "Yugo" as part of their name; both phenomena are unthinkable in Slovenia or Croatia. Large numbers of Serbs still visit Macedonia for business, pleasure, or black marketing with no visible public resentment against them or their use of the Serbian language. Macedonia's President is Kiro Gligorov, a former Communist. The state is ruled by an unstable multi-party coalition government in which politicians switch party affiliations frequently, with a hint of violence here and there. The president of Macedonia's parliament alleged that an assassination attempt has been carried out against him.

Some United States political leaders and media commentators have bolstered an impression that Macedonia is in danger of Serbian aggression. It is true that some marginal voices within Serbia call for protection of the minority population of Serbs within Macedonia (someone even coined a term for an enclave of Serbs within Macedonia, "Makedonska Krajina"—a term that directly parallels the name for disputed Serb regions in Croatia). Others issue reminders that the great medieval Serbian emperor Dušan set up his court in Skopje, the present-day capital of Macedonia, and ruled over many Macedonian areas. In the minds of some Serbs this constitutes a historical precedent for a Serbian-ruled Macedonia. But there is little evidence that the present Serbian regime wants Macedonia. Only one scenario for a Serb takeover of Macedonia seems plausible, and even that one is unlikely: if Serbia were to conquer all former Yugoslav republics in a bid to re-create the failed Yugoslav state, Macedonia would likely also be on Serbia's menu.

In order to discourage Serbia from such a dubious aim, small units of UN forces, including a small contingent of about 350 U.S. soldiers, are now in place in Macedonia. Such an expansion of the Balkan wars would probably arise only if war broke out between Serbs and Albanians in the Kosovo province of Serbia—which borders Macedonia. A sketch of that scenario might be as follows: If Orthodox Serbs, who are outnumbered by Muslim Albanians in Kosovo by a ratio of nine to one, were to massacre Albanians in an attempted insurgence there, then Albanian relatives and friends from Macedonia and Albania proper might decide to aid their compatriots, and in doing so would pull the nations of Serbia and Albania into the conflict. Neither Orthodox Greece nor Muslim Turkey could stand idly by if their co-religionists were in need of allies. Nor would Bulgaria be able to avoid the fray, since Turks would have to cross their country in order to get into the action. Thus, the presence in Macedonia of a token UN force seems plausibly to indicate that even more countries could also be plunged into any conflict in the region. Indeed, if the present Balkan conflict is not contained north of

Macedonia, we have the ingredients for a possible world war. While there is no imminent danger of this course of events taking place, it is a sufficiently scary possibility to seriously concern many governments.

Until February 1994, when Greece unilaterally imposed a commercial blockade of Macedonia, tensions between Macedonia and Greece were like so much "hot air." Many Greek politicians, professors, clergy, and millions of Greek citizens have been agitated, and they have poured into the streets of Salonika, Athens, and Washington waving flags in a frenzy against Skopje; they use the name of the capital city to designate the entire state since they cannot bring themselves to call it Macedonia, even if qualified by adjectives, such as "Slavic Macedonia." Pseudo-erudite manuscripts are churned out by Greek professors, pious sermons preached by Greek priests, and fiery speeches uttered by Greek politicians about alleged threats to Greek existence. The behavior of the Greek intelligentsia once more confirms the general and probably well-deserved reputation of professors as oddballs, clergy as patsies, and politicians as demagogues. Militarily speaking, at this point Greece could have Macedonia for breakfast and not even belch, but in spite of their rhetoric Greek leaders know that it surely would be a liability rather than an asset for Greece to have to contend with a poor land peopled with poor Slavs. The entire confrontation seems to point more to some Greek complexes—and to, possibly, a guilty historical conscience for having forcibly Hellenized their own Slavic minority—than to a genuine threat.

The Macedonian-Albanian conflict is quicksand that could devour both nations. Ethnic Albanians officially make up 25 percent—unofficially, 40 percent—of the new republic's population. Macedonians have been increasingly terrified by the skyrocketing birthrate of the Albanians, who still maintain the traditional 10–15 child families, while the Slavic Macedonians and Serbs have reached the European average of two children per family. Demography is the time bomb of former Yugoslavia. When Serbs and Macedonians raise the issue of the higher Muslim and Albanian birthrates, the latter complain of genocide and oppression; when Macedonians and Serbs take measures to assure control of what they regard as their territory, Albanians who reside on the same land cite the size of their ethnic group and call for implementation of democratic principles of self-governing and majority rule. Two Albanian parties are active in Macedonia, the Party of Democratic Prosperity and the People's Democratic Party, and they form an oppositional coalition that causes plenty of headaches for Macedonian politicians.

THE ROLE OF RELIGION IN MACEDONIA

To parry the perceived Albanian threat—that Albania will try to annex the western part of Macedonia—Macedonian politicians turn to the Macedonian Orthodox Church for help. In most of the twentieth century the Orthodox Church in Macedonia had been under the authority of the Serbian Orthodox Patriarch in Belgrade. However, already under Tito's regime and with his blessing, if not prodding, the Macedonian Orthodox hierarchy and believers occasioned a schism which is unresolved to this day. The Macedonian Church claims autocephaly; namely, total canonical self-governing and independence—a development that no other Orthodox church in the world has thus far been willing to recognize. More recently, the Serbian Church has gone so far as to reluctantly offer the Macedonian Church autonomy within the scope of the Serbian Church, but even this concession does not satisfy Macedonian aspirations.

The new Macedonian constitution affirms religious freedom and separation of church and state. (The Macedonian Orthodox Church is the only religious community explicitly mentioned in the document.) Jordan Boškov is a young parliamentarian of the Macedonian Internal Revolutionary Party, which has the largest bloc of elected deputies in the parliament. He is faithfully Orthodox and is dissatisfied with the present church-state arrangements defined in the constitution, which he deems to be a vestige of Communism's attitude toward religion. He argues that instead of providing for church-state separation, the Orthodox Church's place within the state must be reestablished following the Greek model. It would be natural, he says, for the Macedonian state to care for the Church's needs and, in return, for the Orthodox Church to support the state according to the ancient principle of *symphonia,* or harmony between the secular and the religious spheres.

According to Boškov, the Orthodox Church is the hinge of the Macedonian nation; there should be lively interaction between religious and political authorities, yet with a clear division of responsibilities. The Orthodox hierarchy, he claims, was regretfully indifferent to Macedonia's parliamentary debates when it was trying to establish a new identity apart from Yugoslavia, and it did not make a strong bid to ensure that its central social role be conceded. Boškov believes that Orthodox religious education should be given in all schools, that at each public festive occasion an Orthodox Church representative should be present, that laws should clearly and tightly regulate religion, and that God's name should be mentioned and God's help acknowledged in legal acts of government. He also believes in pan-Orthodox cooperation under the leadership of the Ecumenical Patriarch of Constantinople (Istanbul). Boškov (and probably most Macedonian politicians and citizens) unambiguously rejects the American model of church-state separation, although he has admitted that Macedonia's Albanian politicians have voiced objections to his views.

The present exarch, Metropolitan Mikhail Gogov, a leading personality in the Macedonian Orthodox Church, was a political prisoner for six years during the Communist era. He is a former married priest, whose wife died, making it possible for him to be ordained a bishop. Having served Macedonian Orthodox congregations in Australia, he speaks fluent English, which he began learning in prison. Metropolitan Mikhail contends that it is only normal that a sovereign state have an autocephalous church, a goal toward which he is striving. He claims that the Serbian Orthodox Church causes the most trouble, particularly when it recently appointed its own bishop in the city of Tetovo, where the Macedonian Church already has a bishop. Mikhail claims that prior to democracy's arrival the Macedonian Church's relationship with the country's Muslims was normal, but that now the Albanian parties are provoking conflict. Mikhail had been nominated to become Macedonia's President, for which he had even the support of the Muslims, but he decided against it, citing the needs of the Church.

The Roman Catholic Church in Macedonia is small, and its bishop, Joakim Herbut, is a Ruthenian from the Vojvodina region. He was trained in Zagreb, and most of the Church members under his jurisdiction are Albanians in Macedonia and Kosovo. Even smaller in number are the Protestants in Macedonia, of whom, through a quirk of history, Methodists form the leading church. I visited several villages in the Strumica region on Macedonia's Greek-Bulgarian border and found several where Methodists are nearly as numerous as the Orthodox. In one village the new steeple of the Methodist church is higher than that of the Orthodox—something that probably does not sit well with the established Church.

Macedonia's Methodists are the product of American missionary activity in European Turkey in the latter half of the nineteenth century. They warmly received me (not only because I am a United Methodist pastor), and the visit was especially meaningful for me since I had written about this religious group in my doctoral dissertation. This was my first chance to witness in person those about whom I had written. They fondly recalled the visits of my mother, who had preached among them; they also recalled how they had escorted her on muleback through huge snowdrifts when she was stranded once by a winter storm in the 1950s. Macedonian Methodists are concerned about the power wielded by the dominant Orthodox Church, but they are far more free now than under the Communist regime, which erected tremendous obstacles (to put it mildly, for one pastor was murdered and one was incarcerated for four years) to impede their work. They seemed optimistic about their future as they prepared to live in greater autonomy from their sister church in Vojvodina, with which they still form an organizational unit.

THE ECONOMIC AFFLICTIONS

Economically speaking, Macedonia has plenty of reasons to worry, although, almost inexplicably, it has a stable currency, whereas that of neighboring Yugoslavia has gone through the roof. The climate is oppressively hot and dry in the summers, the land mostly mountainous; the crops of 1993 were burned to a crisp by a three-month-long drought. Some of the villages I visited had no water at all, which caused a serious health hazard. We drank buttermilk and bottled drinks, but both animals and people were clearly suffering from the water shortage. The water table had dropped so drastically that wells dug to nearly 300 feet still yielded nothing. Deadly confrontations have arisen between villages for control and diversion of streams.

With no mineral resources and an untrained labor force to serve its only partially developed industrial sector, it is hard to see what Macedonia has to offer in exchange for its many needs. Essentially, it is an underdeveloped country with a very low standard of living. Landlocked, it could profit from transit tourism and trade, but now that Serbia is under an embargo such traffic has come nearly to a standstill. The one sector of society that has blossomed is that which is devoted to breaking the embargo and establishing international black-market schemes.

Macedonia is likely to become heavily and perhaps permanently dependent on international relief. As part of the former Yugoslavia it was the recipient of such assistance from the richer republics through a policy of federal resource sharing. I cannot think of how this might be done now. Macedonia is a potential dependency that lacks a sponsor. The question is who can afford them.

CONCLUSION

The problem for both Slovenia and Macedonia is that they are so small that they do not have a critical mass of people who might produce sufficient first-class leaders in various fields. Using an analogy from sports, President Milan Kučan wondered aloud whether his nation has enough players to field a competitive team. Macedonia is even worse off. Both nations are threatened by possible revanchist demands by well-established neighboring countries—Italy and Austria, and Greece, Bulgaria, and Albania respectively. Both have been lucky thus far not to have an extended war on their territory, but neither country is completely out of danger. And both seem willing to resurrect the tradition of a dominant Church following a model of church-state relations that may jeopardize both pluralism and religious freedom.

CHAPTER 11

CROATIA: NEITHER WAR NOR PEACE

The almost empty bus en route from Ljubljana to Zagreb encounters little traffic nowadays. Just a few years ago, the trip would have meant a standing-room-only bus ride in bumper-to-bumper traffic. Then there was no international border between the cities, only a state line that did not interfere with the flow of people and merchandise. Now the bus stops at a grandiose Slovenian border station complete with flags flying and Slovenian border guards and customs officers decked out in brand-new uniforms. Everyone's passports are checked, visas are issued, car trunks are examined.

Several hundred yards down the road the bus stops a second time at a fancy Croatian border station—flags and new uniforms also on display. Croatian visas are stamped into passports. A Bosnian boy who is returning home after visiting relatives in Slovenia lacks the proper papers. He looks about ten years old. His luggage consists of a nearly empty plastic shopping bag, and he is penniless. The guard wants to take him off the bus, but the boy pleads that he must return to Bosnia to help his mother. His father, he says, has been killed in the war. The Slovene bus driver convinces the guard to let the boy transit across Croatia. Later, when I give him a few dollars for food, the boy tells me he is sixteen. It is hard to know whether he is telling the truth. In any case, I am glad my journey ends in Zagreb. Even the thought of traveling on to Bosnia is dreadful.

Zagreb shows no evidence of war except for the young men in camouflage uniforms who head toward the train station carrying duffel bags. Are they heading to one of many front lines where

Croat forces face rebel Serbs, the antagonists only flimsily separated by UN forces? Or are they destined for Bosnia and Herzegovina to assist Croat forces battling both Serbs and, as of late,
Muslims? The Zagreb media are full of war accounts—about a
fourth of the new state is held by Serb rebels—but the city is
peaceful and seemingly prosperous.

Prior to the outbreak of the Serb-Croat war Croatia was affluent—just a notch below Slovenia and Austria. Annually, foreign
tourists outnumbered the local population. Hard-currency income raised the standard of living and helped generate numerous
hotels, motels, bed-and-breakfast lodgings, restaurants, buses,
boats, and the other trappings of a tourist economy. Now foreign
tourism has practically ceased. Only some coastal regions such
as Istria and cities such as Dubrovnik (bombarded early in the
war) have gradually begun to attract a trickle of foreign and domestic tourists. Their return to the Adriatic coast helps assure
others that a once popular vacation spot is safe and peaceful.
Elsewhere all available lodging is crowded with refugees—hundreds of thousands of them from both Serb-occupied Croatia and
Bosnia.

Resentment toward the refugees is not uncommon. Locals
claim that they ruin the hotels and especially that the wealthy
refugees spend unseemly amounts of money as they sit idly in
cafés all day. Why don't these monied exiles go back to Bosnia
and fight the Serbs? the locals complain, expressing the age-old
resentment of the have-nots against the haves. (The same resentment toward war refugees simmers in Serbia as well.)

Croatia's political scene is volatile. The Croatian Democratic
Union, which swept into power at the first free election in 1990,
remains the preeminent political force. President Franjo Tudjman, a former Yugoslav Army general turned dissident, is the
party's and the country's dominant personality. Most citizens
support him, claiming he is a genuine democrat; others, especially the media, see him as an autocrat. Tudjman hails from
the same region as Marshal Tito, Zagorje; he also shares Tito's
penchant for pomp and circumstance and for being the final arbiter on all matters of state, major or minor. Recently he has surrounded himself with a cabinet made up mostly of Herzegovinian Croats; many observers believe that they are responsible for
leading Croatia to take a more belligerent stance toward parti-

tioning Bosnia with the Serbs. These cabinet members are also said to be in favor of annexing the newly created Croatian Republic of Herzeg-Bosnia headquartered in Herzegovina's capital city, Mostar.

News in Croatia brims with details of political intrigues between and within the numerous parties. Within the Croatian Democratic Union the right wing is battling the moderates. Nasty accusations bordering on slander fill pages of the daily newspapers, most of which are controlled by Tudjman. Only the iconoclastic *Feral Tribune,* whose masthead resembles the international *Herald Tribune,* pokes mercilessly at the pretensions of the nationalistically intoxicated political elite.

At least outwardly, however, some of the Croat nationalist euphoria has subsided. No longer is every shop window pasted with posters assuring passersby that "God Protects Croatia." Flag waving has not ceased altogether, but citizens are beginning to realize that independence will not be easy.

Overall, Croatia's economy is in grave condition. The Croatian dinar, the name of the new currency, is highly inflated. Products are readily available but are expensive. Quarrels continue over the slow pace of privatizing former collective property. Generally the trend is to turn over former socialist property to the new state's control rather than to privatize, and great political battles are waged over who will be appointed to run the state enterprises. Likely, the positions present the possibility of financial rewards whether over or under the table.

The whole process of privatization has been rife with corruption, according to accusations made in the press and the courts. Some Croatians have charged that state enterprises are first deliberately ruined financially in order to lower their value. The same managers who wreck the companies then buy them up at bargain prices, using money that they had earlier siphoned off from the same business. A remarkable scam if true. Reportedly the practice is common in all former Communist countries.

In order to get a job or have access to social benefits one must obtain a *domovnica,* which certifies that one was born in Croatia or that one is an ethnic Croat. The latter requires involved genealogical verification. Unsurprisingly, the regulation leads to discrimination against Serbs and Muslims. However, despite intense hatred toward both groups—Serbs especially, Muslims only more recently—it is a great exaggeration to say that there is wholesale persecution of Serbs and Muslims within Croatia, just as it is a lie that all Croats are persecuted in Serbia. Nevertheless, Croatia has its own ethnofascists, as does Serbia. In Croatia these groups harass and bully those whom they perceive as enemies, and the government offers no effective protection. Croatia may aim to be a democratic state bound by law but it has a long way to go.

Despite the obstacles, small groups of intellectuals are working hard to create the conditions for a Croatian state typified by law and democracy. Most of these intellectuals are decidedly anti-Tudjman and feel that they would do a better job at governing. A remarkable publication produced by them is the quarterly *Erasmus*. The journal, supported by an international foundation, gathers writings by gifted scholars and artists who are dedicated to the promotion of genuinely democratic principles. It assumes correctly that people must be educated for democracy rather than merely proclaimed to be democratic. Last December this same group organized a low-key roundtable dialogue with a group of Serb intellectuals from Serbia and the Serb-held regions of Croatia and Bosnia. The meeting's first day was tense and full of recriminations, but later it yielded to very constructive conversations. The gathering was eventually a success and the participants decided to continue—the next round to be in Serbia (reportedly, the Serbian organizers are encountering great obstacles in Belgrade). Dissident journalists from Serbia made a high-profile visit to Croatia in winter 1994 that included reception by senior government officials in Zagreb, indicating that slowly Serbs and Croats are recognizing that they must find a formula for living at least *next to* each other, if not *with* each other.

Such efforts contrast sharply with the work of some Croat nationalist scholars and journalists. The so-called "scholarly" journal *Social Research*, for instance, claims to be both objective and ethical, yet finds nothing wrong with vilifying Serbian history as a whole while it self-servingly explores the causes of the current war in Croatia in one of its issues. Scholars such as those behind *Social Research* represent mirror images of Serbian nationalist scholars who take up the pen to demonstrate the genocidal nature of the Croats and, by implication, the permanent danger they pose to the Serbs. Such intellectuals on both sides ceaselessly sow their hatred. Their lack of fundamental human decency and honor is truly distressing.

Tudjman's ethnocentric slogan, "Croatia for Croats," rather well sums up his opposition to a vision of Croatia as a civil society organized for all citizens regardless of ethnic origin. The slogan, it is safe to say, has done nothing to allay the fears of Serbs living in Croatia. Beyond the slogan, attempts to revive some of the nationalist symbols popularized by the *ustashe* (Croatian fascists active during World War II)—now, once again, admired by a portion of Croatia's right wing—have given Serbs even more reason to resist any idea of Croat independence. Such Croat neofascism has been welcome fuel for Serbian nationalist hatreds. The vicious war between Croats and Serbs in Croatia, 1991–92, cost over 10,000 lives; it continues to smolder and could break out at any time.

Prospects for the resumption of the Serb-Croat war, despite the cease-fire, are real. Violations of the cease-fire by both sides take place regularly on nearly all fronts, especially around Knin and Zadar. Croat regulars appear to be involved in the Bosnian war, though the government officially denies it. Officials say that any Croat soldiers fighting in Bosnia are Bosnian Croats who had joined the Croatian Army to fight the Serb aggression, and who have now returned to defend their homes—an explanation, not incidentally, that corresponds exactly to the version Serbian President Milošević offered regarding the Yugoslav Army's role in the Bosnian conflict.

Croatia aims to restore to itself all the land that belonged to it when it was a Yugoslavian republic. A conversation I had with a man who shared a train compartment with me was instructive. He had already fought the Serbs in Slavonia, and he was resigned to fighting again in a bigger war "against the Orthodox." In this comment he voiced an ethnoreligious assumption common throughout the region: Serbs are equated with Orthodoxy and Croats with Catholicism. When I asked him whether he was a churchgoing Catholic, he said that while he drinks coffee daily with the priest who lives next door, he himself has no reason to attend church since he is a good man. Whatever Catholicism means to this man, he obviously reflects little understanding of his Church's teachings. Yet, ironically, and tragically, he wears his decidedly vague Roman Catholic identity as a badge of loyalty for which, curiously, he is willing both to kill and to die.

Paradoxically, the current Balkan wars are religious wars fought by irreligious people. A major renewal of warfare in Croatia is a very real possibility. If that occurs, relations between Roman Catholics and the Orthodox will suffer horribly.

In the meantime, the close relationships maintained between the Roman Catholic hierarchy and Tudjman and his Croatian Democratic Union have cooled. Franjo Cardinal Kuharić visibly parted ways with Tudjman when he disagreed with the President's policy of annexing Herzeg-Bosnia in exchange for ceding central Bosnia to the Muslims. Cardinal Kuharić, as well as the Croat Catholic archbishop, the bishops of Bosnia, and the influential Franciscan order, declared that the idea of annexation spelled the abandonment of a millennium of Croat life in Bosnia. The religious leaders declared themselves in favor of Bosnia and Herzegovina's integrity, without going into detail as to how this was to be achieved in the face of relentless pressure to wipe the republic off the map.

Official Croatian political response to the Cardinal was predictably vicious, but so far both the Pope and Cardinal Kuharić support the Bosnian Catholic prelates in their perception that a partitioning, and hence destruction, of Bosnia would be a retreat of Catholicism from territories in which it established itself centuries ago. The Roman Catholics also see the establishment of separate Serb units within what has been Bosnia-Herzegovina as an advance of Orthodoxy in a westward direction.

The degree to which the notion of territorial advance or retreat still instructs the religious consciousness in the Balkans is remarkable. Many people on all sides of the conflict still speak of expelling/advancing Muslim, Orthodox, or Catholic life when they have in mind primarily the presence and coming to power of an ethnic group. Few clergy escape the ethnoreligious trap. One who does is Jovan Nikolić, a retired Serbian Orthodox priest in Zagreb, who in utter and bewildering honesty recounts Serb atrocities in Croatia and bemoans the numerous Catholic churches destroyed by the Serb extremists. On the Roman Catholic side, Vjekoslav Bajsić and Živko Kustić, both Catholic priests, are able to provide subtle analyses about the tragedy which has happened to their people and their neighbors. They are aware of the deep ambiguities and contradictions which characterize Croatian history.

Croats, including Croatian religious leaders, have been deeply traumatized by the total destruction of the city of Vukovar and countless villages; by bombardments of Dubrovnik and Zadar; by the interruption of rail and road service within their country; and by the occupation of Croat territories. The Church's response to these and similar events has not always been consistent. In some instances the Church's counsel was pastoral: it sought to address and soothe unmerited suffering and it urged patience and restraint from revenge. Cardinal Kuharić has publicly said that if they burn down your house, do not burn down theirs; if they steal your property, do not steal theirs. Yet at the same time the Roman Catholic Church glorifies Croat history and virtues and promotes the notion that Catholic Croatia forms Western Christendom's most important bulwark against the hordes from the east.

Several years ago, Croats celebrated the 1200th anniversary of the region's conversion to Christianity and its steadfast loyalty to the papacy. For nearly a millennium, after the native dynasty died out, Hungarian and then Austrian kings and emperors ruled these lands, often with little regard for Croat aspirations. When Croats joined Yugoslavia after World War I, they hoped that their national aspirations would be fulfilled in union with other southern Slavs—only to discover the great discrepancies in expectations and outlook among these.

Croatia's later longing for complete sovereignty was tainted by fascist extremism during World War II, which, according to some, went beyond extremism to genocide. As yet, Croats have not reconciled the deep conflict between their aspirations and the excesses associated with their attempts to achieve them. Unfortunately the churches in Croatia have not contributed enough to a process of reconciliation—both within Croatia, and between Croatia and its neighbors. As usually happens in most countries, Croatians confront the paradoxes of their history through denial and the redoubling of national chauvinism. In their own minds they are oriented toward Western Europe. Yet their behavior is often characterized by petty (but often lethal) Balkan argumentativeness, cruelty, and quarrelsome intrigue. Like their neighbors, they can be very narcissistic. What Croatia needs most now is a period of peace that will allow the nation's citizens to discover their collective and political soul in the, for them, novel environment of freedom and independence.

From a sheerly political standpoint, when Croatia engaged in a bitter fight with Bosnian Muslims in 1993 it squandered much of the world's sympathy (including the propaganda advantage) that formed when it was perceived as the victim of Serb aggression. The images of Croat-held Muslims in concentration camps and the destruction of cultural and religious monuments, particularly in Mostar, not only clouded the Croats' reputation but brought them to the verge of provoking UN-imposed sanctions. Such sanctions would be devastating for Croatia. (Croats themselves, for the most part, are no more able to admit to the role of aggressor than Serbs were; they blame the entire Balkan conflict on the Muslims and Serbs.)

It is highly questionable whether the Clinton administration's effort to create a loose confederate union between Croatia and the Croat- and Muslim-held parts of Bosnia will result in a workable structure. The Washington Agreements were based on proposals formulated by a gathering of Bosnian Croats in Sarajevo in February 1994, in which they opted against partitioning of Bosnia-Herzegovina but were in favor of a federal state within its presently recognized international boundaries but in which great autonomy would be given to cantons. The Washington Agreements satisfied for the time being both Muslim and Croat demands, and the war between them ceased. Additionally, such a federal Bosnia-Herzegovina was to enter a confederate agreement with Croatia which would then open the road for this unit to benefit from European integration. The idea is to win over the Serbs to join this agreement. However, Bosnian Serbs are likely once again to see even such a loose union as threat-filled maneuvering by the other two ethnic groups and the agreement may yet be the source of further vicious fighting rather than quieting of the war. Still, one precondition for ending the war in the Balkans is ending warfare between Muslims and Croats. Another is for Croats to look beyond the constraints of a sheerly utilitarian political standpoint. They must find leaders in both the secular and religious realm wise enough to elevate them above pettiness, vindictiveness, and a false sense of superiority to a more universal and morally responsible vision of Croatia's role in Europe. Creating a law state, a democracy, a civil society are imperatives for Croatia if it is to escape the vortex of ethnoreligious national chauvinism.

CHAPTER 12

ENDING THE WAR

The picture painted in the previous chapters is very complex and depressing. Yugoslavia continues to defy our longing for neat schemes. The combined impact of all the grief in the Balkans tends to inflict a feeling of fatalism by reason of the crushing weight of tragedy heaped upon tragedy. If there were simple answers to the problems, surely, they would have found them long ago. But to say there are no simple solutions does not mean that there are no solutions. Analysis does not have to create a paralysis, as some fear. To start with, no war lasts forever; the present warfare will also end. The question is whether it will end sooner or later and in what shape the region will be after it ends. This chapter explores a number of alternative courses of action and proposes an approach toward peace. It will first explore options which do not involve major foreign involvement, and then consider options which do call for foreign intervention. Recent approaches will be critiqued, and some suggestions toward ending the war will also be offered.

DOMESTIC ALTERNATIVES TO END THE WAR

Let us start with the presumption that the international community wishes to stay on the margins of the wars in the former Yugoslavia. Humanitarian aid will continue to be provided not only by private and religious relief organization but also by governments. It is estimated that such aid costs the international community annually four billion dollars. Foreign governments attempt to contain the war so that it does not spread regionally. In this case one can envision several possibilities. Some of them are clearly preferable to some of the combatants.

Generally, Serb political leaders and a great portion of the Serb public are against foreign intervention. They believe that its absence favors their cause, since their recent victories are in part a result of the lack of assistance given their enemies. The Croat and Muslim leaders favor foreign intervention provided it is directed against the Serbs, because they perceive that it gives them a chance to reverse the course of the war. Several scenarios are possible based on the premise of little or no foreign intervention.

The first scenario that one can envision is that one of the combatting parties wins the war. The most likely winner would be the Serbs. They are the most numerous and are by far the best armed. They have a clear national goal, i.e., to keep all Serbs in a single state. This could be achieved by uniting the Serb Krajina (of Croatia) and the Serbian Republic of Bosnia with the federation of Serbia and Montenegro. Serbs are resolutely fighting for a corridor across Bosnia in order to provide for contiguous land access to all Serb-controlled land as they seek to avoid a situation analogous to Armenia's separation from Nagorno Karabakh. As victors, they might allow the survival of a minuscule Bosnian Muslim state. A smaller Croatia would be acceptable to them and they might allow Croatia to annex a part of Herzegovina (which Croats named Herzeg-Bosnia). No additional border corrections have been demanded publicly by Serb politicians (except very minor ones from Macedonia). They have also shown interest in trading with Croats for a slice of land adjacent to Montenegro in order to gain access to the sea, and in return they would grant a wider buffer zone around Dubrovnik. Serbs would then likely pressure non-Serbs to depart from the territories they hold. This has been called humanitarian resettlement, but the opponents of the idea equate it with ethnic cleansing.

This scenario envisions the war ending with the capitulation of Croats and Muslims. Serbs have gained a Great Serbia in exchange for having lost the former Yugoslavia. The Serb victory and subsequent grudging international acceptance confirms that even in our own time there is no more effective way of achieving one's ambitions than winning on the battlefield. Serbia emerges as the largest Balkan country and henceforth plays a decisive role in the region. The Milošević government or some other nationalist dictatorship holds power, having proved that fascist policies paid off by having unified all Serbs in spite of great challenges and costs. Muslim and Croat refugees would not be permitted to return to their former homes located in Serb-occupied zones.

The second scenario is the economic and military collapse of Serbia. Being totally exhausted by sanctions and war expenditures, and facing the prospect of an internal civil war, the Serbs concede territories which they won in the war to Croats and Muslims after having lost some crucial battles in a renewed Serbo-Croat war and to Muslims after the arms embargo is lifted for Muslims. Several hundred thousand additional people are killed and millions become refugees. Most flee to Serbia, but many stream abroad, where they comprise a disgruntled emigrant population. The Serb flight from Croatia and Bosnia-Herzegovina results in the ethnic cleansing of Serbs from territories in which they lived for centuries, while those who remain are reduced to the status of persecuted minorities. Kosovo Albanians secede and Kosovo is annexed to Albania. Serbia's government changes and Serbia agrees to humiliating conditions which include war reparations of the size that it could not recover in a century. Croatia and Bosnia are likely ruled by euphoric nationalist governments.

The third scenario is to allow the war to burn itself out while the international community makes certain the war is "contained." Seeing that all three sides still have the will and the means to fight, the international community permits them to do so with the sure knowledge that they cannot continue forever. If the Israelis and Palestinians could finally come to the recognition that neither can have *everything* it wants, perhaps the three Bosnian ethnoreligions would reach a similar conclusion. A stalemate might develop. Intermittent warfare and peace overtures would probably ensue until the republics were exhausted, with up to a million killed.[1] The whole area could slip, at least figuratively, back to the stone age. By that time all sides would be willing to accept one of the formulas offered at the beginning of the conflict. Ethnic cleansing would take place and the results would separate Croat, Muslim, and Serb nation-states, the size of each determined by the final positioning of their armies. An un-

---

1. This is not an outrageous figure—that many were killed in Yugoslavia during World War II.

easy peace would come for a generation or two, until someone again lighted the fire for another round. All sides would have become cynical about the rest of the world not having cared enough to step in and help disengage themselves at an earlier time. Some politicians would pay for their belligerence and intransigence; some war criminals would be executed. However, most would escape judgment as there would be little chance of capturing them. The people would be even more disillusioned with political processes and look for some savior to resolve their problems. The great powers abroad might be satisfied that they did not have to sacrifice too many of their resources and only a few of their armed forces. Another holocaust would have taken place. Seeing the casualties, the world might say "Never again" to genocide, but would placidly accept further genocides in the Caucasus, Africa, Near East, former Soviet Union, or the Indian subcontinent.

A fourth scenario is that the heat of warfare in Bosnia cannot be contained in spite of the verbally expressed concern by the great powers. Instability and destruction there and in Croatia destabilize neighboring countries and the war spreads perhaps first into Serbia, then to Macedonia and Albania, and finally sucks in Greece, Turkey, and Bulgaria. Seeing that the peoples of the former Yugoslavia are engaged in mutual destruction, other countries with territorial ambitions come to the aid of their "favorite" Yugoslavian national minority and may be unable to restrain themselves from seizing the opportunity to expand their own borders. In addition to the above-named countries, Hungary and Italy may become involved. Let's say that this scenario might take place whether UN or NATO military intervention does not or does occur. Consequences of action or inaction are unpredictable. A regional war would be costly not only to participants but also to NATO because it would greatly strain the alliance. The outcome of such a war is completely unforeseeable, because great powers would most surely become involved.

A fifth scenario is a drifting toward the establishment of interest spheres in the Balkans.[2] Germany becomes the patron of Slovenia and Croatia, Turkey the patron of Muslims (Bosnia, Sandžak, Kosovo, parts of Macedonia and Albania), and Russia

---

2. Ali L. Karaosmanoğlu, "Crisis in the Balkans," United Nations Institute for Disarmament Research, Research Paper #22 (1993), p. 17.

the protector of Serbs, Montenegrins, and Macedonians. This is reminiscent of political-influence spheres which have already long since inflicted misery upon the local populations, but because each of the local ethnic nations is in need of allies, it will gravitate to ancient power players. The Balkan region continues to be a zone of conflict between both client and patron states. Balance-of-power policies replace collective-security schemes, endangering the concept of the "new world order." World politics becomes chaotic.

All five of the above scenarios would take a minimum of three years but might last as long as a decade or two until the end result is achieved.

FOREIGN MILITARY INTERVENTION

There are both scenarios of war and of peace based on foreign intervention. First, the scenarios of war. There are several alternatives in which foreign military intervention might lead to a sharp escalation, bringing about World War III.

The first is that the ultimatums to the Serbs by NATO and the UN are unsuccessful, and that after bombarding Serb military positions around Sarajevo or other UN-protected cities the war escalates. NATO forces expand their bombardment but Serbs strike back. They perceive that NATO has sided with the Muslims and Croats, and similar interpretation of the intervention is given to the public by NATO governments. Instead of coming to the negotiation table the Serbs redouble their efforts and self-destructively attack all peace-keeping forces, shooting down allied planes. In order not to be perceived as toothless, NATO retaliates and expands bombardment against Serbia itself. Serbia pleads for help from its allies, Russia and Greece. The Russian government acts to stalemate the UN and receives China's support as China is allergic to intervention into internal affairs of states. The Russian Army, even without the express approval of Yeltsin, sends "volunteers" to help Serbia—all with the vociferous support of Vladimir Zhirinovsky, who has already visited Serbia, Montenegro, and Serb-held parts of Bosnia and issued warnings that NATO bombing will be a declaration of war against Russia and be the start of World War III. A less dire alternative is that relations between the West and Russia are strained to the utmost, canceling the cooperative relationships that have developed since 1989.

At this point, NATO either backs down and looses face while Serbs and Russians proclaim victory, or it fights on and a much wider conflict breaks out. NATO ultimately wins (with strong German support) and imposes its solution in the former Yugoslavia. The precedent is set for other NATO interventions in geostrategic danger zones, especially in regard to Russia's relationships with its neighbors in Europe or Asia.

The second scenario is that Muslim countries, seeing that the genocide of Slavic and Albanian Muslims continues, may not restrain themselves, but intervene militarily. The most likely candidates would be Turkey, Libya, Egypt, Iran, and Algeria. Since Turkey has been encouraged by the West to become a regional power and Turkey has traditional aspirations to the Balkan peninsula, Turkey spearheads this involvement. Serbia and Croatia rush large contingents of their regulars to support their compatriots' combat with the Muslims. They appeal to their respective allies, who are bound to respond because they too fear a large Muslim presence in Europe and cannot allow Croats and Serbs to be brought to their knees. UN troops on the ground turn on each other, e.g., Jordanians (Muslims) against the Ukrainians (Christians). Chaos prevails. The Muslims are forced to retreat. After tumultuous sessions in the UN, a final international conference imposes a settlement on Yugoslavia after hundreds of thousands have lost their lives and a multitude of countries are in a state of agitated antagonism.

There are also international scenarios which do not involve large-scale military operations by outsiders.

The first one is that the West crushes Serbia with combined economic sanctions and military pacification. A change of political leadership takes place in Serbia, and it agrees to give up all aspirations to unite Serbs outside of Serbia—although it promises to be their protector. In Serbia, nationalist forces are still active and another dictatorship, which muzzles opposition to the regime, is established. Croatia and Bosnia-Herzegovina are established as sovereign states, and because of the local hatreds the Serbs are ethnically cleansed in these areas and/or withdraw to Serbia. To make room for them, the Serbs in turn drive out their non-Serb population. Painfully slow development toward democracy takes place in all former Yugoslav republics. Economic recovery is also slow, with Slovenia and Croatia succeeding while the others became economic basket cases and depend perennially on economic aid.

A second peaceful solution is that the war slowly burns itself out. The leaders of the various states begin to tire of prolonged warfare and become increasingly receptive to a barrage of peace activism, both domestic and foreign. The number of human casualties is more than catastrophic. Someone (e.g., Owen and Stoltenberg or their successors) chances upon a formula that now becomes acceptable. New, more amenable leaders have emerged in the meantime by means of either a *coup d'état* or elections. Karadžić, Milošević, Tudjman, Izetbegović—some or all of them are gone. The new leaders sign a peace treaty, which all, except minor renegade groups, uphold. The renegades are controlled by both the UN peacekeepers and the respective governments. Gradually, near-normal relationships are restored between the successor states. It is already the year 2,000 and the world is relieved that peace has dawned at last after years of genocide have inured everyone.

The above are all possible scenarios. *No one* knows which dangers lurk behind any alternative. Any move may misfire. Unpredictable consequences may emerge and tip the uneasy balance of power in a world that claims to have an international community but in which the word *"community"* is more an illusion than fact.

All the above scenarios take into account that it will take an inordinately long time to wind down the war and that there will be unacceptably large casualties in that winding down. The states of the region would, after the winding down, remain devastated and unable to join the community of nations as productive members for a long time to come.

A more decisive alternative is needed.

MY PROPOSAL TO END THE WARS

Criticism of Past Policies

Ever more gruesome pictures from Bosnia crowd our sensibilities. One day it is the killing of 60 and wounding of 200 at a market in Sarajevo. Another day it is Croats and Muslims destroying Mostar. Next, it is corpses of Croat villagers massacred by Muslims. Then it is reports of thousands of Croat Army regulars crossing from Croatia to aid their compatriots. The Bosnian Serbs withdraw temporarily under threat only to redouble their aggression when they see that their action goes unpunished. Endless peace talks take place, each ending unsatisfactorily as one side or the other torpedoes the process. Hopes for ending the war rise only to come crashing down again.

Since 1991, the United States government and the rest of the international community have reacted with revulsion and threats to intervene. Then, almost immediately, they have backed away saying that such intervention is not in their national interests. At the same time, instead of the European unity that was announced for 1992, European countries blocked each other's move at practically every turn. Germany and Austria took a pro-Croat and pro-Slovene stance, though to their credit they expressed great disapproval of the Croat Army operating in Bosnia-Herzegovina. France and Great Britain have watched German moves apprehensively. Having their units among the peacekeepers, these two countries were blocking air strikes against troops encircling Sarajevo and other Bosnian cities. But, repeated atrocities made the French and British generals and governments aware that more decisive steps must be taken. Unfortunately, they found an American government reluctant to get engaged on the ground, and without such involvement there is really no effective way to separate the warring sides.

An economically and militarily weakened Russia looks at NATO with mistrust as the Western military alliance ventures for the first time outside its own defense zone without consulting the Russians. Historical friendship with Serbia and cordial relations between Russian and Serb generals, as well as Russia's own geopolitical aspirations to remain a major world power, prompt Russia to map out its own sphere of interest. The immediate neighbors of former Yugoslavia have very contradictory interests *vis-à-vis* the new states. Europe is in a state of profound discord and impotence in addressing the crisis.

The United States, after being burned by the Somali intervention, has assumed an isolationist mood. Prior to the 1992 elections Bill Clinton criticized George Bush for taking an aloof position on Bosnia, only to settle basically for the same approach once he himself was elected. And predicted material, political, and military costs to the United States seemed too high. U.S. military leaders took a cautious attitude: "We do deserts, we don't do mountains," was the humorous but cautious assessment. There has seemed, to Americans, to be no adequate reason to recommend any action beyond expressing dismay over repeated outrageous incidents. Furthermore, in the name of *Realpolitik*, senior officials have stated that we must not act out of outrage but only out of clear national interest. Only a few junior State Department officials have quit over policy disagreement. Having seen the reports of cruelties, they felt that it was not in the interests of this nation to bury its head in the sand and avoid decisive action in order to halt the most massive butchering in Europe after World War II.

Public opinion, which does play an impact on policies in Western countries, has tended toward non-interventionism. No one wanted to see young men and women become bogged down in the primitive and dangerous Balkans. The vast majority of people, in Europe and especially in the United States and Russia, have little understanding about who these groups are and why they fight with such determination. Skillful politicians can usually manipulate public opinion into supporting armed intervention in the name of peacemaking or national interests, but in this case there are too few tangible rewards to be gained and too much to be lost; hence, caution has prevailed. What's more, worldwide economic stagnation, which hit Europe especially hard, has made all Western countries look inwardly. The war in the Balkans is a pesky distraction, one to which they turn unenthusiastically.

Wearily they issue threats from time to time, with very little resolve to implement them. The threats are directed almost exclusively against Serbs. The Milošević regime is criminal if for no other reason that it allowed the Serb name to become synonymous with barbarianism. Never in history have Serbs been more maligned than they are now—and much of it for good reasons. The constant coupling of the words "Bosnian" and "Muslim" have by now cemented the erroneous conviction in the West that all Bosnians are Muslims, when in fact Muslims are a minority as compared to the Christian Serbs and Croats of Bosnia, fully as Bosnian as the Muslims.

Editorials and politicians alike call for the United States to punish Serbs—and Serbs alone—although only the day before the same newspapers may have reported that Croats injected into Bosnia perhaps as many as 20,000 army regulars in clear violation of UN declarations. (The same papers also reported initial successes of the Muslim-led Bosnian Army of 200,000 soldiers, which outnumbers but does not outgun both the Serbs and Croats.) Yet no serious discussion has taken place in favor of UN sanctions against Croatia. I am not arguing for an embargo against Croatia; I argue for removing it in Serbia (see Chapter 9). In Croatia the results would be the same as in Serbia; namely, innocent people would suffer while state policies would be affected only slightly.

Many argue that Bosnia is an internationally recognized state and that the Muslim-led government should not be forced to accept a peace treaty which it does not think is in its interests. In order to level the "playing field," arguments are made for the lifting of the arms embargo on Bosnia; if necessary, unilaterally by the United States. This would result in a U.S. violation of a UN resolution that we initially supported. If the U.S. could get away with such an action, why not others? How can one lift an arms embargo on Bosnia and benefit only the Muslims and not the Croats and Serbs of Bosnia?

Since 1990 the so-called "international community" has issued well-meaning resolutions, empty threats, and followed these up by not much more than humanitarian action. However, since the Saturday Massacre of February 5, 1994, which resulted in 68 dead and two hundred wounded in a Sarajevo market place, a convergence of U.S. governmental, NATO, and UN attitudes has emerged. Presuming that the attack was caused by the Serbs, ultimatums were issued to Serbs to withdraw. Air raids were threatened—something that, a few days earlier, Western military experts said to be ineffective if used alone. President Clinton excluded the use of American ground troops. Hope was expressed that the bombing threat would lead to more successful negotiations. However, no Western strategy was devised regarding what such negotiations were to accomplish except whatever the three sides—Muslims, Croats, and Serbs—agreed upon. And herein lies the hitch: the three sides have such irreconcilable ambitions that, *on their own*, they will clearly be unable to agree.

In a statement to television's CNN on February 10, 1994, Britain's Lord David Owen stated a view not raised by U.S. officials; namely, that the NATO threat of bombardment should apply not only to the Serbs on the hills surrounding Sarajevo but also to the Bosnian Army. The danger was clear, however, that the Serb withdrawal would only be used by the Muslim-led Bosnian Army to recapture territory rather than to bring about peace. The Muslims are by now convinced that only a victory on the battlefield will assure territorial corrections, and this can be expected if they arm themselves while Serbs and Croats are restrained. Thus, instead of prohibiting the creation of borders by conquest we might sanction it, regardless which local army wins at the battlefield.

It appears that by February 1994 the UN had resolved not to permit the strangulation of Sarajevo. NATO became serious about using at least its air power to intervene in Bosnia. For two years the city had been strangled, yet Western government officials until 1994 still argued as to whether it had been strangled enough to protect the city from total destruction.

A Proposal for Action

The argument proposed here is based on ethical and religious concerns rather than political exigencies. The political will to implement it may not exist. But there is an ethical imperative that genocide must stop, not only in Sarajevo but also elsewhere in Bosnia and in other parts of former Yugoslavia. Power must be used to prevent the incessant carnage in the Balkans. All three sides must be made to cease hostilities. We must not react only to what is documented by cameras. The Saturday Massacre will likely be avenged by Muslims by the cutting of throats of innocent Serbs in remote mountain villages and none of us will know about it. Retaliation in the Balkans is usually swift and always sure. Morally, of course, retaliation is not as great a sin as the initial crime, but in Bosnia it is difficult to trace who started the endless series of killings centuries ago. This depressing truth must not, however, lead to our inaction. At some point the cycle has to be broken.

Coercive diplomacy needs to applied by all those countries that have responded to the outbreak of these late-twentieth-century wars in the Balkans. Peacekeeping is not enough, since there is no peace to keep! *Peacemaking, by diplomacy, but if neces-*

sary, by military strikes against those unwilling to comply, yet not exclusively directed against one side only, is the only effective way to bring the butchery to an end. Lt. Gen. Michael Rose, commander of the UN forces in Bosnia, declared in February 1994: "We were not sent to stop the war. We're in wrong configuration for that. We're in wrong number for that."[3]

Herein lies the problem. The international community has *not* decided to end the war. Once it does, it can do so. Massive international military action is needed primarily in Bosnia, but also in the region overall. First, one needs to demythologize the idea of the invincibility of Balkan warriors. It is true that they generally tend to go to war enthusiastically and die without complaint. But in this case a tremendously large number of young men of military age of all nationalities are evading enlistment. Many would welcome UN intervention. Therefore, the parallels with World War II, when the resistance to Hitler engaged a large number of Axis divisions in the Balkans, are not really applicable, because Hitler came to occupy; the UN and NATO will not.

The military action should not be against Serbs alone, although the Serb extremists should be the main target. A UN ultimatum against further warfare, enforced by NATO, should be issued to all three sides, forcing them to the peace table for *serious* negotiations. This would satisfy Russian and Greek objections and assure that UN troops in the area would be more protected because their implementation would be seen as evenhanded.

United States and Allied responses to injustices of the Balkan wars need to be just and decisive, but *proportional* rather than simple-mindedly unilateral. It is true that the Serbs committed the most aggression and the worst atrocities and that the Muslims suffered the greatest losses. It is also true that the Serbs kept attacking targets in Goražde and elsewhere when they promised a cease-fire. This had to be stopped, and the first bombs were dropped on Serb positions around Goražde on April 11, 1994. That intervention was so feeble that it failed to convey the intended message that no military attacks would be tolerated on protected zones.

---

3. Barbara Demick, "U.N. Commander Gives Encouraging View of Truce," *Philadelphia Inquirer*, February 13, 1994, p. A19.

The larger issues cannot be rectified by attacking only Serbs—as if the United States were a Croat-Muslim ally. Even if Serbs were to sustain a defeat (which is probable), it does not mean that peace would come to the region. All three sides must be forced to accept peace rather than merely be urged to agree on it by themselves. None of the three sides believe that they have achieved the goals for which they are fighting. Warriors who feel themselves to be aggrieved are not going to make voluntary concessions as long as they still believe they can achieve more on the battlefield. A peace must be imposed from the outside and all three sides coerced to agree. Those believing that such involuntary acceptance will not succeed do not know history. For centuries Balkan states have been made to reluctantly agree to decisions made at peace conferences (e.g., San Stefano and Berlin), conferences not convened by them. They did not like this but accepted it because it was better than continuous warfare.

From the moment when Yugoslavia began to dissolve, the international community applied unequal standards to the various new states. This aggravated rather than soothed the emerging problems. One injustice is not solved by another. The international community, if it can at all get its act together rather than be divided into spheres of interest akin those of 1914, must use equity and proportionality. *All* who committed atrocities and showed inflexibility must bear the consequences. War criminals of all three sides must be tried!

In 1989 there were still some ways to keep a multi-national Bosnia-Herzegovina together. Today it may be too late, even though it is still the best of all options. By now the majority of Serbs and Croats seem disinclined to live in a common Bosnia, except perhaps as a loose cantonal confederation which would have a questionable future, if for no other reason than that no precedent exists there for the creation of cantons. Croats and Muslims may be persuaded to live together, but Serbs will want to hang on to what they now control, which is 60 to 70 percent of Bosnian territory. The Muslims tend to vacillate. During peace negotiations they press for 5 to 10 percent territory additional to what is being offered in order to agree. When the United States threatens to attack the Serbs, they ask for a unified Bosnia-Herzegovina within the 1991 borders and demand that Serbs be given nothing because what they have taken was gained in war.

Croats are at times satisfied with the 17 to 18 percent of Bosnia-Herzegovina territory which corresponds to their numerical strength, but at other times they feel that they would be locked out of most of Bosnia, where they have lived for ages.

The dynamics of development seems to favor the ultimate partition of Bosnia. If Yugoslavia could be partitioned, why not Bosnia? It was clear to anyone who knew Yugoslavia that when Yugoslavia fell apart there would be a war in Bosnia-Herzegovina that would probably lead to its partition (at least for the time being). Because of that, one must—backed by a threat of force—offer to the three sides a map with which none of them will be happy but which will give enough advantage to each side so that they will be willing to settle for it. We know that the Muslims have legitimate interests. So do the Croats. What we are least willing to recognize is that Serbs, likewise, have legitimate claims and grievances. *An imposed solution that satisfies at least some of the claims of all three will be much better than letting them go on fighting incessantly.* If the plan includes the fiction of a Bosnian federation, so be it; although the logic of future development is likely in the direction of greater integration of Serb cantons with Serbia and Croat and even possibly Muslim cantons with Croatia. It is important not to deprive any of them so drastically of a proportionate territory that, several years later, the war breaks out all over again.

Bosnia-Herzegovina is clearly a case where one cannot do what is *absolutely* right and simple. Here one must resort to choosing the lesser of evils. An international conference on Bosnia should be the first stage of a process that needs also to address the question of Croatia and Kosovo. Assertive proposals for delineating borders and insisting on protection of minorities within such borders must be made. If the Albanians of Kosovo so wish, parts of Kosovo should be allowed to incorporate themselves into Albania, making certain that Serbia's holy places are left within the borders of Serbia. The Croats may have to settle for a state without the Knin Krajina; it is one of the poorest regions of Croatia and not worth fighting over. But a large number of Serbs there may decide they will be better off in Croatia, provided their rights are guaranteed.

Fairly large migrations, or exchanges, of population may need to take place due to humanitarian concerns. Some may call this ethnic cleansing. At least this time it would be socially coercive and internationally supervised rather than the result of murder, rape, and destruction. This is a morally superior approach. It is less costly than a protracted war. It would be a worthy U.S. strategy, replacing the current tactical waffling. It is something both the U.S. government and military could support. It is also something that religious bodies worldwide could advocate in good conscience.

When Germany was defeated in World War II, Allied troops were left to carry out a process of de-Nazification. A contingent of UN soldiers fortified by peace activists skilled in conflict-resolution techniques must be stationed in various parts of Yugoslavia to help eliminate or reduce ethnofascism. Many parts of the former Yugoslavia will have to become temporary wards of the UN—UN protectorates although not necessarily in the legal sense. Sanctions should be lifted and those former Yugoslav states willing to cooperate with the European Community should be assisted to incorporate into the Community and be helped to rebuild their economies. Civic groups that work toward pluralism should be assisted to promote their ideas and be given a chance to lead in a process of democratization.

Though, at present, hatred is so intense that it is difficult to get Serbs, Croats, Muslims, and Albanians to talk to each other, small democratically inclined groups have already begun doing so. Hatred is not an eternal condition. The peoples of former Yugoslavia, like all neighbors, need each other. Necessity is the mother of invention. Gradually, very gradually, neighboring peoples and states learn again to work with each other, not out of love but with suspicion and caution. International train and automobile traffic will be allowed again to traverse the region. Tourists will come again. Business contacts will be reestablished. Slovenes will service the machines that they built before the war and will sell other products. For that they will buy meat from Vojvodina and pepper and peanuts from Macedonia and medicine from Croatia. Automobiles made in Serbia will find their way into Bosnia and Macedonia. Greeks, Turks, Iranians, and Albanians will truck goods back and forth to Western Europe across the former Yugoslavia. The Orient Express will again go from Paris to Istanbul via Zagreb and Belgrade. Relatives and friends will be making telephone calls again between Croatia and

Serbia. Intellectuals and academics will find ways to improve contacts with one another and work on common issues. Theologians will seek ways to establish an interfaith dialogue. Interfaith dialogue centers may emerge in some cities, notably in Sarajevo. Religious communities will find theoretical and practical resources to act as peacemakers rather than as supporters of war; ecumenism will slowly reemerge. All of this will not take place by the end of the twentieth century, but it will not be far into the twenty-first when the former Yugoslav people will thank the international community for having found the political will, military strength, and financial means to make them stop fighting.

There will be pockets of former Yugoslavs among whom bitterness and hatred will persist. Incidents of ethnic murder will take place from time to time. In a democratic society the free press will give space to charlatans who will try to incite hatred. But sufficient cooling off will have taken place so that that hatred will not be quite so extreme after the republics have extricated themselves from each other as when they were still engaged and did not know how to break away in peace. The social psychosis will have subsided and greater sanity will prevail. They will know that any other behavior will lead only to national suicide. Frustrations and tensions will still run high as people will disagree about how to approach each other, but this will be expressed by means of political processes rather than violence. Most difficult will be dealing with the economic and public health catastrophe. However, economic needs will drive them to acceptable political behavior in order to qualify for international assistance.

All of the former Yugoslav states will want to join the European Community, and Europe will offer acceptance under stringent conditions. The preconditions for admission will be the willingness to develop a democracy, to protect the human rights of all, to cooperate economically, and to grant the free movement of people. Consultation must replace intimidation. The dream of brotherhood and unity may have been shattered, but a nitty-gritty grappling with the frustrations of interethnic relations can bring an acceptable level of tolerance. Individuals may even be able to rebuild relations on the basis of cordiality.

Religious groups, both domestic and international, will have the task of detoxifying society. For this they are well suited; all of the religions intrinsically possess healing abilities for fractured individuals and societies and they are present in nearly every city and village. Messages of dealing with the enemy in ways that make coexistence possible can be found in the scriptures and traditions of all religious groups. In the past, religious leaders considered the pastoral task of protecting and nurturing *only their own* communities their paramount task. They neglected nurturing positive attitudes toward the "other" or "outsider." Now they must realize that ecumenism and interreligious dialogue—if merely for selfish reasons—must play a greater role, because the degree of mingling has become so great that the well-being of the "other" has a direct correlation with the well-being of our own group.

The peacemaking responsibility of religious communities in Yugoslavia have not been sufficiently utilized and were not considered a mainstream task. In peacemaking the domestic religious communities can receive a significant support from the international groups and agencies both in know-how and in dedication. It may well be that peace in the former Yugoslavia will not come by some decisive strategic move of the great players in this tragedy but, rather, by the small, incremental steps of millions of "the little people." The Yugoslav drama is, indeed, a confrontation of good vs. evil, except that the delineation between good and evil does not run along ethnic lines. Rather, it runs within each community and even within each person, in whom there lies the capability of forging human links of interethnic cooperation as well as murderous ethnic hatred.

Agape (forgiving love) must overcome hatred. Since the latter is more easily aroused than the former, it will require that the good of God prevail in the soul of each person.[4] I know of no other word to describe the ability to overcome the hurt of losing members of one's own family and to deal with the hatred that consumes the killers of another ethnic group except to label it "miraculous." I have seen it embodied in a young Muslim scholar from Sarajevo whose father and sister had been killed in this war yet who has not responded by hatred toward the Serbs.

---

4. For helpful hints about practical approaches to peacemaking in the former Yugoslavia, see the work of Gerald Shenk and David Steele, *God with Us?: The Role of Religion in Conflicts in the Former Yugoslavia.*

In that sense, peace in the Balkans will be a miracle of God, who will use as divine tools all those able to forgive rather than to avenge.

It is not our task to create or predict the future. But we need to establish optimal conditions in order to make a better future possible. Cessation of interethnic warfare in the Balkans is the precondition for determining whether the people of that peninsula enjoy a peaceful future or a permanent holocaust.

CHAPTER **13**

AND THE WAR GOES ON

By August 1994 none of the many "turning points" in the Yugoslavian warfare helped resolve the basic conflicts that caused the outbreak of the wars. None of the contending parties attained their strategic objectives nor did they become satiated with waging war. Despite having signed cease-fires of limited duration and having shown cautious willingness to consider proposals by external mediators, *all sides continued relying mostly on military means* to obtain their political and ethnoreligious goals. Since none of the antagonists are able to win a decisive military victory, the conflict is settling into an interminable low intensity war, which threatens to escalate sharply with each failure to find an accommodation. Serbs, Croats, and Muslims continue to arm themselves, each under the illusion that ultimately they will accomplish their goals by means of defeating their enemies. Ozren Žunec, a professor of sociology and philosophy at the University of Zagreb, provided a very sober analysis of the threat of renewed warfare between the Serb-held Knin Krajina and the Croatian Army, joining Peter Gailbraith, the American ambassador to Croatia, in warning that such a venture would have catastrophic consequences for both sides.[1] He points out the folly of Tudjman's contention that the Croatian forces could rapidly liberate their lost territory and emphasizes that for Croatia political solutions that encompass the development of democracy are the only reasonable assurance that rebel Krajina Serbs can be suc-

---

1. Ozren Žunec, "Hrvatska u sukobu niskog intenziteta," *Erasmus*, No. 7 (Zagreb, May 1994), pp. 46–63.

cessfully reincorporated into Croatia. What is true for Croatia holds true for the other states.

The American contemplation of lifting the arms embargo and supplying the Bosnian Government Army with heavy weaponry so that they can defend themselves plays into the hands of the Bosnian government's hope that they can retake territories occupied by Serbs. The Bosnian general Rasim Delić declared that the nature of the Muslim strategy is changing from a defensive war to a war of liberation—another sign that long-range guerilla warfare is a likely prospect.

On the surface the "51–49 Plan" of the so-called Contact Group (consisting of the United States, Great Britain, France, Germany, and Russia) may seem a step in the direction advocated by the author of this book (in Chapter 12) by which the international community might end the war. This formula, which was agreed upon at a Summit in Italy in early July 1994, advocates the acceptance by all three warring parties of a unitary Bosnian state, while the internal division of territory would give the Muslim-Croat federation 51 percent of specified territory whereas the Serb area would be restricted to 49 percent (the Serbs having to yield about 20 percent of the territory which they occupied during the war). The Croats and Muslims reluctantly agreed to the "51–49 Plan," but the Serbs turned it down, causing the Muslims to retract their earlier consent. The Serb reply also caused division between the sponsoring Great Powers as to whether the response was unacceptable (the U.S. position) or provided further negotiating possibilities (the Russian position). Once more the international community was unable to find a common approach to the chaotic situation in the Balkans.

The proposed 51–49 solution—which looks good on paper—is not likely to be acceptable to any of the three parties in the long run unless the threat by the Great Powers was to become so formidable that short-term compliance would ensue. All three sides have already complained that the 51–49 proposal is "unacceptable," "unjust," "rewarding aggression," "legalizing ethnic cleansing," etc. At a minimum the result will be endless haggling over maps, land resources, corridors, roads, access to the sea, and so forth.

The continued war and the resulting anguish and impoverishment provide little hope for the advancement of democracy in the region, which is a precondition for the long-range settlement of the Balkan crisis. The opposition parties are weak and, with few exceptions, are also based on ultra-nationalistic premises. There are hardly any serious "programmatic political parties," that is, parties that have concrete plans to solve burning social problems or that advance the interests of a segment of the population other than the nationalist cry to rally the entire population for continued "defense of the homeland." Even analysts from among the opposition concede that they have been marginalized and disunited. The parliaments of all the former states of Yugoslavia have become powerless because the *de facto* organizing principle in all of the new republics has become an absolute presidency that strives to depict the political opposition as undermining the effectiveness of defending the country during war.

A monumental struggle is being waged between the forces of evil and the forces of good with all the earmarks of a morality play. The territory for which they vie are the souls of average citizens. The conflict is between those of all nationalities who are bellicose and who fan the fires of war in order to spread it to territories not yet affected and those who resist mutual "ethnic cleansing."

The warmongers continue to incite hatred. At a rally of *chetniks* in Podgorica (the capital of Montenegro), held in the spring of 1994, the huge crowd roared songs such as *"Ubićemo, zaklaćemo ko sa nama neće"* (We are going to kill, we are going to cut the throats of any one who won't join us) and *"Muslimanka sva u krvi, Srbin joj je bio prvi"* (The Muslim woman is all bloody; a Serb was the first to ravish her). The Croat crack unit "The Tigers" counter with a song in which they boast they will strip off the skin of *chetniks.*

The migration of hatred—which was first evidenced in the late 1970s in Kosovo and then spread to neighboring Serbia and Montenegro, and then to Slovenia, Croatia, and Bosnia-Herzegovina—continues its southward journey. Serbs, Greeks, and Albanians visibly increased their threat to the territorial integrity of Macedonia in the summer of 1994.

Opposing these formidable evil trends and giving a little cause for hope are small groups of people who battle hatred with truth, objectivity, and peacemaking. An increasing minority of domestic and foreign scholars and journalists are showing evenhandedness in analyzing the causes and the development of the war—a necessary prerequisite in finding a solution. The small non-governmental peace groups continue valiantly to buck the tide by spreading the culture of nonviolent conflict resolution. The *Erasmus* circle, for instance, organized a sequel to the Zagreb dialogue between Serb and Croat dissident intellectuals by sponsoring a fruitful dialogue between Croat and Muslim independent intellectuals in Sarajevo on May 3–5, 1994. While such small peace groups and the few anti-nationalist opposition parties have little chance of actually providing a present alternative to the governments, at least they are holding up a moral vision based on reconciliation and cooperation.

The most that one can expect at this point is *the creeping normalization of life* through a series of cease-fires and lowering of the intensity of "ethnic cleansing." An extension of "neither war nor peace" (like the one prevailing in Croatia) is preferable to a raging war, though the fragile nature of such a "settlement" is obvious.

Tragically *the most promising option has been irretrievably lost.* The best option for all the South Slavic peoples and other minorities living among them was Yugoslavia—with all its flaws and blemishes. The future offers only worse alternatives that cannot serve the well-being of all the peoples. The future will always be a zero sum game; what is good for one ethnoreligious group is bad for another. Infinitely more tragic is that the chance for a common future for the peoples of the former Yugoslavia has been gambled away by means of mutually attempted exterminations.

Optimally the peoples of the former Yugoslavia need to start again from the beginning, from another point zero, and find a new theory and praxis of cooperation. But no such beginning is on the horizon. Memories of injuries and injustices which are to be avenged in new rounds of bloodletting are set against the as yet unpersuasive hope of democratic evolution which might diminish the lure of revenge. Amid these contradictions and fierce fighting, the still tiny forces of renewal and regeneration of the Balkan societies may yet give rise to peacemaking that will restore sanity and cooperation. The odds for this are not good but the only humane alternative for well-meaning people is to devote their efforts toward that goal.

SELECT BIBLIOGRAPHY

Ali, Rabia, and Lawrence Lifschultz, eds. *Why Bosnia?: Writings on the Balkan War*. Stony Creek, CT: The Pamphleteer's Press, 1993.

Balkan War Report (incorporating Yugofax). London: A Bulletin of the Institute for War & Peace Reporting.

Banac, Ivo. *The National Question in Yugoslavia: Origins, History, Politics*. Ithaca and London: Cornell University Press, 1992.

Clissold, Stephen, ed. *A Short History of Yugoslavia*. Cambridge, Eng.: Cambridge University Press, 1966.

Cohen, Lenard J. *Broken Bonds: The Disintegration of Yugoslavia*. Boulder, San Francisco, Oxford: Westview Press, 1993.

Čuvalo, Ante. *The Croatian National Movement, 1966–1972*. East European Monographs. New York: Distributed by Columbia University Press, 1990.

Denitch, Bogdan. *Ethnic Nationalism: The Tragic Death of Yugoslavia*. Minneapolis and London: University of Minnesota Press, 1994.

Djilas, Aleksa. *The Contested Country: Yugoslav Unity and Communist Revolution*. Cambridge, MA: Harvard University Press, 1991.

Dragnich, Alex N. *Serbs and Croats: The Struggle in Yugoslavia*. San Diego, New York, London: A Harvest Book, Harcourt Brace & Co., 1992.

Drakulić, Slavenka. *The Balkan Express: Fragments from the Other Side of War*. New York and London: W.W. Norton & Co., 1993.

Filipović, Zlata. *Zlata's Diary: A Child's Life in Sarajevo*. Intro. Janine Di Giovanni; trans. Christina Pribichevich-Zoric. New York: Viking, 1994.

Glenny, Misha. *The Fall of Yugoslavia: The Third Balkan War*. New York and London: Penguin Books, 1992.

Gow, James. *Legitimacy and the Military: The Yugoslav Crisis*. New York and London: St. Martin's/Pinter, 1992.

Gutman, Roy. *A Witness to Genocide*. New York: Macmillan Publishing Co., 1993.

Helsinki Watch. *War Crimes in Bosnia-Herzegovina*. New York: HRW, 1992.

I Dream of Peace: Images of War by Children of Former Yugoslavia. Preface by Maurice Sendak. Intro. by James P. Grant. New York: Unicef/Harper Collins Publishers, 1994.

Jelavich, Barbara. *History of the Balkans: Twentieth Century,* Vol. II. Cambridge, Eng.: Cambridge University Press, 1983.

Jelavich, Charles and Barbara. *The Establishment of the Balkan National States, 1804–1920.* Seattle and London: University of Washington Press, 1977.

Kaplan, Robert D. *Balkan Ghosts: A Journey Through History.* New York: Vintage Books, Random House, 1993.

Lees, Michael. *The Rape of Serbia: The British Role in Tito's Grab for Power, 1943–1944.* New York: Harcourt Brace Jovanovich, 1990.

Magaš, Branka. *The Destruction of Yugoslavia: Tracking the Break-up 1980–1992.* London and New York: Verso, 1993.

Martin, David. *The Web of Disinformation: Churchill's Yugoslav Blunder.* New York: Harcourt Brace Jovanovich, 1990.

Meštrović, Stjepan G., with Slaven Letica and Miroslav Goreta. *Habits of the Balkan Heart: Social Character and the Fall of Communism.* College Station: Texas A & M University Press, 1993.

Mojzes, Paul. *Religious Liberty in Eastern Europe and the USSR: Before and After the Great Transformation.* Boulder, CO: East European Monographs, Distributed by Columbia University Press, 1992. (See Chapter 12, "Yugoslavia: A Study in Ambiguity.")

Naythons, Matthew, and others. *Sarajevo: A Portrait of the Siege.* New York: Warner Books, 1994.

The Other Balkan Wars: A 1913 Carnegie Endowment Inquiry in Retrospect, with a New Introduction and Reflections on the Present Conflict by George F. Kennan. Washington: Carnegie Endowment, 1993.

Prstojević, Miroslav, et al. *Survival Guide.* Sarajevo: FAMA, 1993.

Ramet, Sabrina P. *Nationalism and Federalism in Yugoslavia 1962–1991,* 2d ed. Bloomington: Indiana University Press, 1992.

Religion in Eastern Europe (bimonthly). Formerly *Occasional Papers on Religion in Eastern Europe).* Rosemont, PA.

Rode, Martyn. *The Breakup of Yugoslavia.* New York: Macmillan Children's Book Group, 1994.

Shenk, Gerald, with David Steele. *God with Us?: The Roles of Religion in Conflicts in the Former Yugoslavia.* Uppsala, Sweden: Life and Peace Institute, 1993.

Singleton, Fred B. *Yugoslavia: The Country and Its People.* Cambridge, Eng.: Cambridge University Press, 1992.

Stojanović, Svetozar. *Communist Implosions, Nationalist Explosions.* Lawrence: University of Kansas Press, forthcoming.

Thompson, Mark. *A Paper House: The Destruction of Yugoslavia.* New York: Viking, 1992.

INDEX